THE MIGHTY DEAD

Communing with the Ancestors of Witchcraft

by Christopher Penczak

COPPER CAULDRON
PUBLISHING

CREDITS

Writing: Christopher Penczak

Editing: James St. Onge

Proofreading: Shea Morgan, Lisa Curley, Cindy Kirby, Thomas Oakspear Joyce, Stephanie Lehnert, Claire Manning, Tina Marie Van Orden

Cover Design: Derek Yesman

Interior Art: Christopher Penczak

Interior Design & Publishing: Steve Kenson

For more information visit:

www.christopherpenczak.com

www.coppercauldronpublishing.com

ISBN 978-0-9827743-7-3, Second Revised Printing

Printed in the U.S.A.

"There is a part of the Inner Planes, the Other World, which is called Witchdom. There you may learn much, if you can contact it. There are spells and chants, dances and music and such woods and streams as delight the hearts of witches. Witchdom has a temple, in that all sacred places on this earth have their astral counterparts. Nothing is lost, but much is stored deep."

—JOHN BRAKESPEARE

ACKNOWLEDGEMENTS

A very special thanks to my many friends, fellow teachers, elders and the authors whom I know only through their books and art, who opened me to the ways of the ancestors or deepened my knowledge and experience: Christopher Giroux, Alaric Albertsson, Matthew Venus, Matthew Sawicki, Joe and Doug of Otherworld Apothecary, Emily Jones, Raven Grimassi, Stephanie Taylor, Maxine Sanders, R.J. Stewart, Orion Foxwood, Michelle Belanger, Christian Day, Jimhal Difiosa, Peter Paddon, Ian Corrigan, J.M., Catherine Yronwode, Dolores Ashcroft-Nowicki, Andrew Wood, Alberto Villoldo, Evan John Jones, Carlos Castaneda, Cora and Victor Anderson, Doreen Valiente, Robert Cochrane, Alex Sanders, Gerald Gardner, Austin Spare, Dion Fortune, Aleister Crowley, Alice Bailey and H.P. Blavatsky.

Thank you to my friends, family and Temple for their support in this work, and in particular to Steve, Adam, Ron, Alix, Rama and all of the Temple of Witchcraft.

To Rosalie as her spirit guides me onward.

To my ancestors; to those of blood, to those of milk and to those of breath and bone and flesh and to those of the stars, I thank you.

To the First Witch, the Last Witch, and All Witches In Between.

OTHER BOOKS BY CHRISTOPHER PENCZAK

City Magick (Samuel Weiser, 2001)

Spirit Allies (Samuel Weiser, 2002)

The Inner Temple of Witchcraft (Llewellyn, 2002)

The Inner Temple of Witchcraft CD Companion (Llewellyn, 2002)

Gay Witchcraft (Samuel Weiser, 2003)

The Outer Temple of Witchcraft (Llewellyn, 2004)

The Outer Temple of Witchcraft CD Companion (Llewellyn, 2004)

The Witch's Shield (Llewellyn, 2004)

Magick of Reiki (Llewellyn, 2004)

Sons of the Goddess (Llewellyn, 2005)

The Temple of Shamanic Witchcraft (Llewellyn, 2005)

The Temple of Shamanic Witchcraft CD Companion (Llewellyn, 2005)

Instant Magick (Llewellyn, 2005)

The Mystic Foundation (Llewellyn, 2006)

Ascension Magick (Llewellyn, 2007)

The Temple of High Witchcraft (Llewellyn, 2007)

The Temple of High Witchcraft CD Companion (Llewellyn, 2007)

The Living Temple of Witchcraft Vol. I (Llewellyn, 2008)

The Living Temple of Witchcraft Vol. I CD Companion (Llewellyn, 2008)

The Living Temple of Witchcraft Vol. II (Llewellyn, 2009)

The Living Temple of Witchcraft Vol. II CD Companion (Llewellyn, 2009)

The Witch's Coin (Llewellyn, 2009)

The Three Rays of Witchcraft (Copper Cauldron Publishing, 2010)

The Plant Spirit Familiar (Copper Cauldron Publishing, 2011)

The Witch's Heart (Llewellyn, 2011)

The Gates of Witchcraft (Copper Cauldron Publishing, 2012)

Buddha, Christ, and Merlin: Three Wise Men for Our Age (Copper Cauldron Publishing, 2012)

The Green Lovers (editor, Copper Cauldron Publishing, 2012)

The Feast of the Morrighan (Copper Cauldron Publishing, 2012)

Forthcoming

Ancestors of the Craft (editor, Copper Cauldron Publishing, 2013)

The Waters and Fires of Avalon (editor, Copper Cauldron Publishing, 2013)

TABLE OF CONTENTS

Table of Exercises

Table of Figures

INTRODUCTION

The Mighty Dead are arguably one of my most pivotal experiences in the practice of Witchcraft, revitalizing my path and work in ways that I never dreamed. Ironically, I found them —or perhaps they found me—when I thought I was leaving the path of the Witch and delving into more "spiritual" practices. Sometimes you must leave a tradition to truly find it, to bring the seemingly foreign knowledge of the wasteland beyond back to your roots, and realize that hidden within is fertile soil for your own regeneration.

In the mid-nineteen nineties I hit what I now affectionately refer to as the "Wiccan Wall." It's a realization many of us get—that there are only so many spells books, wheel of the year books, and moon ritual books you can read before you start to go mad or get exceedingly bored. While I now understand the impulse of every author to write a basic magick book—as we each feel we have something important and unique to say—when that's almost all of what you have (and that's how I felt at the time) you look elsewhere for your inspiration.

I had completed my training in basic forms of Witchcraft and psychic development and had opted to not go the way of the formal British Traditional coven scene, observing too much in terms of politics, control, and submission. For a tradition said to be training in a transpersonal and transformative mystery, I didn't really see its effects in terms of the personal development and maturity of the practitioners I knew. (Thankfully, I have since met some amazing Traditional Wiccan initiates.) So I delved into the realm of healing. Psychic healing was the experience that solidified the reality of the magickal principles of the Witch for me and, learning the lore of the Witch as the Cunning Man and Wise Woman, I realized that while magickal associations of herbs and gems were widely known, few of my peers and teachers were working in the vocation of the metaphysical healer. I wanted to find people who were.

My search led me to the modern New Age movement. I began with the energy healing system of Reiki. Soon I was introduced to crystal healing, flower essences, vibrational energy medicine, and eventually discovered my love of herbal medicine. It was a strange mix of the very clinical and the most outlandish ideas. I met those described as light workers, ascensionists, and Shamballa healing practitioners, and would only later find out through deeper research they sprang from the Theosophical fount of wisdom started by Madame Blavatsky and Alice Bailey—contemporaries of the modern occult revival of the Golden Dawn, which in turn influenced Wicca.

At the time, I thought I was possibly leaving Witchcraft and Wicca for something deeper and more concerned with personal and planetary healing and spiritual philosophy, rather than simple folklore and the personal gratification of spellcraft. While I tried on these new labels, I didn't quite give up my sense of being a Witch, and found that my habit of wearing black and a pentacle disgruntled many of my new peers and teachers. Being a rebellious button-pusher at heart, it only encouraged me to keep them rather than cast them away as I was advised. Still, my experiences seemed to be pulling me away from the crooked path of the Witch.

In the deeper visionary and healing workshops, we were guided through experiences to connect with the "masters," the ascended beings of Theosophical and New Age lore. There is quite an established pantheon of such spirits, with pseudo-historic origins. In the workshops, everyone around me experienced the wisdom, healing, and guidance of figures such as Quan Yin, Mother Mary, Master Jesus (known as Sananda to his "close friends" communing with the inner planes) or the alchemist Saint Germain. A quick internet search will give you a wide range of channeled teachings attributed to these beings and many more that are part of the spiritual hierarchy.

When the sharing circle got to me, I had no tales of familiar masters to relate to the group. In my visions, I met an old woman from Cornwall, and another from Ireland. I found healing with a man from medieval Germany, a priestess from Greece, and several temple members from ancient Egypt. There were a few who defied familiar cultural associations, but were all very Pagan, all sorcerers or cunning folk of one kind or another, and all decidedly non-famous when they chose to tell me their names. They were not the typical spirit guides one might find on a journey, but seemed to evoke the same experiences and qualities of these other masters my fellow students experienced in a different context. Dare I say they were the ascended masters of Witchcraft and Paganism? I perplexed those of my new community, as almost all of the world religions were represented in the ascension mix—Judaism, Christianity, Islam, Hinduism, Buddhism, Taoism, Shamanism—but very little that would be classified as Witchcraft.

I soon discovered many of the same problems that caused me to avoid the British Traditional Wiccan covens were also present in my New Age community, albeit under different guises and veils. Issues of control, submission, and people suffering from delusions stemming from over-identifying with archetypal forces led me to leave, synthesizing what I experienced into my own brand of Witchcraft and eventually teaching it to those who asked.

Once again firmly anchored in my Witchcraft identity, I dove deeper into the roots of British occultism from my survey of Theosophy. I was exposed to things that were hidden from me before hitting my Wiccan Wall. I reread the classics, with a greater context and better understanding than I had when I was in my twenties. I saw evidence of the Masters of Witchcraft, Paganism, and Magick in all of these writings. Aleister Crowley and Dion Fortune gave great illumination on my experiences. Most notably, material associated with the Clan of Tubal Cain sparked my imagination. An old article on the Tubal Cain group of traditional Robert Cochrane witches summoning a past "Witch master" in a cave caught my interest. When the description from their descending tradition, known as 1734, described the "Hidden Company" as those past spirits that gather around the ritual circle, I immediately knew and recognized the experience as something I had felt many times before. I spoke with students and associates of the Inner Convocation traditions of author R.J. Stewart working with the material and traditions of his teacher, occultist and author William Gray, and recognized elements, with a slightly different veil, of my own experiences.

Finally a circle in the woods with a pair of more traditionally-minded Witches, where questions were viscerally answered and verified and I recognized and equated the spirit faces within their company with spirits whom had contacted me, the pieces of the puzzle fell into place. The way became clear and my craft deepened in relationship to these Mighty Dead. It is in that spirit of deepening our practice as Witches that I share this with you. May you deepen your own Craft with it.

CHAPTER ONE
WHO ARE THE MIGHTY DEAD?

Who and what are "the Mighty Dead"? Why are they important? And how do you commune with them? All of these questions are explored in detail, but each is a mystery. As you go, you will find your own answers to these three questions, as my answers will not necessarily be your answers.

The simplest understanding of the Mighty Dead is that they are the sanctified dead. They are the holy dead. While modern Pagans live in a world where we see everything as holy, as everything has an indwelling spirit or spark of divinity, when we call these spirits sanctified, we are setting them apart from what we would commonly think of as the dead. They have reached some state of holiness differentiated from their peers.

Every religious practice has some tradition recognizing this category of spirit, though the terms might not be clear or explicit. Every religion has those souls who have, to some extent, "succeeded" in the given goals of the path. They become examples, guides and teachers to others on the path, separating them from those who simply died without this level of success or wisdom.

THE EASTERN MASTERS

The most commonly understood expressions of these concepts are found in the New Age lore rooted in the Theosophical foundations of Madame Blavatsky, Alice Bailey, and those who followed them, such as controversial authors Godfre Ray King, Elizabeth Claire Prophet, or Joshua David Stone. They, in turn, are based on concepts of the Eastern masters, particularly of the bodhisattvas.

Generally speaking, as the different forms of Buddhism have their particularities, a bodhisattva is one who wishes to attain Buddhahood not just for the self, but by their compassion for every living sentient being. Bodhisattvas are often considered enlightened beings existing in a transhuman state between human consciousness and full attainment of the nirvana of union with the all and dissolution of the self. Many seekers on the path take the bodhisattva vow to attain Buddhahood for all. One of the most famous stories of the bodhisattva is of Quan Yin. She is about to reach nirvana and enter into no-self, but hears the cries of mothers and children across the world. Her compassion has her delay her own full enlightenment to remain behind until all sentient beings can reach it as well. From this state of betweenness, she is able to answer the prayers and support multitudes in a way she cannot when incarnated fully in one body, place, and time.

Likewise in the East is the concept of the Taoist immortals, those who have achieved their immortal state of being, bodily or spiritually, through Taoist practices such as inner and outer alchemy. They are depicted as wizards, sorcerers and adepts of magick with superhuman abilities beyond their immortality. They are immune to heat and cold, do not need food, and never get sick. They retreat to mountains in the west of China under mysterious circumstances, but can appear to guide those on the path seeking knowledge. While virtuous in their own way, the attainment of their immortality is more dependent upon occult technique than piousness. They are humans who have transcended the limitations of humanity. Like the masters of Blavatsky's Theosophy, it can be difficult to ascertain if their proponents believe they are physically and bodily incarnate, or simply within a transcended body of light, intangible in the physical world.

THE VENERATION OF SAINTS

In the Christian traditions, the closest we have to the bodhisattvas are the saints. From this tradition's standpoint, Christ dwells within the saint, whether the saint is alive or dead. From a metaphysical perspective, we would say that the individual has attained Christ consciousness, a state of unconditional love not unlike the compassion of the bodhisattva. These individuals can mediate the energy of the Christ force to others from "heaven," under very archetypal forms, leading to calling upon the saints for blessings such as healing, protection while traveling, or finding lost objects. Usually miracles are associated with the life of the saint. Often the names of Pagan gods, such as Bridget, were converted to the names of saints when the Christians took over a culture where the god's worship would not be denied. They simply changed the focus and theology, while keeping the folk traditions and holidays. While the Catholic Church, among others, recognizes and venerates saints, from an occult perspective many who are recognized are not necessarily true adepts of Christ, and many who are never known and recognized can be.

HEROES AND DEMIGODS

In the Pagan traditions, these sanctified dead are harder to see. One can claim the demigods are like the bodhisattvas, saints, and masters, and in many ways they are. To the average storybook reader the heroes of Greek myth are different in origin than the heroes of the occultist. In the interpretations of the Greek philosophers, such as Thomas Taylor's notes on *The Description of Greece* by Pausanias, *Volume I-III,* based upon the philosophies of Pythagoras and Plato, there are three orders of souls who perpetually attend the gods—angels, daemons and heroes. While the angel is the intermediary spirit between the gods and the worlds, the daemon is the intermediary connection between a human's conscious self and the higher worlds. Some consider the daemon the familiar spirit or guide while others see it as a personification of the Higher Self.

Heroes are those souls incarnated in human form that turned from contemplation of the temporal to the eternal and then dedicated themselves to serve the gods. Heroes move towards certain gods, certain archetypal qualities, and in so doing, are identified with a particular deity, giving rise to the idea that the figure was a demigod, literal son or daughter of a particular divinity. We are all the children of the gods, and all have the opportunity to become demigods on the path of evolution. Because of this, many who are uninitiated mistake the heroes for incarnated gods, but the heroes simply act as the worldly agents or vassals of the gods to whom they are most attuned. One need only look at the story of Hercules, demigod son of Zeus, with esoteric eyes to see a coded story of initiation through the twelve labors of the zodiac, generating his seemingly superhuman abilities and ending with his flaming, poisoned body consumed and the light of his divinity revealed. He ascended to Olympus to live alongside the gods. The heroes are said to be served, not by the common familiar spirit, but by an elevated or exalted essential daemon that most of humanity cannot experience since they cannot turn from the senses and the temporal view of the world to experience the eternal.[1]

We can see another view of the sanctified dead in the Norse Einherjar. Their name means "lone fighters," and they are the souls of men chosen by the Valkyries for their valor and bravery in battle. Half of the dead are chosen to go to Valhalla in Asgard for Odin, and the other half go to Freya's hall, Sessrúmnir, in her sacred field Fólkvangr. I think it's important to think of the Einherjar, demigods, and heroes as sanctified dead. In our modern metaphysical spirituality, we envision those reaching enlightenment and sanctification as entirely peaceful, pacifist and vegetarian, but the cultural factors of spiritual virtue contribute to the process, as each virtue is particular to the time and place. It's interesting to think of sword and axe wielding warriors and heroes, venerated for their bravery and battle prowess, reaching a condition similar to the compassionate bodhisattva or loving saint.

Likewise, the Priest-Kings of many traditions, most notably the ancient tradition of the Egyptians, where the religious leader is also expected to be a warrior and strategist. Egyptian occultist and ceremonial magician Florence Farr speaks to this concept in her work that would later become the book *Egyptian Magic.*

> *"Mild saintliness was by no means the ideal of the Egyptian Priesthood. Intense practical interest in the life of their country, and the ennobling of natural functions, drew a sharp contrast between them and the ascetics of India and Christendom."* [2]

While turn of the century Egyptology has fallen out of favor with true Khemetics with a greater academic understanding of ancient Egypt, she makes a sound point worthy of reflection for us today.

THE OCCULT REVIVAL

It is only in the occult revival of the late eighteen hundreds and early nineteen hundreds that the image of the Eastern masters begins to widen. One of Blavatsky's masters, known as Master Rakóczi or simply as Master R, was considered a European alchemist. He is equated with, or confused with, the popular figure of the alchemist and magician Saint Germain, though many believe Rakóczi was Germain's teacher. But their presence in this mythos showed the validity of spiritual traditions beyond Hinduism, Buddhism and ancient Egypt among the Theosophists.

Since that time, New Age masters from Judaism, Christianity and, most importantly, native and tribal traditions, such as White Eagle, have been experienced by channelers seeking to share their wisdom. The communion with native elders juxtaposes nicely with native concepts of spirit lodges composed of the grandmothers and grandfathers, aunts and uncles of ancestors passed.

And interestingly enough, the term lodge is used in both tribal medicine teachings and Masonic style ceremonial magick.

Not long after the rise of Theosophy came the occultism of The Hermetic Order of the Golden Dawn. This order of ceremonial magicians said it was in spiritual contact with the "Secret Chiefs." They represented an invisible hierarchy of adepts, guiding the visible outer hierarchy of mortal magicians. In fact, the Golden Dawn's ranking system had ten grades, and the three upper offices were filled by these masters, corresponding to the supernal triad on the Tree of Life. Samuel Mathers, a founder of the Golden Dawn, stated the following in a lecture to the Members of the Second Order in 1896:

> *"As to the Secret Chiefs with whom I am in touch and from whom I have received the wisdom of the Second Order which I communicated to you, I can tell you nothing. I do not even know their Earthly names, and I have very seldom seen them in their physical bodies....They used to meet me physically at a time and place fixed in advance. For my part, I believe they are human beings living on this Earth, but possessed of terrible and superhuman powers....My physical encounters with them have shown me how difficult it is for a mortal, however "advanced," to support their presence....I do not mean that during my rare meetings with them I experienced the same feeling of intense physical depression that accompanies the loss of magnetism. On the contrary, I felt I was in contact with a force so terrible that I can only compare it to the shock one would receive from being near a flash of lightning during a great thunder-storm, experiencing at the same time great difficulty in breathing...The nervous prostration I spoke of was accompanied by cold sweats and bleeding from the nose, mouth and sometimes the ears."*

He, like Blavatsky, believed in their physical reality, but could one adept at magick have had a visionary experience, an altered state that was easily confused with physical, third dimensional reality? I know many mystics, myself included, that have questioned our sanity and the validity of visions that appeared to be so real.

Occultists then and now suspected the Secret Chiefs of the Golden Dawn were one and the same with Theosophy's masters of the Great White Brotherhood. They chose two different tracts to help manifest the shift to the New Aeon, from a more Eastern perspective and a Western one.

The Great White Brotherhood's classic name is still in use but supremely dated by its time. The original sentiment was meant to be inclusive. Great White was used in terms of the union of all colors reflected out into the world. Brotherhood was used in the sense of humanitarian love, a collective brotherhood/sisterhood of humanity. The potentially perceived racial and gender bias causes issues with the term today. Many Theosophists prefer the term Lord (and Ladies) of Shamballa, indicating a connection to the mythic city of enlightened adepts in the East.

Ceremonial traditions that broke off from the Golden Dawn had their own Secret Chiefs, under the name of Inner Plane Adepts, the Withdrawn Order, the Secret Masters and the Illuminated Ones. Many of the pioneering occultists of the era are now considered to be part of this inner world order.

Aleister Crowley, the most famous breakaway from the Golden Dawn, reluctantly started his own religion of Thelema with himself as the prophet, formed the Order of the A∴A∴, often known as the Silver Star, and took over the Ordo Templi Orientalis, or O.T.O., transforming it into a Thelemic organization. This is a small bit of what he said about the Secret Chiefs in the collection of letters *Magic Without Tears*, Chapter IX:

> *"They can induce a girl to embroider a tapestry, or initiate a political movement to culminate in a world-war; all in pursuit of some plan wholly beyond the purview of the comprehension of the deepest and subtlest thinkers… But are They men, in the usual sense of the word? They may be incarnate or discarnate: it is a matter of Their convenience."*

In this letter from *Magick Without Tears*, Crowley goes on to address the concerns one would have about these Secret Chiefs – including a delusion created by a "master" who is not confident in his own decisions, and must base them upon "invisible chiefs" that lower initiates do not have access to for dispute. Since so much of the Golden Dawn's self-revealed history is called into question, with its secret *Cipher Manuscript* and unverifiable charters obtained from lodges in Germany, many doubt that Mathers had any supernal contact with these beings. Yet Crowley, who broke away from Mathers and eventually created his own, believed in them, viscerally described contact, honestly wrote of his doubts, and faced the questions of others. Perhaps when we shift the view from the suspect motives of Blavatsky and Mathers to the more direct experiences of Alice Bailey and Aleister Crowley, we get a more honest and less superhuman view, one taking place in higher dimensions rather than in flesh and blood. Would these discarnates not be the sanctified dead from ages past, with enough power, or "might," to make themselves known so clearly?

INTRODUCTION TO THE MIGHTY DEAD

The first reference I know to these entities in modern Witchcraft and Wicca comes from Gerald Gardner, the founder of Gardnerian Wicca, the root of modern British Traditional Wicca, which he supposedly based upon the fragmentary teachings from the New Forest Coven, along with world folklore, British occultism, and the ceremonial magick of both Aleister Crowley and medieval manuscripts such as *The Key of Solomon*. In his public works, *Witchcraft Today* and *The Meaning of Witchcraft*, Gardner makes references to the Mighty Dead. It took me by surprise in the rereading of the books, as none of the Gardnerian Witches make much mention of them, nor do the publicly available versions of the Book of Shadows. Having many Gardnerian and Alexandrian friends now, if this was a teaching that was emphasized in Britain in the fifties and sixties, it is neglected now. They became prized gems on my search for the history of the Mighty Dead and convinced me that there was some form of legitimate folk tradition passed to Gardner, despite what many of his modern critics say today. Though I must admit the skeptic can argue that he simply was aware of the concept through the writings of Aleister Crowley and Dion Fortune, with whom he was more than passingly familiar.

When referencing the cycles of life, death and rebirth, Gardner outlines the general ideas of reincarnation, but specifically gives another option, that of the Mighty Dead, who he compares to saints and demigods.

"It would seem to involve an unending series of reincarnations; but I am told that in time you may become one of the mighty ones, who are also called the mighty dead. I can learn nothing about them, but they seem to be like demigods - or one might call them saints." [3]

After teachings on the Charge of the Goddess, he described one of the benefits of being admitted to the circle (coven) as being introduced to the Mighty Dead.

"I am forbidden to give any more; but if you accept her rule you are promised various benefits and admitted into the circle, introduced to the Mighty Dead and to the cult members." [4]

Again he compares the Mighty Dead to the Christian saints and references prayer and payment to the Church as a method of Christian magick. He goes on to describe the reciprocal nature between the Witches and the gods, as they both need each other.

"Yet you must not ask Him directly for what you want, but pray to some saint, who is a dead man, as we understand it, though one whom we would call the mighty dead, and you must give money before you can hope to receive favour." [5]

In his book *The Meaning of Witchcraft* he described them as the Mighty Ones, sometimes a term used for the gods, other times for the guardians of the four directions, but here, clearly for the Mighty Dead. He described them as the "Old Ones" of the Witch Cult, and for the first time described a special place for other Witchcraft initiates, breaking the cycle of rebirth outlined previously. One can assume that reaching this "favored place" confers status as one of the Mighty Dead.

> *"The modern witches believe that at death the "Mighty Ones", the Old Ones of the cult, come for faithful followers and take them to a favoured place among other initiates who have gone before."* [6]

The "promise" of British Traditional Wicca, as depicted in *The Descent of the Goddess* prose in the Gardnerian Book of Shadows, is to fulfill love.

> *"To fulfill love, you must return again at the same time and at the same place as the loved ones; and you must meet, and know, and remember, and love them again. But to be reborn, you must die, and be made ready for a new body. And to die, you must be born; but without love, you may not be born."*

Implied in this is to be reborn into the Witch Cult, find it, find your loved ones in the cultus or tribe, remember your love, and love them again. Once bonded through initiation, you return time and again to the sacred magickal arts.

A critique of modern Wicca is that Wiccans of both a traditional stripe and those of more eclectic ways do not honor and commune with the dead often or deeply, as Witches of more ancient traditions did up to the Medieval period. For some, Witchcraft was synonymous with necromancy and the work of graveyards. Today's Witches work with the dead only on Samhain, when the veil is thin. While this can be true for many of us, it's changing. Many come to Wicca due to experiences with ghosts and hauntings, leading us to work with discarnate spirits and ancestors more often. Some come to us now through the teachings of spiritualism, seeking something with a deeper philosophy and initiatory nature. Shamanic traditions with their death walkers and psychopomps are finding their way into modern Witchcraft. My own bouts with Theosophy and spiritualist channeling techniques led me right to the Mighty Dead, and here we have, encoded in some of the original works on what would later be known simply as Wicca, subtle teachings on the nature of the Mighty Dead within our Craft.

THE WITCH MASTERS OF TUBAL CAIN & THE HIDDEN COMPANY

Robert Cochrane, Magister of a Traditional Witchcraft group known as The Clan of Tubal Cain, described a full ritual of the Witches of Warwickshire in a magazine article, depicting something quite different from a Gardnerian Wiccan circle. The very visceral ritual apparently included the meeting of an anonymous Witch master through a rite of sacrament, with wine, apples, and dancing held within a cave with the focus upon a skull and a sword.

"I become aware of everyone else in the clan as if they were in me. I can feel them all. A strong feeling that someone is standing where the skull is impinges my mind. Immediately we begin to thrust our will towards it, probing, questioning, a sensation of the stranger increases immensely. We know who he is. My heart gives a bound of fear and joy together. We intensify our will until it is like a bridge of iron, our total concentration is upon him. We can actually see green lights flashing on and off around the skull. "Master, Master" I can feel the group calling him. Blue light twists and spirals in the centre. We work harder and harder still, our minds hurting with the intense effort. The light coalesces into the shape of a man, cloaked like ourselves. Wave after throbbing wave of power pulsates us. A feeling of exhilaration erases our tiredness, he exudes strength and wisdom. We greet him." [7]

While it is possible it was a manifestation of some god the Witches worked with, it more likely seems to be a spirit of a passed Witch, dressed like the Witches gathered for the circle. The first sense is a "stranger" and then the "shape of a man" in the flashing lights. These seem to depict more human and less transcendent forms of spirit. He manifests the qualities of power, strength, and wisdom, and inspires both fear and joy.

Cochrane was a contemporary of Gardner's, yet publicly despised him. Supposedly he coined the term "Gardnerians" as a pejorative to differentiate them from the "real" Witches of hereditary and clan stock, who did not seek publicity and fame in the way Gardner did, and took it upon himself to show another view of the Craft to the growing occult community. Ironically, many Gardnerians now use the term to be exclusive, often claiming uninitiated solitary Wiccans as not true practitioners.

It appears that if Gardner knew little about the Mighty Dead, beyond their existence and the fact that the circle will connect you with them in some fashion, Cochrane had a formula for communing with individuals from the dead in a group setting, even if he didn't use the term Mighty Dead.

One of my first illuminating experiences with the Mighty Dead was from reading work from one who worked with Cochrane, Evan John Jones. In *Witchcraft: A Tradition Renewed,* it struck me with this passage:

"…there is another form of manifestations which was best summed up by an American member of the clan. She called it the Hidden Company. In this case, the Hidden Company she was referring to is not so much seen as felt and partially seen: the hazy forms that seem to be part of the working but are out on the rim of the circle. This phenomenon is not something which happens immediately but something that builds up over a period of a year or so. It is as if these spirits have gradually accepted the workings of the group of coven as something linking to their past life and ways. To what extent they are attracted to the group or if the group attracts them is one of those unanswerable questions. All that can be said is that they are there and that they are a recognizable part of the coven worship and workings.

In a sense, although density and direction of the coven are in the hands of the working members, there is a distinct feeling that to a certain extent the group is directed by the Hidden Company. Not in an obvious way; but there is that definite air of subtle influence being brought to bear on the members. In long-established groups, very often any new member goes through a psychic vetting. In the case of an unsuitable member, there is a definite sense of hostility and rejection of that person by the Hidden Company. To ignore this will in time lead to the weakening of the contact between the two worlds; and should disharmony continue within the group, eventually contact will be broken off. The one thing that should be stressed about this particularly form of contact is that it is not a personal contact through one person. Nebulous and ill-defined though it may be, the presence of the Hidden Company is one that is felt by all and recognized by all. In this sense, the Hidden Company are perhaps the guardian spirits of the coven." [8]

With that, I felt myself filled with such excitement. I had seen the hazy forms around the edges of my circles for a while, solitary and group, without ever really knowing who or what they were. They were not the guardians of the directions, nor were they the gods. They were clear and tangible, but offered no direct communication. It was only once I had a name, a purpose for them, that they began some communication with me, slowly and hesitantly, and that I began to relate them to my Theosophical experiences of Witch "masters." In a later anthology book, Jones goes on further, elaborating on the Hidden Company:

"When it comes to the 'Hidden Company', a name first coined by some American clan members, we are looking at a modern name for what is actually a very old phenomenon. The Hidden Company, as we see it, is more than the old spirit guardians of both clan and coven. Mind you, there have been some disputes

about the Company's precise nature. Are they souls of past witches attracted back to this world by the coven's workings or are they, as some think, souls that have passed through many incarnations and no longer have to return to bodily existence on Earth? Are they indeed 'enlightened souls' that dwell in Gwynvid, that special place of existence that we all hope to gain someday? Or are they, as I personally believe, the souls of past clan members responding to the call of like to like and blood to blood? It is a question that we never resolved and in the end it boils down to personal belief. The only thing that anyone can be sure of is that the Hidden Company exists." [9]

He later relates the Hidden Company to the "watch" that calls the Horned God, referred to in one of Cochrane's poems, *This is the Taper that Lights the Way* with the lines *"…That fetches the watch. That releases the man. That turns the mill…."* [10]

Since then, I've found variety of groups connected with the Clan of Tubal Cain or its offshoots, such as the American 1734 Tradition, that use the term Hidden Company for the beings guiding these specific groups, those of Traditional Craft, or Witchcraft in general. I have found this term to be my favorite, even more so than the Mighty Dead, for it confers the sense of companionship, guidance and spirit family – ancestors of spirit if not always of blood. We use both the Mighty Dead and the Hidden Company interchangeably in the Temple of Witchcraft. When I've described these passages in lecture to students, I am warmed by the few faces that light up. They too, are now given a name for and understanding of something they experienced, but no prior book or teacher had really established.

JACK AND THE MOTHER OF WICCA

Doreen Valiente started her occult career as the High Priestess of Gerald Gardner, famously rewriting much of his Book of Shadows. Gardner fit the traditional lore he received together with bits of occultism from a variety of sources, including Aleister Crowley. Valiente immediately reorganized the material, along with a few other sections, and suggested new material be written to replace it. She reworked The Charge of the Goddess, noting the influence from Charles Leland's *Gospel of the Witches*. Later, she had a falling out with Gardner over his publicity, "old laws," and the appropriate age of the High Priestess, and began working with Robert Cochrane in the Clan of Tubal Cain for a time. When things deteriorated in that group, she worked with The Coven of Atho and later compiled and pioneered even more lore in her writings.

Doreen is affectionately known as the mother of modern Wicca and, with her writings, did a lot to encourage new Witches and support the formation of the Pagan Federation in London. She was well known for her compassion, humor and level head in a time of flamboyant personalities and ridiculous arguments.

Between the years 1964 and 1966, she made psychic contact with the spirit of a deceased traditional Witch named John "Jack" Brakespeare, who lived in the early 19th century.[11] John, also going by his Witch name Nick, supposedly led a coven in Surrey, and while in the state between waking and dreaming one night, she saw a vision of robed Witches led by John in a field by moonlight. Though they were sporadic, these communications proved fruitful. John made contact to pass on true old ways to Doreen, something she had sought through both Gardner and Cochrane.

The following prose and wisdom was attributed to John, as recorded in *The Rebirth of Witchcraft*:

> *Black spirits and white,*
> *Red spirits and grey,*
> *Come ye, come ye, come ye that may.*
> *Throughout and about, around and around,*
> *The circle drawn, the circle bound.*

It is a verse to cast the circle, using the colors traditionally associated with the four winds.

> *"John Brakespeare returns from Witchdom. There is a part of the Inner Planes, the Other World, which is called Witchdom. There you may learn much, if you can contact it. There are spells and chants, dances and music and such woods and streams as delight the hearts of witches. Witchdom has a temple, in that all sacred places on this earth have their astral counterparts. Nothing is lost, but much is stored deep."*

This is a teaching on the inner planes paradise of Witches, what Doreen compared to Heaven, Paradise, Summerlands, and the Happy Hunting Grounds. To me it sounds like what I later learned as the Grove of the Hidden Company.

> *"Witches today waste much time on unnecessary matters. You think these things important, but they are trivialities. Look to Witchdom for your answers. Do not mix up East with West and end nowhere. Toledo held many mysteries that you seek. But do not stuff your heads with book-learning. Get down to practice. It is easier to sit reading a book than it is to practice; but reading books nourishes only the thinking mind. It is the Inner Mind that needs to feel its own strength. Dip into the Pool of Memory and find treasure."*

This is John's advice on focusing on what is important and working with information from sources other than books.

"Do not be in a hurry. Find few people and good. When the full moon is out, you can come close to Witchdom. The rays of the moon have power, when they bathe the earth with its light. It is the window, in more ways than one. You too can see through the window." [12]

Some double meanings in a teaching about the Moon and the window are found here. The Moon is a gateway to seeing and entering "Witchdom."

Perhaps a mix of Gardner's and Cochrane's teachings, plus Valiente's own treasures from the Pool of Memory, was the right combination to unlock a new stream of lore from Witchdom.

AN EMPTY CHAIR FOR THE KING OF WITCHES

Alex Sanders is quite possibly the most active of the famous dead Witches of the Wiccan revival. It makes sense. He was a showman, flamboyant and liked attention, but he also had a sincere desire to teach, to heal, and to share the magick. Ten years after his death, a group of Alexandrian Witches made contact with him as documented in the book, *A Voice in the Forest: Spirit Conversations with Alex Sanders* by Jimhal DiFiosa. Since then, I know a number of people who have experienced contact, myself included, after befriending his ex-wife Maxine. I don't know anybody having such a good time with Gerald. Though I'm sure Doreen is chatting some folks up out there, they tend to be quieter about it.

Alex Sanders was known as the King of Witches. While he too sought publicity, more so than Gardner, it was an unfortunate title given to him by the groups he worked with, to simply signify King of their Witches, not of all Witches, since the title earned him ire amongst other Witches of every stripe and added to his image as egotistical. Though he had desires of summoning the Witches of old when a child, he found himself offering his body so the "powers could speak through him" regarding the initiation of covenmates Maxine and Paul.

"The results were astounding. A voice was heard, that of a middle-aged man who called himself Nick Demdike. In broad Lancashire accent sprinkled with oath, he claimed to have been a Lancashire witch in the early seventeenth century. He had been thrown into gaol but before being taken, had flung his athame into a brook near Whalley Abbey where it lay rotting to this day. Nick laughed rudely at Alex's predicament and declared that he should do as he was told and initiate the pair, and that they would need to be bound to the art—he called it "Wicca", the old English name for witchcraft—as fast as possible." [13]

After the trance ended, the coven went searching for, and found, the knife. Alex found the experience exhausting, and felt it better belonged to Spiritualism, which he gave up for Witchcraft. He later got over it and agreed to repeat the experiment, but Nick would only come when he had something to say, refusing to be conjured by the coven. "Assured that he would not have his energy sapped by trivial chatter, Alex was never again loath to offer his body to the long-dead witch" though generally he was not in favor of bothering the dead if they were not seeking to speak with him. Was it contact with the Mighty Dead or simply one of the dead who happened to be a Witch? I'm not sure, but there was obviously something profound about the encounter and subsequent relationship that was life changing. Nick appears to have guided the development of the coven not unlike the Hidden Company, though in a more direct and personal way. But I would expect nothing less from Alex Sanders. For the direct, personal, and more flashy would suit him and his coven, and he carries on in that tradition as a spirit. At the end of his life he took a deeper interest in the practices of Buddhism, attempting to rectify his mistakes, so his ability to commune in this way, akin to a Bodhisattva for Witches, is not a complete surprise.

In *A Voice in the Forest*, Sanders's spirit suggested placing an empty chair in circle for him. This is an interesting practice, as it shows up in quasi-Masonic style orders, as a place for the Invisible Master guiding the group. I'm sure with his background Sanders would know that in life, and I think it's great that many Witches are doing just that for him. He's become an invisible master and patron saint for many of us. Not too shabby a move for the former King of the Witches.

THE MANY NAMES OF THE MIGHTY DEAD

Ultimately this lore shows us that one can become the Mighty Dead through the practice of the craft, or perhaps the practice of any true spiritual system of empowerment and mysticism, in opposition to dogma and belief. Remember Dion Fortune's words explaining the inner plane masters:

"What you are now, they were once. What they are now, you can be." [14]

It is an invitation to follow. It can be helpful to look at the wide range of spirits and entities we can collectively associate with the Mighty Dead. Purists from the camp of hard polytheism would say that each is its own "tribe" with its own chiefs. Each tradition has its own separate clan and family of masters. There are overarching collectives for greater world religions, and then specific groups tied to specific lineage traditions. While the bodhisattvas serve all those approaching Buddhism, there might be specific groups of bodhisattvas for specific lineages of Buddhism. The

Mighty Dead apply only to the Witch Cults, and specific groups of them guide specific traditions and covens. The Mighty Dead or Hidden Company of the Clan of Tubal Cain and its offshoots are different than those guiding Gardnerian Wicca or the Temple of Witchcraft.

Theosophists would look at the multidimensional nature of enlightened consciousness, where there is no separation, and believe in a collective and connective awareness that simply manifests in different families and tribes, based upon the assumptions and predilections of the mystic approaching them. One large collective of enlightened souls is working together. Those who came to their enlightenment through Buddhism might be focused on manifesting that way. Those who approached it through Christianity are manifesting as saints. And those sorcerers, priestesses and cunning women are manifesting in the Witchcraft traditions as the Mighty Dead. Collectively they are all reaching out to all the traditions of this time, in a joint effort to usher in the new aeon, and will work with whomever will work with them, whose purpose is in harmony with their own.

In the end, much like the gods, their nature is a mystery we need to explore, and no one approach has exclusive claim to the truth for us all. The truth is in the experience.

Ancient Ones

This is a general term for the illuminated masters (and sometimes various elder gods) that can apply to any culture or tradition. The term is specifically used in the Cabot Tradition when making a libation of the Waters of Life to the powers. *"A libation to the Gods and the Ancient Ones. Ishi Baha!"* The deities of the tradition are seen not as personal manifestations of transpersonal powers and phenomenon, but as the ancient human ancestors who have been deified.

Ascended Masters

This Theosophical title is most popularly used in the New Age movement. The name "ascended" can be a misnomer, for while their consciousness has expanded, and many traditions view them as ascended to the heavens, many in the Witchcraft traditions see these beings as existing in the Underworld, or in a realm aside to ours. Directions really are of little help in dealing with issues of consciousness, as they exist in a direction that cannot be pointed to.

Awenyddion

While technically the Welsh term *Awenyddion* can refer to a bard divinely touched by awen, when awen is used as a metaphor for enlightened inspiration, an Awenydd (singular) is one who is animated by such power. They are illuminated with wisdom, wit and vision. In the Temple of Witchcraft, awen through the Three Rays of Witchcraft is seen as a major step in the enlightenment process of becoming one of the Mighty Dead, so Awenyddion is a proper term for these entities.

Bodhisattvas

A bodhisattva is one who wishes to attain Buddhahood for the benefit of all sentient beings. It can refer to a being already leading an enlightened existence, or one heroically dedicated to such an existence for all. Often one has attained enlightenment but delayed it to aid others. Many bodhisattvas are depicted as supernatural beings existing in a liminal state rather than flesh and blood.

Born from the Nameless Religion

This is a cross cultural reference that indicates the attainment of a religious insight beyond any one religion, particularly any one dogmatic religion. It has been applied in the traditions of Witchcraft as well as the indigenous religion of Tibet. Their wisdom is born from no religion and all religions.

Buddhas

Refers to these spiritual immortals as Buddhas from a Buddhist perspective, simply meaning one who is truly awake. For many, it is the equivalent of Christ Consciousness, but in Theosophy, the role and office of the Buddha was elevated higher than that of the Christ. Buddhas are considered generally above bodhisattvas in more traditional forms of Buddhism, for they have attained enlightenment, not delayed it.

Cuccilatii

The Hooded Ones or Hidden Company of the Clan of Tubal Cain as referenced by Evan John Jones and Shani Oates in *The Star Crossed Serpent.*

Christed Ones

Mystical Christianity and New Age lore with Christian overtones refer to masters in terms of achieving Christ Consciousness, or the Christed Self. In terms of ceremonial magick, the level can roughly equate with minor adepthood at the consciousness level of Tiphereth. In more ancient terms, a Christ or Messiah, is a King, and can refer to the sovereignty of an adept.

Circle of Enlightened Beings

This is a general term used in modern Buddhist traditions to relate the bodhisattvas to other similar entities from different cultures, also acknowledging the already inherent enlightened nature of all things, yet to be made manifest.

Company of Illuminated and Blessed Kings and Heroes

This is a term used in the traditions of R.J. Stewart for the spirits of past kings, heroes and wise ones from the Western Mystery Traditions. [15]

Company of the Watchers of Avalon

A term used specifically for those spirits associated with Avalon/Glastonbury, guiding its use and development from a collective consciousness. Modern figures such as Frederick Bligh Bond and Dion Fortune are included in this Company, as well as more ancient figures such as the spirits of Merlin, the Lady of the Lake and the monks of the Glastonbury Abbey. This group consciousness works in both a Pagan and Christian paradigm, just as the later Grail mythos does.

Dream Assembly

A term popularized by the book *The Dream Assembly* by Howard Schwartz that can refer to Hassidic masters of a high aptitude, perhaps bordering on the enlightened disembodied masters. Dream Assembly can also be associated with the Rosicrucian group Fama Fraternitatis for an astral gathering in the "House of the Holy Spirit."

Einherjar

The Einherjar are the "lone fighters" of the Norse tradition, those chosen by the Valkyries of Odin and Freya for their valor in battle. They are valiant mortal warriors ascended to the halls and fields of Asgard, the heavens, to dwell with the gods, earning their place through bravery, valor and honor in the Norse culture.

Elders of the House of Israel

A Kabalistic term for the elders both corporeal and possibly non-corporeal in the Jewish traditions. The guiding spirits of the tradition.

Enlightened Ancestors

A simple and non-culturally specific name for the sanctified dead.

Grand Array

In medieval trial transcripts of the Witchcraft persecutions, the Devil was described to be in his "grand array," or the Man in Black's ritual garments and mask. The term has sometimes been used to reference the Mighty Dead, perhaps because an array is a systemized arrangement of objects. These beings form a greater pattern collectively through a systemized arrangement of their collective consciousness.

Great White Brotherhood

The Great White Brotherhood, also known as the Great White Lodge, is the term popularized by Theosophists for the Ascended Masters of the Spiritual Hierarchy of Earth. Often originally depicted with Eastern leanings giving a nod to the Shamballa mythos of Tibet, with the addition of more multicultural New Age channelings and teachings, the Great White Brotherhood is now depicted far more multi-culturally than ever before. Accordingly, every great sage, seer or wise person is ascribed membership into the lodge.

Gwynwyddigion

The Gwynwyddigion or Gwynwydden are "men of sacred knowledge." While technically referring to living corporeal beings, bards, sages and magicians, in *The Barddas of Iolo Morganwg*, this level of sacred knowledge, of the whiteness or illumination of the otherworld, with the same root "gwyn" as many of the deities and faery folk of myth, can indicate a level of illumination with that knowledge akin to the masters.

Hidden Company

The Hidden Company is the named used by those associated with the Clan of Tubal Cain and the American 1734 Tradition. The term was coined by American members of the Clan according to Evan John Jones, and since then has been adopted by a variety of Craft groups, primarily those identifying with Traditional Craft, pre-Gardnerian forms of Witchcraft uninfluenced by the modern New Age traditions, retaining their connections to the land, ancestors, and folkloric traditions. Other similar, but more generic names include the Hidden Masters, Hidden Ones or the Company of Hidden Ones.

Holy Ones

This simple title refers to the holiness of these beings, though not particular to any one tradition or time. Interestingly enough the Holy Ones are references in Christian myth to the

Watchers, the angels, and some would say also the fallen angels, giving them association with the Fey and other spirits of the land.

Hooded Ones

This is another name for the Hidden Company in the mythos of the Clan of Tubal Cain, as found in the book *The Star Crossed Serpent,* by Evan John Jones and Shani Oates. Most likely a reference showing that the Clan of Tubal Cain sees itself as a "robed" tradition of Witches, distinguished from Gardner's skyclad traditions of British Traditional Wicca. Interestingly the same hooded and robed imagery is emphasized in Crowley's image of the inhabitants of the City of Pyramids (see **Chapter Nine**).

Illuminated Ones

The Illuminated Ones, The Company of Illuminated Ones, and the Illuminare are all names for the ones who bring light or enlightenment to others and the world. Illuminare specifically is the name of the "ascended masters" consumed by fire, now burning with pure light, as shared by author Veronica Cummer in her book *Sorgitzak: Old Forest Craft.* They illuminate others.

The Mighty Dead often get equated with the Illuminati, which coming from the same root word can refer to several different things, from beneficent ascended masters, a historic enlightenment secret society and even to a secret shadow government ruling the world through economics, fear and violence, with roots in ancient alien races and modern conspiracy theories.

Immortals

This is a general title for any adept attaining immortality be it spiritual or physical.

Inner Convocation

The Inner Convocation can refer to both the inner plane meeting place and the assembly of entities gathered there to work with priestesses and priests of our world. It is based on the work of ceremonial magician William Gray, made public in his pamphlet *The Rite of Light* in 1976 and continued on by his student R.J. Stewart and his own initiates.

Inner Plane Adepts

Inner plane adepts is a general occult or ceremonial term for the sanctified dead, acknowledging they have turned from the outer planes of form to the inner planes, at a level of adepthood, rather than as seekers. In Qabalistic terms, the title Adept refers to various ranks of those who have achieved consciousness of the ethical triangle, either Tiphereth, Geburah or Chesed. Some distinguish these Adepts from the more enlightened spirits of the higher sphere of Binah.

Invisibles

Invisibles is a cross cultural term that can refer to spirits in general, particularly in the context of Voodoo, or an unseen gathering of illuminati. Often more in reference to the members of an informal society of philosophers and scientists, as depicted with the historical term The Invisible College. The Invisible College lent inspiration to chaos magician and occultist Grant Morrison's depiction of a multicultural, multi-tradition group of spiritual freedom fighters and the higher forces and "ascended masters" employing them in a war against darkness and control in the comic *The Invisibles*.

Justified Men

This is a variant title of The Order of Just Men and Women Made Perfect. A Qabalistic reference to the Body of Saints.

Khou

In the Egyptian tradition, when the Khou is justified or sanctified, it is known as an Illuminated One. It is the luminous immortal ego self, also associated with the Yekh or Akh. When debased this self can become a demon.

Kings and Queens

The Kings and Queens, Secret Kings and Queens, or Company of Kings and Queens is a Western Mystery tradition term referring to these secret chiefs' spiritually royal status, establishing personal and communal sovereignty in their work.

Lords and Ladies of Shamballa

The Lords of Shamballa, and more recently the title of the Lords and Ladies, or Ladies and Lords, of Shamballa, is another Theosophical title used for the ascended masters. It is often considered a more politically correct term in place of the Great White Brotherhood. The collective consciousness of the masters is considered the enlightened city of the Shamballa, also known in a more corrupted form as Shangri-La. Each master is a citizen in the spiritual city that is the capitol of our spiritual "government." It is given a physical location in the East, from Tibet to India. The favored title for the ascended masters in the Shamballa Reiki-Healing traditions.

Maggid

In the exoteric world, the Maggid refers to the traditional Jewish preachers as opposed to the Rabbi-scholars. They worked with the people through question and answer or lecture, and were quite popular in Eastern Europe. In esoteric circles, such as those described by Gareth Knight in *Magical Images,* the term is synonymous for the inner plane contacts mentioned in early Qabalistic writings.

Master Men and Gray Ladies

The Master Men and Gray Ladies are a possible occult reference to the ascended masters, being gender inclusive, and referring to the men much like Master masons or masters of the lodge-temple in terms of initiatory progression, and the ladies being associated with the gray ladies of fate, the various aspects of the goddess as weaver and bringer of fate, including the Norns, who are a larger group of spirits than just the famous three equated with the Greek Fates and Wyrd Sisters. At the level of consciousness of the Mighty Dead, one is a master builder of life and the life developing on the world, and capable of influencing, or weaving fate.

Mighty Dead

The Mighty Dead is the term used in Witchcraft traditions, particularly in British Traditional Wicca descended from Gerald Gardner, though the term has become popular in a wide variety of modern Wiccan, Witchcraft and Neo-Pagan traditions, particularly the Reclaiming and Anderson Feri Traditions, to refer to our sorcerous ancestors, rather than blood ancestors. Sometimes the Mighty Ones is used in place of the Mighty Dead.

Mighty Ones

The Mighty Ones can refer to a wide variety of entities. Sometimes they are simply used synonymously with the Mighty Dead. Other references see them as a collective term to include generally five orders of beings: the Elementals, Angels/Archangels, Mighty Dead, Watchers and Deities. For some, the Watchers are synonymous with the Archangels. For other traditions, they are the Grigori, the fallen angels. For many traditions, the fallen angels are akin to the elder Faery races, the angels within matter. Still others relate them back to the Mighty Dead alone, as the Mighty Ones are the children of the Watchers/Grigori, the Biblical "Sons of God" who mate with the "Daughters of Men." Their giant children were the first of the Witchblood and are our eldest ancestors of spirit.

Mukammil

Mukammil means "Perfect Master" in the teachings of Indian master Meher Baba, one whose soul is conscious of itself as God, and uses this knowledge and divine attributes for the advancement of others. Unlike the Perfect Ones, the Perfect Master has disciples. While Baba says there are five Mukammil upon Earth at any one time, incarnated physically, similar Sufic teachings state there is only one. See *Qtub*.

Nemo

This is a Thelemic term for a saint, a "no man" that dwells in the City of Pyramids and a reference to Aleister Crowley once he crossed the abyss and became Magister Templi. See *Saints*.

Odiyya

In the Hindu teachings found in the book *Kali's Odiyya: A Shaman's True Story of Initiation* by Amarananda Bhairavan, an odiyya is described as a sorcerer who has transcended the clutches of space-time, mind and body through mystical practices. Not everyone can become an odiyya, only sorcerers. These odiyyas were once human. However, there are also woodland odiyyas with no human origin, able to manifest a body in the physical world as desired. They appear akin to Faery sorcerers from the realms of nature. Perhaps when one becomes a true odiyya, they are in communion with these beings. It appears to be akin to the masters, in a more tribal, shamanic or sorcerous form of Hinduism and Kali worship when depicted in this text.

Like the odiyya, there are the aghori, mystics who transcend horror, disgust, fear and loathing through their bizarre rituals. The aghori can work with the odiyya. Bhaikari odiyya are underworld sorcerers. Some of these beings had a human life, and others did not, but they act as predators, almost vampires, particularly seeking out humans in transition from life to death and mystics unaware of their presence in a ritual state. The "good" odiyya fight the underworld odiyya much the same way the European Benandanti fought the Malandanti in Northern Italy during the "night battles," or the ascended masters working against the "dark brotherhood" of anti-masters in modern ascension.

Order of Blessed Souls

This is a Qabalistic term referencing the Ashim, or Flames of Fire, the Order of Angels associated with the sephira of Malkuth, the Kingdom, or the terrestrial world of Earth and the physical universe. Unlike the angelic orders of the other spheres, these "angels" are considered Earth's angels because they come from the Earth, not just the heavenly kingdoms. They are the "Souls of the Just Made Perfect," implying they are prophets, masters, demigods, heroes or saints, taking the role of "angel" to help those on Earth.

Order of Just Men and Women Made Perfect

Another Qabalistic phrase referencing the saints, Masters or Order of Blessed Souls, used most by the practitioners of ceremonial magick, particularly those in the Golden Dawn style of teachings.

People of the Secret

This is one of the lesser known names used in early modern occult literature for the Spiritual Hierarchy or Secret Chiefs of the Mystery Traditions. Used by Edward Campbell writing under the name Earnest Scott, in a book of the same name, *The People of The Secret*. Much like Blavatsky's vision of the masters, these Secret People would seed new ideas into human populations to guide consciousness and evolution. Strangely Edward Campbell's area of expertise was not apparently esotericism but the training of wild animals.

Perfect Ones

Also known as Kamil in the teaching of Indian master Meher Baba, these beings have realized their soul as God and are conscious of creation, yet they do not use their abilities in creation. Usually indicates an incarnated individual moving towards becoming a Mukammil. Meher Baba says there are fifty-six at any one time upon the Earth. In Celtic traditions, Caer Fredwyd, one of the various Celtic "castles" or "mounds" in the otherworld, is translated to the Castle of the Perfected Ones, Castle of Carousal, or Castle of Mead. Many take it as a reference to the realm of the Ascended Masters.

Perpetual Assembly

This is a term used in the work of R.J. Stewart for the company of kings, queens, priests, and priestesses of eternal light. They are the Perpetual Assembly in the Inner City of Light.[16] They gather continuously and without rest at the inner city in devotion to the light.

Principal Ones

Principle Ones refers to the work of Maria Sabina, the famed healer who used psilocybin mushrooms in her healing work as a *curandera*, or traditional healer of Mexico. She had a vision of six or eight Principal Ones coming to her and showing her a book of wisdom. She soon realized it was her book, and she knew all of its contents by memory. The Principal Ones showed her, and she became one with them.

Qtub

Also spelled Ktub, Qutub, and Kutub, *Qtub* is an Arabic word technically referring to the center, an axis or point around which things revolve. Most commonly an astrological or spiritual access point, or both. It also refers to a perfected spiritual master in the Sufic traditions with a spiritual hierarchy around him, mediating the teachings of Allah to the world. Some think of the Qtub as primarily corporeally present, while others see this figure as non-corporeal and spiritually present. This is akin to the spiritual idea of the master of masters, the Brahatma, or King of the World in Shamballa and Agartha teachings, in their most positive sense, rather than some Gnostic concepts of the imprisoning archon or World King. The Qtub would be considered the head or leader of the saints, attended to by various spiritual ministers, guides, and interestingly enough, four for the "four corners of the globe," not unlike Wiccan quarter guardians. They are in collective communion, but ruled by the wisest, the point around which all others revolve like a pole star. Qtub enters the Witchcraft mythos through the controversial neo-Sufic author and contemporary of Gerald Gardner, Idries Shah, as well as from a book of poetry by Witch Andrew Chumbley, simply entitled *Qtub: The Point.*

Saints

Saint is a term used in Christian traditions for those mystics who are "in Christ," whether they are in heaven or upon the Earth. From a New Age Christian perspective, a saint is one who is in "Christ Consciousness" or the quality of consciousness often equated with an ascended master.

In Thelemic cosmology, a saint is defined as one who has crossed the Abyss and spilled their blood into the Cup of Babylon with the blood of all saints, and now dwells in the City of Pyramids under the Night of Pan. They are considered a Magister Templi, or Master of the Temple. In some Qabalistic theology, such masters leave the body behind when crossing the Abyss. In Crowley's Thelema, a "Master of the Temple" can retain their body as they continue the path of evolution and enlightenment.

Secret Masters

This is a simple title for the masters, beyond culture or tradition. Like many other titles imply, they are secret because they are hidden, unknown to the masses. Only the occultist or initiate seeks them out.

Shadow Company

Shadow Company is another name for the Hidden Company in the Clan of Tubal Cain. The Clan tends to see them not as enlightened or ascended in the sense of never needing to incarnate again, but simply as the souls of past witches attracted to their workings as ancestral guardian spirits of the clan.

Those Who Promised

This is a modern Buddhist term, referring to those who made the bodhisattva promise.

Tzaddikim

Found in Jewish mysticism is the tale of the thirty-six secret kings and queens of the world, thirty-six righteous individuals who shoulder the world upon their backs. Due to their work, the world continues to exist. Without them, we would spiral out of control. They are known as the Tzaddikim. While the assumption is that they are corporeal beings of explicit holiness, they appear to have some of the qualities, such as secret kingship or queenship, as the ascended masters, and "rule" the world through their actions unseen. They are sometimes associated with miracles, and in other lore they are anonymous and unknown, with no outward signs. They are Qabalistically associated with Yesod, the lunar sphere, as the foundation of the world, while traditionally masters are associated with Tiphereth, Chesed or Binah.

Wisdom Keepers

Wisdom Keepers is a general name used most often in reference to Native and Tribal traditions of the Americas. Sometimes it refers to living medicine people, while in other esoteric circles, it references ancestral spirits who guide the current generation of leaders and healers. Wisdom Keepers, along with other entities known as "keepers," are found in the neo-Peruvian initiatory teachings of Munay-Ki.

Withdrawn Order

The Withdrawn Order is the nameless order of holy ones described in the teachings of W.E. Butler in the book, *The Lords of Light.* The term is also used in the teachings of author David Goddard, in his books *The Sacred Magic of the Angels* and *Tower of Alchemy.* They are decidedly immaterial, but close to the material plane, able to influence and teach under the appropriate conditions created by a lodge. They act as intermediaries for the greater spiritual orders "above" them in a sequence of orders within orders described like Jacob's Ladder. They are considered a planetary lodge of Earth, rather than one based within the stars. They oversee the work of primarily the Western Mystery traditions from this perspective.

Xian

Xian is the Chinese word used for the Taoist immortals. It literally refers to one who is spiritually immortal, meaning transcendent or enlightened, and has over time, come to mean one who is also physically immortal and superhuman, someone who has attained the status of a celestial being. Xian is equated with saint, sage or rishi and can imply a hermit, recluse, alchemist or wizard. Sometimes the term is given to what others today consider to be mythic creatures – faeries, witches, djinn or fox spirits. In Taoism, there are a set of eight famous immortals renown over the others, who were said to have been born in the Tang or Song Dynasty, living on a group of five island mountains in the Boahai Sea.

So many names they have. So many forms in which they may appear. Individual or group, defined or diffuse, they all point to a similar phenomenon. One of the first teachings on the masters that I received from my Theosophical New Age community was that the name didn't matter. You can call them anything you'd like once you establish contact. As you reach out to them, if you're ready, they will reach out to you. If you're not, then it will be empty. Other spirits and guides will work with you to prepare you for them. At the time, I was introduced to the Lords of Shamballa with the old name that bothered me so much: The Great White Brotherhood. When it was my time to lead ceremony, with my own perverse sense of humor to guiding me to test if this "it doesn't matter what you call them" teaching was true, I called out to the Big Black Sisterhood. They responded! They were right; the name doesn't matter as much as the spiritual connection, even though my teachers were less than thrilled with my choice. But I believe the masters of the Mighty Dead like a little humor. I don't think they reached enlightenment by being too serious. Ours is a religion of "mirth and reverence" according to the Charge of the Goddess.

Why are the Mighty Dead "mighty"? Why is the accumulation of magickal power a necessary component of this path? Many would consider the accumulation of power contrary to the path of enlightenment. In some Hindu traditions, the *siddhis*, the powers, are a distraction on the path. But in some views of Tibetan Buddhism, one must accumulate magickal power before becoming a Buddha. If you become a Buddha without magickal power, you won't be able to help anyone else on the path to enlightenment. Power, along with love and wisdom, are necessary qualities to join the ranks of the Mighty Dead.

1 Hall, Many P. *The Blessed Angels.* The Philosophical Research Center, Inc. Los Angeles, CA: 1996 and *Lectures of Ancient Philosophy.* Tarcher/Penguin, New York, NY: 1984.

2 Farr, Florence, *Egyptian Magic.* The Aquarian Press/Thetford Press Limited: Thetford, Norfolk, UK: 1982. p 16-17.

3 Gardner, Gerald. *Witchcraft Today,* Chapter 2, p 18.

4 Gardner, Gerald. *Witchcraft Today,* Chapter 3, p 24.

5 Gardner, Gerald. *Witchcraft Today,* Chapter 3, p 24 Chapter 13, p 91.

6 Gardner, Gerald. *The Meaning of Witchcraft,* Chapter III, p 49.

7 Cochrane, Robert (Roy Bowers). *Witches' Esbat.* New Dimensions Magazine (Vol. 2, No 10) November 1964.

8 Jones, Evan John with Doreen Valiente. *Witchcraft: A Tradition Renewed.* Phoenix Publishing, Custer, WA: 1990. p. 39

9 Jones, Even John & Robert Cochrane, editor Mike Howard. *The Roebuck in the Thicket: An Anthology of the Robert Cochrane Witchcraft Tradition.* Capall Bann Publishing, Somerset England 2001. p. 127.

10 Jones, Even John & Robert Cochrane, editor Mike Howard. *The Roebuck in the Thicket: An Anthology of the Robert Cochrane Witchcraft Tradition.* Capall Bann Publishing, Somerset England 2001. p. 135.

11 Guiley, Rosemary. *The Encyclopedia of Witches, Witchcraft and Wicca.* Infobase Publishing: 2008. P 354.

12 Valiente, Doreen. *The Rebirth of Witchcraft.* Phoenix Publishing, Custer, WA: 1989. Pp 113-114.

13 Johns, June. *King of the Witches: The World of Alex Sanders.* Coward-McCann, Inc., New York, NY: 1969. Pp 95-97.

14 Fortune, Dion. *The Cosmic Doctrine.* The Aquarian Publishing Company, London: 1949. p. 9

15 Stewart, R. J. *Advanced Magickal Arts.* p 175

16 Stewart, R.J. *Advanced Magickal Arts.* P 145

Chapter Two
Death and the Afterlife

Almost all cultures honor the dead. Their practices may seem similar or strange to us today, but each treated the dead with honor. One need only look at the wide variety of funerary practices to see the transition from life to death has been eternally important. The culture's understanding of the afterlife and the mechanics of how to get there, how it works, and what is needed or appropriate in it shapes their funerary practices. What was possible or naturally observable in the process of death in a region also shaped beliefs about death and the afterlife.

Starting in the Middle Stone Age, we find burial practices not unlike our own, with bodies interred in the Earth with grave goods, or treasures. We presume these items were beloved objects that should not be passed on, offerings to the spirits of the land, or items the deceased would need in the next life. Flowers, jewelry, painted decorations upon the body or bones are all common. When one looks at many of our ancient Pagan monuments, such as Stonehenge, their use might have had more to do with the dead and burial practices than most Pagans today would like to admit. We have no real understanding of what they believed the afterlife to be, though looking at surviving tribal peoples at a similar level of technology, there might be a belief in a world of spirit entered through the land.

ANCIENT PAGAN CIVILIZATIONS

When we look at ancient cultures that we consider to be sophisticated, their practices are not all that different. While we erroneously believe the Egyptians to be obsessed with death, because so much of what we know about them comes from the elaborate tombs of kings, life was just as important to them as the afterlife. Due to the natural desiccation of the body within sandy graves, creating natural mummies, the royalty and priesthood sought to perfect the process by creating the mummification and embalming process. Based on what we know of Egypt, there is a belief in life after death, though many consider it a bodily life, where grave goods were needed and the body must be properly prepared if one wants the immortality of the afterlife. One could argue if the ancient Egyptians believed the physical corpse would get up and have a life, or whether it was a talisman to preserve consciousness in the otherworld. Some, particularly kings, can reach a state of deification, apotheosis, after death and unite with the gods, and they become worshipped like the gods. The way to the realm of the dead was no easy journey, and a specific type of magick, a guide book filled with words of power and charms, known as the *Egyptian Book of the Dead* or *Book of Coming Forth by Day*, including material from the earlier *Pyramid Texts* and *Coffin Texts*, guided one through the dangers of the afterlife. The underworld itself, or Duat, was said to be ruled by the first Pharaoh, Osiris, a vegetative and solar god associated with death and resurrection. If one made it through the perils of the journey, judgment was faced. The deceased had to state the forty-two negative confessions to the judges, maintaining that these forty-two sins were not committed. The heart must be weighed against the weight of a feather on the scales of Ma'at, and if it fails to pass, if it's too heavy, it's fed to Ammit, the devouring creature, and their afterlife would end. If they passed the test at the scale of Ma'at, of truth, Anubis would lead them to the afterlife with Osiris, and they would be vindicated. Many of the spells of *The Book of the Dead* were to prevent anything from going wrong in the judgment, implying magickal skill was more important than moral action.

Fig. 1: Weighing of the Heart

In the New Age world there is a lot of speculation about the true understanding of the dead in Ancient Egypt. How much of what we know today was meant for the masses? Were the priests privy to some greater insight? Were many of the ancient temples and pyramids really initiation chambers to enlighten someone prior to death and not tombs, as orthodox Egyptology maintains? Does the creation of mummies, preserving the body, hinder rebirth and karmic release, trapping the soul, as many Eastern traditions would suggest, or does it confer some sort of favor, freeing you from the bonds of reincarnation to attain godhood? We might never know what the ancient Egyptians really believed or what is an accepted occult truth.

Today some fear that the preservation of the corpse keeps us locked in our bodily identity, what we will learn as the Middle Soul or Middle Self (See **Chapter Five**), and slows the process of enlightenment and reincarnation, trapping many spirits as ghosts, chained to the body. Others believe the mummification process helps one ascend to the realm of what we now call the Mighty Dead, without further need of incarnation. The Egyptians had a complex understanding of the soul, and of magick, so who are we to judge? Did they believe in reincarnation as some suggest? If so, there is little evidence for it among the mainstream documentation, though it rings a chord of truth for mystics who believe they had past lives in Egypt, myself included.

While lacking the mummification, Mesopotamian burials are not all that different from those of Egypt. In Sumer and Babylon, the dead were buried with grave goods, and more precious items indicating royalty. While common cemeteries are found, most were buried beneath a family dwelling, so the ancestors would be with them directly. The same practice is found in parts of Africa, where the ancestors were buried in a fetal position but upright, in the living rooms of family dwellings. This is possibly an origin to the concept of "standing upon the shoulders of the ancestors" in quite a literal, as well as symbolic and spiritual, meaning. The Mesopotamians had similar understandings of the underworld as a place of the dead, ruled by the dark goddess Ereshkigal and her consort the war god Nergal. Seven layers of the underworld are defined with seven guardians of the gate and, like many other mythologies, an agricultural god would spend half the year in the underworld, in the season of withering, and half in the realm of life to initiate the growing fertile season.

The Etruscans were an ancient and mysterious race populating Italy prior to the Romans, particularly in the area of Tuscany. Like the Egyptians, they took great care in the treatment of the bodily remains, believing that they directly influenced the deceased's experience of the afterlife. While at one point practicing cremation and placing the remains in a house-like urn, some of the most ancient burials were tombs imitating lavishly furnished households. The realm of the dead was somewhat similar to the underworld of the Greeks, Hades. Much of their culture influenced aspects of Roman culture.

Greek tradition has the classic three shamanic realms of an overworld known as the home of the gods, Olympus; the realm of mortals, the body of the Earth mother Gaea; and an underworld known as Hades. When one died, a psychopomp figure, usually the god Hermes, led the soul to the shores of the underworld river Styx. Those not led by Hermes would find the gate guarded by the three headed dog, Cerberus. The soul would have to pay for crossing the river by giving coins to the ferryman, Charon. In the burial practices, coins would be placed upon the tongue or eyes of the deceased, so they would have payment in the otherworld. Upon crossing, they would be judged and sent to either the paradise of the Elysium Field for the pure, or the cruel and painful realm of Tartarus. Those in Tartarus were seen as beyond redemption. Those who were not awful enough to enter Tartarus, but not pure enough for Elysium, would go to the Fields of Punishment, or to the mixed realm known as the Fields of Asphodel. The Romans had similar views of the afterlife, but the ruler of the dead was Pluto, with his wife Proserpina, rather than Hades and Persephone.

While modern Pagans erroneously believe that all ancient Pagans had concepts of reincarnation, we do know that some mystery schools, such as those studying with Pythagoras, were taught about the transmigration of the soul. It is also possible the initiates of the Eleusinian Mysteries, the sacred dramas of Demeter, Persephone and Hades, as well as the Mystery Schools of Orpheus and Dionysus, taught a similar reincarnation doctrine. These initiates were said to be unafraid of death, learning its secrets in their training. Some state that those who reincarnated three times and went to the Elysium Fields each time, subsequently went on to the Fortunate Isles to the west, a concept also found in Celtic myth. But this was not the lore of ordinary Greeks and Romans. There was also the status of heroes and demigods. The hero's soul played an intermediary role between the people and the gods, much like the saints of the Catholic tradition. Demigods are seen as half human and half divine, undergoing some trial to "earn" godhood and a place in the halls of Olympus. Hercules, son of Zeus, is the most famous of these figures, experiencing twelve labors to redeem himself and eventually earn his godhood, though that did not appear to be the initial intention of his quest.

Most of these cultural traditions have in common the cults of death and resurrection in their mystery schools. Figures identified with vegetation or the Sun, sometimes one and the same, including Osiris, Tammuz, Adonis, Dionysus, Bacchus, Persephone and Mithras, undergo seasonal death and rebirth. On the exoteric level, it is a story of cycles and seasons. Why do we have winter? Why do we need to harvest? Why is the world no longer an eternal paradise, but alternating between seasons of growth and rest? These stories try to tell us why. On the esoteric level, the initiate of the mysteries identifies with these gods, becoming one with them. The Egyptians said every man and woman is Osiris. Through this process, they are initiated, or 'born again' and through the perspective of resurrection, join the ranks of the Mighty Ones with knowledge from beyond. In this, they become like our Mighty Dead.

NORTHERN PAGAN TRADITIONS

While coming from the same Indo-European roots as many of the ancient civilizations, the Northern tribal traditions, among people who migrated longer and further than their counterparts in these cradles of civilization and western thought, saw death with some very similar views to those of the Greeks, in terms of judgment and reward. Unlike the Egyptians, the judgment could not be mediated through magick. Burial practices were often funeral pyres, giving the image of the Viking funeral, but usually people were buried in the ground whenever possible. Sometimes kings and warriors were buried in ships, or ship-like coffins, interred into the Earth with typical grave goods of jewelry, treasure, weapons and other valuables. Marker stones, sometimes written upon with runes, were laid out.

In the Norse and Saxon traditions we have some even stronger polarity views of right and wrong as well as good and evil. The Norse universe is divided into nine realms, each with predominant forms of entities. Midgard, or Middle Earth, is the realm we know with humans. There is a general realm where the dead go, those who die of natural causes and life circumstances. This is the realm of Hel, ruled by a goddess of the same name. There are parts of the heavenly realm of Asgard dedicated to the heroes who have been chosen by the Valkyries of Odin and Freya, who are rewarded with an eternal feast until the day of Ragnarok, the Norse Apocalypse. The dishonored dead are said to go to Niflheim or Nifhel. These are the spirits of thieves and murderers. One could argue that like Egypt, there is a form of judgment, though it appears the judgment is often self-created. You would get in Hel whatever you made in life. The sagas tell us when the good god Balder goes to Hel after being shot with a dart of mistletoe, the only thing he was vulnerable to, he is greeted with a feast and blessings.

One realm plays a stronger role in our understanding of the Mighty Dead, and this is known as Alfheim, or Elf-Land. Populated by the spirits known as elves, or faeries to some, many see this realm also inhabited by honored dead transformed by the land and their relationship with these spirits into bright and shining ones. Elf can refer to any disembodied spirit you encounter, from nature spirit to discarnate human. At certain points in folklore, the realm between the dead and the elves gets blurry, as they are both considered to be the spirits in the land, or under the hills. If you bury the dead, are they not the spirits under the hills now? Many ancient "faery mounds" in the British Isles are actually Stone Age burial chambers. Perhaps some of the ancient faeries are ancient ancestors. As the dead grow wise while they merge with the land, they become brighter like the elves. Eventually in British lore, mixing Saxon, Roman and Celtic traditions, Alfheim became Elphame, and associated with the gods of Witchcraft, the faeries and the dead all at once. There were less dividing lines than we have today.

The Druids taught the doctrine of rebirth and reincarnation, at least according to Caesar, giving rise to the legendary battle prowess of the Celts, as they believed they would be reborn. But to the Celt, the rebirth would be along tribal lines, reincarnating among the ancestors. Many of the western lands, particularly western islands, associated with the Faeries, were also realms of the dead. Tir na Nog, while technically not a realm of the dead, is now thought of as such, an earthly paradise beyond the realm of known space. The Tuatha Dé Danann were said to live in Tir na Nog after the arrival of the Irish upon their land. Another paradise of the heroes and soldiers of the Irish was Mag Mell, a land ruled by Manannan mac Lir, and like Tir na Nog, took on less of an afterlife quality and more of an earthly paradise, akin to faery. Eventually these or similar myths became bound up in the Arthurian concept of Avalon, the Apple Island of Faery Women or priestesses where dying kings went to rest before returning to the world.

The concept influences the initial Wiccan image of the afterlife being the Summerlands, a fairly non-distinct, non-judgmental realm where we return to rest and relax with our loved ones, gods and spirits, in perpetual feasting and sex. It's a mix of the halls of Valhalla with the realms of Hel and Elphame. One could look at the Medieval Witch's Sabbat as a corruption of the Summerlands. The Summerlands also lend their name to area of England known as Somerset, wet marshy lands only rendered visible and usable during the warmer, drier summer months.

A popular occult view of the ancient burial mounds in the work of R.J. Stewart is the concept of "sleepers." They are humans who willingly gave themselves to burial to be intermediaries between the human world and the spirit world. They are the ancient dead and mummies found all over the world in unusual sacred sites, sadly most often disturbed by archeologists seeking to understand the past. The sleepers willingly give up their place in the cycle of death and rebirth for a time, bonding their soul-spirit to the land and working at the threshold as a tribal spirit contact for the good of the land and the world. Many are considered to be in these burial mounds of the ancient world, and other sites across the globe. One might argue that the world as a whole has been in such a state because so many sleepers have been disturbed. The later sacrificial cults we find, particularly in South America, are degenerate forms of these practices, when the sanctity was no longer understood and the mechanism to do so was not able to be implemented. The thought to simply placate the land and the gods with blood replaced the deep magick of communication.

A view that might play our most important role in understanding the Mighty Dead in Witchcraft comes from the Welsh branch of the Celtic Traditions. A cosmology that is not vertical, like the Norse world tree, but horizontal, in the form of three concentric rings, was popularized in *The Barddas of Iolo Morganwg.* In this view, the spirit world is divided among three, or perhaps four, realms envisioned as concentric rings. The inner ring, containing the cauldron of the underworld, is Annwn, seen as the most likely cognate to the underworld of other vertical cosmologies. It is the place of beginnings, of first shape and form. The next ring is Abred, the realm of Earth as we know it, or the material plane of existence. It is the realm of seasons, birth, death and humanity. Human-like entities, gods and spirits, can exist in Annwn, but they don't live and die as the men in Abred do, though sometimes one from Annwn can live in Abred and one from Abred can live in Annwn, such as in the story of the Welsh figure Pwyll, who becomes a chief of Annwn. Those who are perfected go onto a realm of Gwynvyd, a realm of perfection and divinity. It is most like the "Upper World" of the vertical world tree. Those who dwell there once dwelled in Abred, but through wisdom and learning they were transformed. On their quest for Awen, for inspiration, they understood the true nature of divinity, called here Ceugant, surrounding all of creation. The Barddas on this topic are written in a question and answer style.

> *Q. Did all, who reached the circle of Gwynvyd after the primary progression of necessity from Annwn, fall in Abred from pride?*

> *A. No; some sought after wisdom, and hence saw what pride would do, and they resolved to conduct themselves according to what was taught them by God, and thereby became divinities, or holy angels, and they acquired learning from what they beheld in others, and it was thus that they saw the nature of Ceugant and eternity, and that God alone could endure and traverse it.* [1]

While written in a more Christianized framework, it points to a deeper magickal understanding beyond orthodox Christianity. A model for the modern Witch, rather than concentric rings is one of different frequencies occupying the same space. Just as radio waves, light, infrared and cosmic rays all occupy the same physical space, they operate on different frequencies. One could say that Annwn, Abred and Gwynvyd all are in the same space, but in different frequencies. When we cast circle and perform ritual between the worlds, those frequencies come closer together. We are able to tune in to more than the dominant human frequency of Abred, and those in Gwynvyd are also able to tune in to us and are able to gather and see what is going on in our circle, creating that first experience of being "watched" by a hidden company of masters. They are observing the nexus created by our rituals, for those in the middle "ring" and physical world are more likely to bridge the gap between all three realms to create such a nexus. Perhaps Gwynvyd is seen as outside of Abred because we feel these presences of masters on the outside of our circle, from beyond looking in, while many of the more familiar underworld spirits seem to manifest inside the circle.

Often the motion of Abred is described as clockwise, or deosil, with the Sun, while the motion of the Annwn underworld is counterclockwise and even Gwynvyd is counterclockwise. To the underworld, the motion is widdershins, against the Sun, but in Gwynvyd, it is tuathal, or with the stars, as the stars apparent motion around the heavenly pole is counterclockwise.

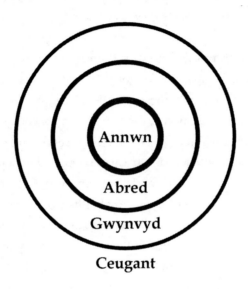

Fig. 2: Three Realms in Concentric Rings

MONOTHEISM

Though part of the greater Western mystery tradition, the view of the afterlife in the monotheistic traditions is not so different from Pagan counterparts in cosmology, but in attitude and later evolution of attitudes towards death. Some of the Judeo-Christian thought on the afterlife were influenced by the dualism of the Zoroastrian traditions of Persia, as a number of concepts are similar.

In the Jewish tradition, there are a variety of conflicting thoughts regarding death and afterlife. Some include simply stopping consciousness as the body passes back to the Earth, or a judgment after death where the accepted live in the "World to Come" or *Olam Haba*. Most do not enter this realm at first, but must review their life and be re-educated regarding their past, or even punished, though the punishment was not eternal torment or damnation. Such punishment was only for a select few who were truly evil way beyond any normal standard of human conduct.

Sometimes the concept of resurrection in the future is implied in the Olam Haba. The term *Sheol* is used for the realm of the dead, either as a realm underground or beyond the world. *Gehenna* is another term for a realm in the afterlife, a place for purification. Some believe reincarnation as part of the Jewish mysticism. Called *gilgul* in Jewish mysticism, reincarnation is the belief that the soul, after death, will be reborn into a new body. The mystical book of *The Zohar* mentions it repeatedly, even if it is only implied in *The Bible*. Today some Jews believe in reincarnation, while many do not.

For most forms of Christianity, the three worlds imagery is readily apparent in the simplified concepts of Heaven, Hell, and Limbo or Purgatory. Though the particular requirements can change depending on the denomination, those who are essentially "good"—followed the teachings of Christ, the rules of the Church, the Ten Commandments, and believe in Christ as the redeemer—go to Heaven, a realm of eternal blessing, peace, and union with Christ and God the Father. Those who disobey the tenets of Christianity go to Hell, a place of torment and pain. The name Hell comes from the Norse Hel, and mixes imagery of the dead, a realm of ice and a realm of fire along with some imagery from Pagan afterlife worlds such as Hades. Those who do not easily fit into either category go to a middle ground, akin to a waiting room, known as Purgatory. Christians believe that the faithful will be resurrected bodily with the second coming of Christ, and funerary practices usually kept the body intact as much as possible, though not to the point of mummification as they did in ancient Egypt. Christian folk magick traditions working with the dead often call upon souls who are considered in purgatory, in need of redemption to "work" their way into heaven with good deeds after death, since they did not perform them in life. The graves of such people serve as ritual sites for spells of protection, healing and legal aid.

Islamic tradition also believes in a heaven, or paradise known as Jannat, with eight levels, and a hell known as Jahannam, with seven levels. Like Christian tradition, Islamic lore also believes in a Judgment Day and the return to an everlasting home. While awaiting judgment, one has a level of comfort or pain depending on their faith and good works as a Muslim. In Islam cremation is forbidden. One must be buried in a grave.

The Judeo-Christian view went on to inspire the Christian Spiritualist Church, and its interest in mediumship and spirit contact certainly influenced the growth of modern occultism. Today many who "channel" the ascended masters use techniques that could be considered neo-spiritualism or pseudo-spiritualism. Rather than focus on judgment, healing and contact with the dead became the primary goal, to both prove life after death and the belief, like many ancient traditions, that the dead generally wish us well and want to help us. The Spiritualist movement then influenced the fusion of Eastern and Western thought through the birth of the Theosophical Movement and its offshoots, marking the major connection with the ascended masters for popular consciousness.

EASTERN AFTERLIFE

Eastern thought of death, the afterlife and particularly reincarnation has influenced modern Neo-Paganism more than most would suspect. Never having an Inquisition, unlike Western Europe, and still having living unbroken native traditions, unlike Egypt or Greece, allows a rich development of terminology, literature and practice among Hindus and Buddhists.

In Hinduism of India, the dominant belief is that the atman, or soul, is indestructible and immortal, and upon death, leaves the world of form and bodies to be reborn, or reincarnated again. The new life is determined by the karma, or actions, of the person in the previous life. Lower life forms are the new life from "bad" karmas, while more auspicious human life, moving upward in the Hindu caste system, is the result of "good" karma, though the eventual goal of the spiritual traditions is no karma, to embody dharma and be free from the world of rebirth as an enlightened master. Between lives, the atman can go through various realms, some described as "hells" to experience purification before moving onward to the next life.

Buddhists, on the other hand, are said to not believe in the concept of a distinct soul as most Western occultists, and even mainstream Christians, know it. The soul as an entity does not exist. But Buddhists do believe in rebirth and karma, which is an interesting contradiction. I had a Buddhist teacher explain it to me with two candles. When you light a new candle from a candle about to burn out, one flame is not reborn to a new candle. That original flame will "die" when it is snuffed out. But the consequence of its life, its energy, is passed on to the new candle flame. The new candle flame is a direct result of the previous one, the rebirth of its "karma" or action, but it is not that separate and distinct flame in a new candle, but something different. Likewise, when the energy of our actions, good and bad, is "reborn" somewhere else, it is not necessarily a separate and distinct soul, but something else that is passed on. Yet for the practical purposes of the Western occultist and Witch, we can think of it as a soul. Perhaps we simply need to think of the soul as less cohesive and individual than most of us do.

In *The Tibetan Book of the Dead*, also known more properly as *Bardo Thodal* or *Liberation Through Hearing During The Intermediate State*, is a bardo text describing transitional states. In this case, it describes the transition of death. In the Bardo Thodal, a series of different afterlives are depicted.

What you focus on upon the time of death determines where you go and the result of your next incarnation. Six "realms of desire" are described:

1. The Domain of the Gods (Devas)
2. The Domain of the Jealous Gods (Titians or Asuras)
3. The Domain of Humans (Manussa)
4. The Domain of Animals (Tiracchānayoni)
5. The Domain of Hungry Ghosts (Preta)
6. The Domain of Hell (Naraka)

Ultimately one is not seeking rebirth, but freedom from rebirth through the eternal oneness of Nirvana.

Cremation is a common burial custom for both Hindus and Buddhists, as the burning of the body speeds up the cycle of rebirth, giving the entity or karmic energy less of an anchor to remain in the world. Tibetan Buddhists, due to the scarcity of wood for a fire and the hardness of the ground, would often practice sky burials where the body would be raised up to be consumed by carrion birds such as vultures.

As more authentic Tibetan Buddhist lore makes its way into the occult circles of west, Witches find that the practices of Tibetan Buddhism and Bön are often in harmony with Witchcraft and ceremonial magick, as compared to more pure or simplified forms of Buddhism. The blending of the Native occult practices of Tibet with Buddhism gives it a character that resonates more with our teachings.

One such teaching working its way into the Witchcraft community is the concept of Tulkus in relationship to the Mighty Dead. A tulku is the reincarnation of a particular lama (Tibetan High Priest/Hierophant/Guru) continuing his work in the next incarnation. Other lamas, and all other beings, are said to not have conscious control over their next incarnation, but a tulku does and can make an announcement of where and when it will be upon death. Those of the order will then seek out the new lama, with tests to prove the veracity of their identity, including having them identify possessions and ritual objects from their previous life. The Dalai Lama is the most famous and well known of the tulkus, though he is also an incarnation of one of the bodhisattvas, Avalokiteśvara. So one can be both a tulku and a true bodhisattva at the same time. Technically the reincarnated tulku is not truly reincarnated, but an emanation of the previous life, as the strict

Buddhist philosophy does not believe in the individual soul. Currently there are over five hundred lineages of tulkus known to Tibetan scholars.

What, if anything, does this mean for our Mighty Dead cosmology? Some British Traditional Wicca practitioners wonder if such a phenomenon will, or should, occur in these lines. If through psychic means we can locate the reincarnations of figures such as Alex Sanders, Gerald Gardner, and Doreen Valiente, and develop traditions for the future to find, re-educate and continue the lineage teachings of the Wicca. Perhaps our own Mighty Dead will establish these lineages like Avalokiteśvara.

While I'm all for deepening the traditions of the Craft, I'm not always certain this would be a good idea. I have visions of a reincarnated Alex Sanders getting a new next life magickal primer from Harry Potter books and movies. Perhaps if those reborn are called to the Craft, they will find it and make their presence in our community known by their actions, not necessarily by omen and tests.

---

1 Morganwg, Iolo. Ed. by J. Williams Ab Ithel. *The Barddas of Iolo Morganwg*, Vol. I., Abred.-Gwynvyd.-Awen., 1862.

Chapter Three
The Ancestors

With an understanding of the Pagan afterlife and its worlds, we must better understand who we are connected to as ancestors and why. Our ancestral connection runs deep and wide, and includes a spectrum between the illustrious Mighty Dead and our relatives of genetic ancestry. Our work includes the whole range of spirits who seek to work with us, and our practice deepens if we understand, acknowledge and work with them.

Each type of ancestor forms a link in the Great Chain of Being, the connecting force between all forms of life enfleshed, and, in my own view of it, the line of connection to the world of spirit. We live in a time when connection is breaking down. The fibers of the web are frayed. By reaching out to many forms of ancestors, we help reweave the connections between the worlds, at least the frayed human world. The natural inclination of ancestral reverence has been discontinued, and we are soul hungry because of it. In some ways, we've broken, or are at least breaking, the chain with the way we currently live. We fear and hate death and prolong life by any means necessary because we lack this connection. We don't feel and see the presence of the spirits of our loved ones in many forms, all around us. Our perception of the spirit world as a natural part of everyday life has shut down because we do not revere our dead, and make them a part of the life of the living.

By understanding and working with a wide range of ancestors, we reestablish something lost for the majority of humans in Western civilization, and thereby provide a stronger foundation for other humans in mystical traditions to reach out across the lines of race, to deepen the connective spirit force between humanity and the animals, plants, minerals, faeries, angels and gods. But if our own house is not in order, if our own tribe is not firmly connected here and on the other side, we cannot properly join with the other creatures of the beautiful garden of the gods.

Like the points of the pentagram, I envision five points of ancestry. The pentagram is a sign of incarnation and excarnation. One enters from spirit into flesh by the five limbs of the human body – two arms, two legs and a head. Likewise it is through the body, the same gate, we exit to return back to the spirit world. They say that a birth in the physical is like a death in the spirit world, as the root of your consciousness shifts location. And a death in the physical world is like a birth, or perhaps rebirth, in the spirit world. This truth is hinted at when one looks at old grimoire diagrams of the pentagram and human form. Each type of ancestor we can experience is like a point in the pentagram, a limb of the greater human family that centers around each of us.

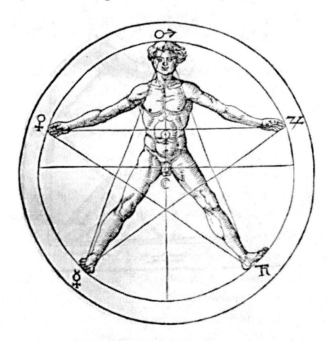

Fig. 3: Pentacle with Human Form

Each of these five forms connects us specifically with one of the three souls found in some Witchcraft traditions. Though the purpose of the three souls and their relationship to the Mighty Dead will be explored fully in Chapter Five, it can be helpful to start our understanding of the three souls, or three selves, in relationship to our various ancestral connections. In their most simple descriptions, the three souls can be described as the Higher Soul or Higher Self, the Lower Soul or Lower Self, and the Middle Soul or Middle Self. They are really the soul, spirit, and personal awareness, respectively.

The Lower Soul is more animalistic and instinctive, and relates to clans, intuition, and unconscious body awareness. The Middle Self is the personality and individual identity. The Higher Self has a more global and universal awareness. Many equate them with the Freudian psychological terms of the Id and Ego and Super Ego, but mystics find those interpretations somewhat limiting as they are more multidimensional than pure psychological terms would indicate.

ANCESTORS OF FLESH AND BLOOD: GENETIC KIN

The spirits who are genetically connected to you are the Ancestors of Flesh, also considered the Ancestors of Blood, or combined as the Ancestors of Flesh and Blood. Some traditions of reverence focus on the matriarchal lineage, also known as the distaff line, because the mothers, grandmothers and great grandmothers are known without a doubt as compared to fathers. The distaff line, referring to a spinning tool often culturally associated with women, is often recited in specific rituals to form a deeper bond with the ancestors of the mother. Our mitochondrial DNA is traced through our mother's genetics, giving us a sense of our global genetic connections. If at all possible, get your mitochondrial DNA tested and traced. Your connections might surprise you, showing how small our global family is, and how far out it reaches.

While matriarchal lines are important, as some believe the distaff is represented in Witchcraft art like a wand, misunderstood as phallic, one should not forget the ancestors known and unknown on the paternal side of the family. The paternal line is sometimes known as the spear or sword line, due to the masculine nature of these tools.

Exercise: Distaff and Spear Lines

Start by doing some family research. Make a family tree. Use whatever resources you have available, but whenever possible interview and record the stories of living family. My family has members write out a book about their childhood memories, relatives, and stories, which is then given as a gift at Samhain to the children, often adult children, of the family.

When you have enough research done, make a list of all your maternal ancestors you can trace. Then do the same for your paternal ancestors. Practice ritually reciting them, like a chant, in whatever way you feel is correct. You can include last names, but don't have to. It's the power of the chain, the links and the remembrance, that is important here. You can use this in future ritual to evoke, conjure, and work with the ancestors of blood.

Due to the tribal nature of our genetic culture, these ancestors connect best through the Lower Self. Through them we inherit our talents, and our difficulties. Many believe we inherit both genetically and energetically from our ancestors, and it becomes our duty to heal what we inherit. As we do, we change at the very least the energy of our DNA, if not as some believe our very DNA, and it heals both forward and backward in time. We are said to redeem them.

The idea rubs many, particularly Americans, the wrong way. They feel they are entirely independent from the actions of their parents and family and should have no blame or responsibility regarding their actions. It's a fundamental misunderstanding and a desire to not accept blame or responsibility. The teaching is not personal. You are not personally responsible, but this is the situation and how you handle the situation you are given is the measure of your responsibility. Like it or not, we all don't start with an equal and fair chance. We simply get a life. Some start with resources, be it financial, emotional, spiritual or mental. Some come into a family with disadvantage, abuse or illness. It's not fair. We can blame karma, environment, genetics and family, but it's not about assigning blame in a personal way. It is simply the reality. The Norse concept of fate, of wyrd, includes the momentum of actions taken before you, by your family, clan and society. You can change the momentum of fate by changing your actions, but some momentum, good or ill, is stronger than others and requires more work. Much like a president who inherits a country's situation, the circumstances are not his fault, nor does he get a "do over" and start again. He must deal with the reality of the situation. It's the job he signed up for, even if it turned out to be different than he thought. Spiritually, our life, whatever it is, is the "job" we signed up for by incarnating.

I know many who undergo great spiritual transformations, and in turn, catalyze their parents and siblings, even if they are not in an active relationship with these family members. In American tribal traditions, the idea extends to seven generations forward and backward, and one living in this wisdom is said to contemplate every action in terms of its result in seven generations.

If we were that forward looking, thinking, and acting, perhaps many of our current circumstances would be different, and now is the time to change, to think in that way, for the seven generations to come.

Exercise: Inheritance

Contemplate your genetic family for a time. Think about their skills and talents. Think about their challenges and outright troubles. Include everything, from the spiritual down to illness and issues with career. When you look truly at yourself, which do you think you also carry? Make a list of what you inherit from your family, particularly your parents and grandparents, as they say it often skips a generation. Look in terms of spiritual views and challenges, mental patterns, emotions, artistic, mental and even psychic talents, physical aptitudes, illnesses and patterns of employment, responses to conflict and phobias. Is it possible to have more compassion for your family when you see more of yourself truly within them and vice versa?

Some will complain that these exercises cannot be done by those adopted, and this is true. While the techniques tend to focus on issues that are specific to blood relatives, they can be adapted to those other groups, such as adopted kinfolk of the milk line of ancestry described below. Also one can perform meditations to connect with the energy and ideas of the blood line, even if no names are known. Such meditations can still intuitively yield what you have inherited from the blood, as it will be remarkably different than those traits, skills and challenges held by the milk line.

ANCESTORS OF MILK AND HONEY: ADOPTED KIN

If our ancestors of genetic connection are known as the Blood Line to some, then our ancestors of our chosen family are called the Milk Line, as they are our adopted kin, or those who have adopted us. The Ancestors of Milk, or Ancestors of Milk and Honey, are those who nourish us, adopt us and treat us like family. I first learned about looking at adopted kin as Milk Line ancestors through the work of author and Celtic shaman Tom Cowan.

Many of us who walk the path of magick are outcast. We do not fit in well with our blood family. Often our strongest relationship with our genetic family is after their physical death, when our connection can be redeemed through our actions. While growing up and living our lives, we must choose our own family. We make our own family, through friends and community, not blood. While blood can give us life initially, like our genetic family, it does not nurture us. Like a small child, we need to be nourished by milk of the loving mother or one who can provide it. It is the milk that keeps us alive, nourishes us and strengthens us to be in the world. Only with this spiritual milk can we grow strong enough to fulfill our purpose in the world.

Exercise: Who and What Nourishes You?

Make a list of all the people who are not blood family who you consider family in your life, living and dead. Who has personally nourished you, and who have you have nourished? What kind of nourishment did they give you? Understand who supports your life and existence in the world, your own mission, beyond your blood kin.

This milk helps shape us in many ways just as much as our genetic heritage does. Many of us realize the issues of nature vs. nurture are equally important, but in different ways. The nurturing we get, and the nurturing we seek out and create for ourselves, is critical in shaping our personality, ethics, morals, behaviors and health. Finding our own nourishment is one of the first acts of self-empowerment and stepping out of victimhood when we do not receive what we need from our genetic family.

Those who are adopted into a family know how powerful adopted family is in shaping the self. In such ritualized adoptions, rather than much of the informal family of friends many of us create, be it a civil legal ritual, or the spiritual adoptions of native rituals, one inherits the whole line of milk ancestry, not just the ones you know personally. In such cases, you would have your own "distaff" and "spear" lines of milk.

Exercise: Recitation of the Milk Line

Repeat the exercise on the Distaff and Spear Lines, but this time, with your adopted family if you should have it. If you are not legally or spiritually adopted, still make a list of names to use ritually from the previous exercise on "Who and What Nourishes You?" Whose family from that list also supports you, even if it is indirectly? Add them to the list. See the web of interconnectivity in which you participate.

There has been a larger movement in Neo-Paganism and a variety of alternative cultures of tribalism, neo-tribalism, or clanism. While I understand the sentiment, sometimes it concerns me as I see the larger ethnic clanism as a source of much difficulty in this world, particularly in the Middle East, and contrary to the Aquarian movement of the next age. Ideally we need to expand our consciousness to think of all of humanity as a part of our greater familial tribe, and not replace genetic biases with chosen societal or religious traits.

While the Milk Line can at first seem like a type of spiritual tribe or clan, as it involves those we have chosen into our immediate "tribe" or familial network, the key to understanding the milk line is in the nourishment and care taking. It's not just a group of people who have something in common, but those who behave as family towards each other. Many throw around the terms "tribe" and "clan" without looking at the deeper responsibilities of it and have an idealized romanticism about the topic.

In terms of the three selves, any of them can be our link to our Ancestors of Milk. They can include those with whom we do share some cultural or ethnic characteristics, if not outright blood. Many ethnic communities do keep that "take care of our own" attitude. Most are those we forge in this lifetime, through the Middle Self, through shared real world experiences and direct communication. Some are from past life incarnations that are not related to our current bloodlines. The global past life connections can play out in the need to take the role of parent, child, sibling or other family relationship, because that is the familiar relationship between those two people through the Higher Self.

It is important to note that many of our bloodlines take on the qualities of the milk line when raising us. One can say that anyone can be a parent, but it takes that loving connection to be a Mom or Dad. But for the purposes of these exercises in this text, the divine line is the genetic or non-genetic connection.

Milk is associated with the blessings of paradise, as the paradise realm of the dead is called the Land of Milk and Honey. Originally it was a biblical reference to the land of Israel in the Old Testament, and referred to the rich agricultural resources promised to the Israelites by Yahweh. It has been adopted into many cultures, including Neo-Paganism, to reference the Summerlands of the dead. Milk and honey are two great blessings, two great nourishments from nature that require human hands to obtain. Rather than just being picked off the tree casually like fruits or nuts, one must ideally raise the cows, nourishing them, and keep the bees, cultivating them. Both reference the level of care needed, just as those of the Milk Line of ancestors care for us, and we care for them. Unlike blood, it is not an automatic connection.

ANCESTORS OF SKIN AND BONE: LAND KIN

The Ancestors of Skin and Bone, or simply the Ancestors of Bone, are the ancestors of place, those who have lived, and those who have died where we reside. Sometimes they are our

Ancestors of Blood and Milk, but our link of bone is through what they leave behind in the land, becoming part of the genus loci, the spirit of the land. These ancestors are connected to the land through the virtue of leaving their matter in the land. When alive, their bodily fluids, waste, flaked skin cells, cut hair and nails end up in the land. As they break down, they become part of the land itself. You have contributed to the land everywhere you have lived and everywhere you have been. This is why these are the ancestors associated with skin. In death, the body is returned to the Earth, and the bones are the last part of the body to break down. Even in cremation, the body is calcinated, burned down to "bone" or white powder, and returned to the land when the ashes are scattered.

The ancestors of place contribute to the spiritual power of a location, and when you are attuned to a place, you attune to these ancestors. You are attuned in some fashion to the ancestors of place where you are born, and many traditions suggest you keep a stone from your homeland with you wherever you travel, as a ritual tool to keep that connection.

You also attune to the Ancestors of Bone where you live. This attunement is becoming harder in the modern era as current embalming methods slow down the return of the body to the Earth, though the energy of the body will still radiate out into the land and gravesite. The fact that most of our food is no longer locally grown prevents us from drawing upon the energy of the place and its associated ancestors. When fruits and vegetables were grown more locally, and animal products were consumed that were raised locally who were fed upon local grains and grass, we attuned to the ancestors of place much more easily. The strange by-product of the globalization of food has become an attunement to the wider web of ancestry from many different places, though the attunement is not to the land where you live, so it's not as strong.

Exercise: Community Research

Learn about the people of your land. Learn about the history of your community through its people—its great citizens, leaders, artists, colorful personalities and eccentrics. What, if any, native people lived in your area, whatever "native" means for your area? We have layers of bone ancestors, all on top of each other. It adds interesting contrast to our spiritual work.

Being a lifelong resident of New Hampshire, and born just over the border on the Massachusetts state line, I have access to New Hampshire's history as one of the original colonies, and its revolutionary war history. Beyond that, the Penacook and Abenaki were found in New Hampshire. Where I've resided was more likely a part of the Penacook tribal areas, along with parts of Massachusetts. They were one of the first tribes to encounter English colonists, and they no longer exist as a separate tribe, having been hunted down by the British with survivors joining other tribes to the North and West of their home area in the Merrimack Valley area. In my own magickal explorations of the ancestors of land, I have encountered warriors and medicine people I can only guess were part of this tribe, or some earlier tribe settlement.

It is through the personal, Middle Self, that one connects with the Ancestors of Skin and Bone, for the personal self is the one who decides to live or stay in a location. The material components of the body are of the personal self, and the land is the Middle World, between the heavenly world and the underworld. Ancestors of Skin and Bone are most likely to help us with issues of the Middle World. They are particularly concerned with issues of the community around them.

Exercise: Grave Exploration

Seek out the graveyards where you live and work. Look around. Listen. See whose grave might call to you. A powerful technique to commune with the spirits associated with the grave is to meditate upon the grave by placing your athame point down into the grave, and drawing up the energy-intelligence of the grave. Through the blade and handle, you will commune with the spirit, but I have to warn you it can be an intimate and sometimes overwhelming experience.

If possible, do any research on the grave, the ancestor, in question. With modern internet resources, it's becoming easier to do such research. Try to find why there might be a resonance between you and that passed ancestor. Why do their bones resonate with yours? In Chapter Four, you'll learn more about how to work with the ancestors through graveyard magick.

Bones are associated with the planet Saturn, the planet of karma, of consequence and wisdom earned through the past. It is the planet of contraction, calcification and crystallization. In fact, along with bones, all the connective tissues and dense proteins are ruled by Saturn. All are forms of manifestation, like the bones, though the bones provide the structure for all else to follow. The skeleton is the frame around which the body hangs. Through the bones, the wisdom is saved and disseminated to the land. From the bones, our blood comes. Through the bones, we can seek these mysteries and wisdoms.

ANCESTORS OF BREATH AND BREAD: STORY KIN

Ancestors of Breath and Bread is a term I use for those departed souls we feel a kinship with due to profession or vocation, art, or interests. They are inspirations to us on our life's path, though they do not share a religious connection. But these people are sustained by the same things that sustain us, our metaphoric breath of life, or bread of life, and that forms a link between us, at least for us among the living. We usually connect to such people through our Higher Self connections, as it's a more global, worldly and less personal connection to them, rather than through blood, or place, the lower and middle selves respectively. There are ancestors from what teacher Tom Cowan calls our Story Line, those who share a similar story, a similar background.

Single mothers might find inspiration in the strong willed, high spirited single mothers of past times, and find an ancestral contact. Professional might feel the inspiration of past successful members of their profession guiding them. Queer, or GLBTQ (Gay Lesbian Bisexual Transgendered Questioning), people will seek out other queer ancestors, particularly those in ancient history, to show their continued presence, or more modern figures fighting for social justice. In fact, a whole movement has begun with the ancestors of Men Who Love Men, due to the work of Andrew Ramer in his poetic book *Two Flutes Playing*. Artists and writers tend to gravitate towards the artists and writers that inspire them, or share similar themes and backgrounds. Musicians tend to flock to past musicians for inspiration.

When I was in college for music, and studying Witchcraft, I made a strong bond to a particular musician who had recently died due to complications from a heroin overdose, Andrew Wood, the singer of a Seattle grunge band called Mother Love Bone. While I loved his music, I strangely felt his spirit guiding me in situations where drugs could get out of hand for me, guiding me out of more dangerous situations. Perhaps I just thought of him in those situations and decided I did not want to die at age twenty-four as he did. Later, as I delved deeper into Witchcraft and the ancestral work associated with it, on a visit to Seattle, I found his grave and had a profound connection with him directly, and he's been on my ancestral altar ever since. While we did not know each other in life, and probably never would have crossed paths, his consciousness directly and indirectly affected mine. We played similar music and liked similar influences. He died when I was seventeen, so we were only seven years apart. It was a profound connection to the Ancestors of Story, of Breath and Bread, as much of the same things sustained us. Today, I feel a strong connection to many authors and occultists, though they might have more cross over in the last type of ancestor, the Ancestors of Spirit.

Exercise: Influences

Review your life and take note of anyone who has passed that you feel has shaped your life or influenced you that is an Ancestor of Story. Who and what inspired your current vocation or hobbies? Who passionately moves you? Who is sustained by what sustains you, and whose work has offered guidance and inspiration as well? Make a list and ponder these potential ancestors of bread and breath.

ANCESTORS OF SPIRIT AND SOUL: PATH KIN

The Ancestors of Spirit are those who walk the same path as we do, more or less. While everyone's path is unique, many of us walk what authors Raven Grimassi and Stephanie Taylor call the Well Worn Path. Referring specifically to Witchcraft, it is the path our Witchcraft ancestors have walked before us, and when we reach a certain point, we blaze a trail upon the Hidden Path. As more make their way upon this secret road, it becomes a bit more worn, guiding those who would come after us.

Those who walk a general spiritual path or tradition as you do can be considered Path Kin, as well as those from a specific spiritual body that you belong. For example, one who is Catholic can look at the entire Catholic Church, and all past members, as spiritual kin, and specifically can feel a connection the members of the local parish who have departed. Likewise, a Witch can feel kinship with the ancestors of all Witchcraft, or those from a specific tradition that Witch is initiated into, such as the Alexandrian line. Those sharing a specific tradition have a stronger lineage bond, particularly those sharing a magickal tradition.

Some Path Kin are closer to the Mighty Dead than others. Those who were magickal adepts in past lives can cross in a more aware state of consciousness, albeit not enlightenment. Here an adept refers to one of higher magickal knowledge and spiritual development, yet below what we think of as the bodhisattvas, saints or Mighty Dead. They become better guides and allies to us, often healers and what are known as a type of Inner World or Inner Plane Contact. Many of the modern occult personalities of the twentieth century present as Inner Plane contacts to their spiritual descendants, such as Dion Fortune. Priests and Priestesses of ancient temples and traditions will remain discarnate, and seek out living magicians to act as conduits for their wisdom and teachings. They can pass threads of knowledge and power to the living, but have their own unfinished business, biases and personal karma to balance. Sometimes even living adepts residing in the past can project themselves into the future and act as inner world guides for us today.

Path Kin can refer to those who are not sharing a terrestrial bond, but a spiritual bond, through what many call the Soul Group, Soul Family, or Soul Tribe. They are a collection of entities incarnating together in various places and times, through the Higher Self as a global incarnation, sharing experiences, lessons, and life. Some Witchcraft traditions refer to this as a Blood Line, not referring to genetic connections, but the Witch Blood, the blood crystallized with light and fire. Other traditions have similar concepts. Theosophically-inclined groups refer to the collective as a monad, extending our souls and personalities into the world. House Kheperu, a Psychic Vampire tradition, also works in the modality of incarnating soul groups. One can think of such groups as the spiritual tribe.

Exercise: Soul Groups and Path Kin

Take this time to think about those who have walked the Well Worn Path before you. Are there any famous or not so famous Witches you know that you have no other link to beyond your spiritual path that you feel are an influence and guide now? Then think about those in your life today with whom you have a strong spiritual bond. You might not share a religious background, but you certainly share a life path together. With these thoughts of soul groups, who do you think in your life could be a part of your soul group? They might also be a part of your blood family, milk line, community or story line. Does the bond go deeper? Do they feel the same way about you? And have any of these figures passed from this world, leaving you here? Do you ever have spiritual contact from them, visitations?

The Mighty Dead can possibly be a part of any of these ancestors, but usually are connected to us through tradition or soul. As modern genetic research proves, all of us are connected via a handful of human families, and can in the end, all be considered ancestors of Flesh and Blood, all a part of the human family. We are all connected in many ways. One race. One planet. One shared collective history. All on the path of spiritual evolution whether we realize it or not. Many different expressions of one.

Only through a true knowledge of our own links can we fulfill our part in the Great Chain of Being. This is originally seen in the classic era as a ladder or vertical hierarchy connecting "God" to the other orders of being. Most often depicted in a Christian context, the basic structure influenced many metaphysical teachings, including alchemy, which sought to change status within the order, transmuting lead into gold. The origin of this concept might come from the eighth song of the *Iliad*, as translated by Samuel Butler, where Zeus says:

Gods, try me and find out for yourselves. Hang for me a golden chain from heaven, and lay hold of it all of you, gods and goddesses together – tug as you will, you will not drag Jove the supreme counselor from heaven to earth; but were I to pull at it myself I should draw you up with earth and sea into the bargain, then would I bind the chain about some pinnacle of Olympus, and leave you all dangling in the mid firmament. So far am I above all others either of gods or men.

This chain was later interpreted not only as the chain of creation, but the chain of initiates. Those who partake in the knowledge of the chain are then influenced by the higher virtues of the gods and spirits of heaven. As we become more conscious of the chain, we move all things towards heaven, or perfection.

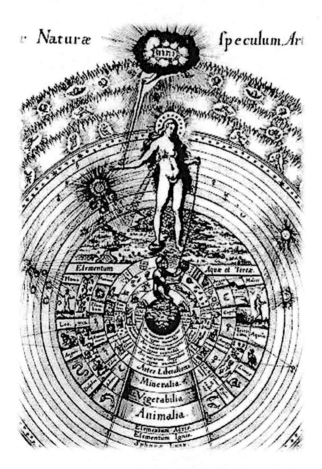

Fig. 4: The Great Chain of Being

In the Aquarian Age, we must re-envision non-hierarchical models of connection, making ladders into loops, into a woven tapestry, as we all work together to turn the Machinery of the Universe, the cogs of spirit, flesh, light, time, space and matter to keep the web alive.

CHAPTER FOUR
WORKING WITH THE
UNSANCTIFIED DEAD

According to some traditions, one does not approach the sanctified dead unless one has already established communion with more traditional ancestral contacts. As Gardner said, one must be introduced to the Mighty Dead. In fact, the dead were often the first spiritual contacts of an individual, before the more cosmic gods. The blood relatives cared about you first and foremost, for they lived on through you. Like good family, they care for your wellbeing, and act as intermediaries between the world of flesh and the world of spirits for you. Many of us today, even the non-magickally inclined, at least initially, still report a feeling of presence, guidance or protection from a deceased loved one. It's a memory of these teachings still operating, even though our current society does not exactly encourage them.

For others, the ancestors of blood do not play the same role of importance compared to the sanctified dead. The sanctified dead, such as the saints in Catholicism, are the intermediaries between the people and the Trinity of God the Father, Jesus Christ the Son and the Holy Spirit. Simple humans are not given much supernatural power just through death, while in many tribal cultures, the distinction between sanctified or deified and unsanctified dead is unimportant. All are with the spirits now. While the focus of this chapter is on the ancestors in general, not the Mighty Dead, the techniques can be used for any ancestral contact.

NECROMANCY

The name for magick with the dead is necromancy. Technically necromancy means "divination with the dead," but over time its meaning has expanded to include many different forms of magick. While due to the popularization of seemingly horrific images from television and literature, some of which do have a historic truth, there are a lot of misunderstandings around the necromantic arts. When I teach a workshop and mention necromancy in passing, without a detailed explanation, I find myself greeted with horrified looks. People assume it is about grave robbing, zombies and the use of cadavers in potions and spells. While there is history to all those practices, any communication with the dead can be considered necromancy. A spiritualist minister or psychic who communicates with those who have passed is technically a practitioner of necromancy. No skull or bones needed. Popular and "wholesome" appearing television psychics who work with passed loved ones are indeed necromancers, even though they wouldn't identify with the word.

Witchcraft in its most classic form has far more to do with the dead than most modern Witches would suspect. While today we equate Witchcraft as an agrarian cult of fertility, it is really a cult of death and resurrection, life and death, not just life. Early historic references to figures that are translated to "witch" were necromancers. In fact, most associations with ancient Witches usually fall under the categories of herbal magicians who could cure or kill; seers, psychics, and visionaries; and spirit workers, particularly spirit workers with the dead.

Early Greek Witches and later Roman ones are associated with graves and summoning spirits. One of the oldest references to Witches in *The Bible*, the Witch of Endor, was technically a necromancer. The deities of Witches are often the gods of the underworld, of spirits or of gateways. Hecate is associated with the wandering spirits of the dead at the crossroads. The Morrighan is queen of phantoms. Osiris is lord of the dead in Duat. The image of the necromancer survives into the Christian period of Europe, when Christian ceremonial magicians, such as John Dee, were often considered "Witches" by the populace due to their necromantic activities.

Fig. 5: John Dee Summoning a Spirit

Technically getting any helpful information, but particularly if it's about the future, is considered necromancy. The idea was that the dead, in the realm of the dead, are beyond the bounds of space and time. Today we might say that the underworld is a matrix for what will happen. Our ideal patterns, from a shamanic cosmology, start in the Upper World, in the perfected pattern of the heavens. Like light and rain, they descend and penetrate the ground, nourishing the seeds of things to come, which then form roots and "sprout" as a physical reality. Or from an occultist perspective, things form on the astral plane first, before they manifest in the physical world.

Good psychics can see patterns on the astral and predict their outcome through the reading of symbols. If you cannot perceive the patterns yourself, you can get similar information by speaking to someone who can. Those who reside on the astral plane, or pass freely through, are also those who reside in the underworld. From this unique perspective, they can see into the past, present, and future, and give us information. But their interpretation can be flawed as a human's interpretation, so particular spirit contacts might be better at certain kinds of information than others. Often a spirit will be good in death with topics they were good with in life. They will be able to interpret that information better than most. You seek out the spirit of a banker or investor for investment advice, or the spirit of a healer, for medical advice. The spirits of Witches and magicians are best for many tasks that fall under the category of magick, just as Witches today might use psychic gifts for investment advice, medical advice, or spiritual advice.

ANCESTRAL REVERENCE

Necromancy most likely grew out of ancient ancestor reverence, creating specialized techniques for those talented at communicating with the dead. In modern cultures today with a Stone Age ancestral reverence tradition, we see that this work is not limited to the necromancers, but a family tradition. The ancestors of a family served as its guardian spirits, particularly as families remained in one home for multiple generations. In the ancient traditions of Sumer and Africa, ancestors were buried in household land, the concept of the house spirit, or genus loci of your home, and your ancestral spirits, together as one.

Today we are less connected to our ancestry. We do not know our family more than a few generations. We move frequently and have no connection to place. Those in the United States have an amalgam of cultures, and I think that can be exciting, but there is also a tendency to lose root cultures. I know my own family lost a lot of its cuisine, music, language, and magick to become more "American" and less ethnic.

This disconnection changes us, and some would say on a fundamental biochemical level. To reconnect with the ancestors, to experience what R.J. Stewart writes about in his classic book, *Underworld Initiation,* is to create a fundamental shift, biological and spiritual. At first, this reconnection can be intensely purgative, as we connect to not only the bliss of our people, but also to the traumas and problems, disasters, migrations, plagues, famines, prejudices and spiritual wounds. We carry them in our blood, and may have no idea they are affecting us. We then sift through layers of memories and knowledge from our history, even back into the dawn of civilization. We sift through thoughts, feelings and desires that might not be our own, but still affect us. As we heal, they heal. As they heal, we heal, and finally in relationship, we receive knowledge, talents and powers for the betterment of both.

To make the commitment to reconnect with our ancestors through magickal means, through the methods of ritual technology, is no easy task. It certainly starts out easy when perhaps compared to other methods of psychic and magickal development, but like maintaining relationships with your family in flesh and blood, it takes work. It takes commitment. You cannot start and then stop and abandon them again. While ancestral reverence can be found in every culture in some shape or form, much of what influenced the modern Witch today comes from powerful, living traditions of reverence, particularly those touched by the African diaspora. Voodoo, both Haitian and New Orleans, Santeria, Ifa and even the folk magick of Hoodoo contribute to our understanding. Some modern Pagans have learned traditions of ancestral reverence in Stregheria, or Italian Witchcraft. Others have explored the traditions of the Celts and Norse. Those influenced by historic re-constructionism usually have a greater reverence for the ancestors, but even in the fertility traditions of British Wicca, we have the highest holy day reserved for the dead, Samhain or Halloween.

Ancestral work restores the balance to the lines of life, rectifying the fairly recent split between our people and our past and the spirits acting as intermediaries. Doing this work redeems those ancestors who are out of balance. It gives them an opportunity to "work" to bring balance to their consciousness. As we explore the anatomy of the soul, we'll discover how different parts of the self are contacted through different means, and have their own "work" to do. Your offerings make the relationship reciprocal.

Some will not be ready for this work. Culturally their consciousness was not prepared for it. Few of us think that we'll be helping others when we die. Some are ill, or injured in life, and while death can heal such things and is beyond the bound of time and space, in some practitioners' experience, my own included, there are different passages of time, but it doesn't mean instantaneous healing. If someone was violent, crazy, or predisposed to hurt you in life, death doesn't mean they suddenly become enlightened. They will most likely still be that way if you commune with them through ancestral magick. Though over time, your own work and the work with other ancestors can trickle to them and change them. I had an uncle who died while we were on bad terms, by his choice. I didn't even think to put him on my ancestral altar. But through a psychic friend who named and described him, he let me know he wanted to be included and wanted to help me in my life, and we've developed a good relationship since, both forgiving each other. Still it was many years after his death, and the situation was not that difficult compared to lifelong mental illness, abuse, or trauma. In those cases, leave such ancestors alone until you get a sign to work with them.

Those that are worked with well are powerful allies for you and the entire family, and some, who go beyond the reach of any one family, might transform their status. In the Voodoo traditions, it's believed that some spirits become intermediaries like the lwa spirits. Are they like the Mighty Dead to the Witches? I'm not sure. Lwa and orisha, while they share qualities with ancestors, are considered a different order of being, though they serve some similar characteristics. While the Masters are often impersonal and group consciousness oriented, the lwa are highly individualistic. But I do believe the reverence of the ancestors helps elevate them towards their own evolution and enlightenment. We help the dead while we are alive in hopes that the living will help us along our next journey when we pass, continuing the great chain of spirit.

WORKING WITH THE SPIRITS OF THE DEAD

The following are techniques for working with the spirits of the dead can be applied in ancestral reverence and in necromancy. Necromancy implies a professionalism and detachment, as the spirits are not personally connected to the necromancer. It is a business arrangement. Some necromantic rituals are done through force, fear or deception of the spirits. That is not the magick I choose to practice, though I admit it can work. Ancestral reverence implies a certain level of fidelity, love and connection, though with the wide range of non-blood ancestors we can work with, in the modern age it can be helpful to look at the entire human family as our ancestors and work for the evolution of all through those whom call out to us.

The following techniques I've found helpful in working with the spirits of those who have gone before.

Ancestral Altars and Shrines

While the terms altar and shrine are used by some synonymously, for the purposes of this work, we shall divide the two into similar, but distinct practices. Ancestral altars are collective workplaces for all of your ancestors, or any of the dead you honor from the various categories. Shrines are for specific ancestors, usually for a short time after death, and are integrated into the greater altar after an appropriate period of time. Shrines help give support to the recently deceased to make a peaceful transition, giving energy and focus to their journey. Altars are places where magickal reverence and work is performed with the ancestors themselves.

To build a shrine after the loved one passes, cover a flat surface with a white cloth. Place a stone to represent the ancestral link, usually white and round, along with a clear glass of water and a constant source of light. Traditionally a seven day candle is used, though many modern practitioners of African diasporic traditions use an electric "candle light" imitating a candle with battery or wall current. Other relics and offerings (See Below) can be placed upon the altar. The shrine is kept for at least three days and up to nine. It is a place for loved ones to talk, remember, share stories, and air grievances and things left unsaid. Regular offerings, as well as love and blessings, help empower the dead to fully cross over in peace. More than one shrine can be made to the deceased. In fact anyone who wants to help with this ancestor can make the shrine just after their passing.

At the end of the period of three or nine days, the ancestral shrine is taken apart and added to the main ancestral altar, for all of the household or temple dead. The ancestral altar is also traditionally covered with a white cloth, though some Witches favor black. If an Ancestor List or book is kept on the altar, add the new name to the list. The stone is added to a box or bowl of stones, one for each ancestor. Offerings are made.

At the ancestor altar you can meditate on the ancestors in vision, speak to them aloud, and ask for help or blessings. Spells asking for the ancestors' aid or protection can be done at the ancestor altar.

Relics

Technically a relic is the preserved remains of someone which is venerated, particularly in the case of a saint or bodhisattva. Many Christian churches required a saintly relic to sanctify the Church. A powerful temple in Sri Lanka, the Temple of the Tooth, is built around the relic of a tooth, believed to belong to the Buddha, with the magickal powers to control the weather. In the ancient world, the body was preserved, such as the mummies in Egypt, but the mummies were not meant to be displayed as they are today in museums, as objects of study or even veneration. But the process of mummification gives an anchor for the spirit to return to the world. To this day in Vietnam, there is a process of exhuming bodies after three years in the grave and ceremonially washing the now black bones and arranging them in a new "home" box to create a powerful spirit home for the ancestor to continue to guide the family as the box is brought home. Some intermediaries in the ancient world volunteer for mummification as "sleepers" in the land. Those who cannot use mummies can use statues and idols. Physical features help the spirit remember and reconnect to its earthly form. Some relics are items held by that saint, such as a shroud, robe or other tool.

For our purposes here, it is the remains of someone's life that creates a link to the energy of that ancestor. Life relics can include pictures, jewelry and other personal objects the deceased owned, notes or letters handwritten by the deceased and even cremated remains, such as an urn of ash. Anything with sentiment that can form a link to the deceased is helpful. Such relics are placed upon the ancestor's shrine, and then integrated if possible into the ancestral altar. With jewelry in particular, if you wish to work with a specific ancestor, wearing the jewelry or keeping it in your pocket will help. Never place the photos of the living on the ancestral altar.

Offerings

Offerings are the method by which we feed our dead. Many think this is silly and superstitious. They are dead. Why do they need to be fed? It's not so much they need physical sustenance, but the spiritual link between us needs to be strengthened, and the offerings made with proper intent help nourish that link. While intent alone can help, certain substances provide a physical anchor and their inherent vibrations are traditionally nourishing and strengthening to the spirits of the deceased. The links of communication close down if they are not fed properly. Ghosts and other spirits can survive if fed. Most ghosts are fed by fear.

Regular offerings should be made at the shrine when working with a newly deceased and with the ancestral altar. When doing specific work or asking for help, offerings should also be made, though many are of the mind that you shouldn't feed the dead until they complete the request. Others believe in thanking first, and then asking for favor. Particular holidays are also excellent times to feed the dead, Samhain (Halloween) being first and foremost. While the Neo-Pagan holidays can be times of offering, if there were other important religious times to your family, who for most of us were not Pagan, then make offerings then. I make many offerings on Christmas

Eve, Christmas Day, Easter and even American Thanksgiving. I usually make my ancestral offerings on Saturday, Saturn's day, also a day of the dead.

Offerings vary in different traditions and cultures. In China, "Hell Money" is burned, sending the "credit" represented by paper money to the ancestors in the underworld. Even representations of houses, cars, and other material goods are burned to "send" them to the ancestors.

Reciting stories of your family, their lore, magick, and history, is a way to feed the ancestors. You are giving them attention. When working with the Ancestors of Bread and Breath, reading their poems, playing their music and reciting their books are a way to feed them, creating a contact to deepen your work. Even reading the favorite poem of an Ancestor of Blood is nourishing. I read Gibran's *The Prophet* aloud for my mother on the anniversary of her death.

Traditional offerings include high-energy items such as light, flowers, incense, and food. Things that are rich in power, often rich in calories, are ideal. Favorite foods and drinks of the deceased can be a very specific way of attuning to an ancestor, or family favorite foods are a way to attune to the whole line. In general, the following are considered powerful and effective offerings:

Candles
Pure Water in a clear glass
Flowers
Starchy Food
Favorite Family Foods
Sweets and Candy
Caffeine (Coffee or Tea)
Spirits (Wine, Beer and hard Liquor)
Incense

Temple of Witchcraft co-founder Adam Sartwell has a specific teaching on the meanings and purpose of the offerings. Light, via the candle, is offered for the spirits to see their way in the spirit world and see their own descendants more clearly. It opens the way to communication. Water and bread are to sustain the spirits. They are the basic staples of food. Incense and flowers, scent, are used to encourage their breath and words, so they can communicate more clearly. And alcohol is to enjoy, a blessing passed between us.

Your own ancestor altar can have an arrangement of candles in a pentagram, for the five types of ancestors – blood, milk, place, story and path kin. You can use red, white, green, yellow or blue, and purple candles, respectively. You can also have a sixth candle for the forgotten, unknown, and unnamed dead.

Some say leave offerings out no longer than a day. Others, depending on the nature of the offerings, leave it out for a week. Food I dispose of after 24 hours. Liquids often stay out for a week, changed every Saturday. Offerings are traditionally buried, or left in nature, but many feel that releasing them to the drains, toilet, or garbage is also satisfactory, as they are now devoid of the spiritual substance. I try to pour liquid offerings at the base of a special tree, as well as many food offerings. Some seem more appropriate to dispose of as garbage due to issues with animals and environment. Others find such disposal sacrilege. Do what you feel is best for you.

Graveyard Magick

There is a lot of controversy around graveyard magick, the use of items from graveyards, and leaving things in graveyards, and I think there always has been, back even to the ancient world. One of the names associated with Witchcraft in ancient Greece was goetia, referring to howling or wailing. First it was the mournful cries of grievers, and then those who were like professional grievers in the community, often older women. The wailing became associated with those performing magick in the graveyard, typically through the use of cursing tablets. Eventually goetia became associated with a form of demon magick in the grimoire tradition, from *The Lesser Key of Solomon*. Witches and heretics were associated with graves, and disturbing graves in the Greek and Roman era, for that was a heinous act. It became an accusation, along with child killing. Though there are enough old world references to Witches and necromancy to make us think there is some connection, it's not all propaganda. Likewise we have survivals of such magick in all manner of traditions of magick and Paganism. One can look at most ancient sites associated with Paganism and find grave sites.

Some of these spells require leaving something in a graveyard, usually under the operative belief that the spirits of the graveyard, the deceased, will take the message/energy/intention to the underworld gods, or act as an ally themselves in your magick. You find that with ancient and modern curse tablets, and even in the Hoodoo spell Fiery Wall of Protection, where a spirit is called upon for aid. Other forms of graveyard magick include taking something from the grave, usually dirt or dust. What graveyard dust is is a matter open for debate, I originally learned it was code for herbs, such as mullein and patchouli, both used for spirit work and both somewhat musty smelling. My teachers taught me that Witches did not take anything from graves, and most in the fertility traditions of British Traditional Wicca do not. One respected priestess told me it would be an anathema for those of the fertility cult to do workings in the grave. Others believe it is literally dust from a grave, swept or scraped off a head stone or monument in the grave, soaked up with chthonic energies of the grave and used in general protection spells or for power. I know a coven of Witches who gently scrape on a gravestone in a Salem, Massachusetts graveyard every few years, to refill their supply. Others still, such as Raven Grimassi in *Old World Witchcraft*, refer to plant matter from the trees in the graveyard as the dust, while those in Hoodoo refer to graveyard dirt, as dirt from a specific grave. The type of person determines what that graveyard dirt is used for in magick. Dirt from a doctor or nurse is for healing. Dirt from a lawyer or judge is for legal success. Dirt from a soldier is for protection. Whatever the person was good at in life has seeped out as power into the land around the body. Grave dirt from a loved one can be used for almost anything, and dirt from a Witch or sorcerer will aid you in your magick. Sometimes the name of the family will help in some way that is not obvious. Dirt from the grave of Michael Strong is for strength. Dirt from an Alex Brewer might help with magick for mead and beer making.

Generally one starts graveyard magick by making an offering to the spirits of the grave at the entrance, asking permission to enter, and knocking three times. Also making an offering or libation of liquor at the tallest grave or monument confers the blessing of the guardian spirits of the yard. This will help protect you from restless spirits, hungry ghosts, unwanted energies and other people in the graveyard. Find the appropriate grave and make sure it is still "alive" or energized. Some people know intuitively. Some people ask with a pendulum. But if there is still energy in the grave, you can use it. Some very old graves visited often can have more energy than more recent graves. The graves of the historic can also have more energy due to the nature of their legend surviving. You must "pay" for the dirt by giving a few coins. I know some who give three to nine silver coins, such as Mercury dimes. Others give pennies, as the copper coins were traditionally placed on the eyes. For some, "real" silver and copper are important, and necessitate a trip to the coin collector store, while others are fine with common currency. If you don't have the coins, offerings and libations of food, drink, and flowers can also work. Dirt is usually taken from the head area, heart area, and foot area, dug with your hands or a spoon. Bottle and label the dirt when home, if it's for future use. Give appropriate thanks to all the spirits you have called upon for aid and protection. A final libation at the gate is never a bad idea either.

It's good, if possible, to converse with the spirit, and ask permission and explain why you need help if you are using it for a specific reason. You can use various forms of psychic contact or mediumship (following) to converse and even get advice on how to handle your problem or situation from the deceased. Along with power, they can have wisdom in their area of expertise. It's also good to get graveyard dirt from both sides of your family if possible, for your own ancestor altar. You can put a pinch into charm bags and potions. The first protection potion I learned to make, in the Cabot Tradition of Witchcraft, suggested a pinch of dirt from the grave of someone you admired for their courage.

Mediumship

Mediumship is the direct psychic contact between a spirit and a medium. The technique was seemingly pioneered by the Spiritualist Church, starting with communication via table knocking or rapping, by the controversial Fox Sisters, though the essence of mediumship was really a resurrection of more ancient Pagan oracle traditions where spirits would speak through priestesses or priests in trance. You see it today in the use of oracular seidr practices of the Northern Traditions, where a spirit from Hel, or a deity, will give a message or converse through a priestess on a high chair. Spiritualism gave rise to the popular séances of the Victorian era, where small groups of people would gather to make contact with their loved ones. The techniques of mediumship were adopted by Madame Blavatsky and the Theosophical Society, and made their way into the modern New Age movement. Today mediumship generally refers to speaking with the dead while the term channeling refers to someone who speaks with spirits other than the dead, usually including the Ascended Masters, as well as angels, aliens and discarnate entities of all types. Channeling can also be a confusing term, due to the use of the word in various energy healing systems, whereby the energy is "channeled" by a practitioner. In the teachings here, a channel is essentially a medium for spirits other than the unsanctified dead. In the original movement of British Traditional Wicca, mediumship, or technically channeling, took a role in the Drawing Down the Moon rites, usually by priestesses with previous mediumship experiences, or a natural aptitude for mediumship/channeling, using the techniques to bring forth the spirit of the Goddess. Such work is called by various names, all with slightly different meanings, including drawing down, aspecting, assuming the godform, possession, and invocation.

While the formalities and structures are usually disregarded today for an intuitive approach, old fashioned mediumship usually required two practitioners at a minimum, a "battery" who also acted as an anchor and a "receiver." The receiver was truly the medium, receiving messages from the spirits. The battery practitioner provided the emotional energy to make contact, and acted as the ground – prompting questions, taking notes and ending the session if it got out of hand. The pairing is akin to what goes on within a coven structure in Wicca, with the High Priestess acting as medium/channel and the High Priest guiding and anchoring the process. Sometimes a small group gathered would also act as battery, be it séance or coven. Their heightened emotions provide a fuel for the work. They would gather much like those of Witchcraft and tribal traditions, in a circle holding hands with the right hand over the left hand. At the height of the séance phenomenon, mediums were said to materialize "ectoplasm," an etheric, but visible substance, from which the spirits would manifest apparitions. The substance would often come out of the bodies of the medium. While mediumship has continued onward, the appearance of ectoplasm seems to have fallen out of fashion for the current generation of mediums.

Mediumship and channeling can be divided into two basic categories. The first is known as conscious channeling. The medium is fully aware and present, albeit in a trance, and simply is repeating a message back out loud to the group. Imagine listening to someone on the phone, and repeating back what they say word for word. While this is considered safer, some feel there is more of a chance for ego to get involved, and the message to be misunderstood. The second is known as full body channeling, or possessory channeling. The spirit takes control of the channel's body. The channel is no longer conscious, or at the very least, is not in the "driver's seat" and is simply observing. The spirit takes control of the voice and movement, and communicates directly. This is considered more dangerous, as many spirits don't know how, or don't remember how, to treat a body and could energetically damage it. Some feel it is more accurate as the spirit is acting directly, while others feel the ego is tied up in the body complex, and no matter what, the spirit is still operating out of the ego and mental body of the channel, drawing upon language, memories, symbols, and idioms of the channel. It's a rare case to have a possessed channel speak a language fluently that they have no conscious knowledge of, though it's not unheard of for various foreign phrases to come out.

While working in partnership, group or solitary, enter into a light trance. Use breath, visualization and/or focused concentration. If conducting it ritually, an altar, offerings, candles, incense and music can help set the appropriate tone and mood. But this can also be done spontaneously at home, in graveyards and walking the woods without any tools. Speak in your mind, or out loud, to the spirit. Listen and feel. How do you receive the spirit's answer? Sometimes they appear around loved ones. You can talk to the spirits of a person before you by gazing around and past the person. Traditionally ancestors of the mother's side of the family appear on the left of the person, and father's side of the family on the right. For some with clairaudience skill, they can be very talkative, replacing the inner dialogue with their own communication. Other times, they show images or convey feelings. Some people receive all three. Often large groups of spirits get talkative. It can be helpful to form the image of a podium or microphone stand in your mind's eye, and ask them to come up one at a time. When done, simply thank them. Release any connections you have to them. Get out of the trance state and ground yourself as needed.

One of my most powerful experiences with this work happened at a graveyard, seeking out a deceased rock star, Andrew Wood. I was able to find his grave through a website and went to pay my respects and commune with him. A creative man before the current advances in technology, he was quite communicative about music and song writing, and amazed at how many gadgets there were for music. Part of me expected that with him being dead, he'd have instant access to all information, or at least not care, but he was like a little kid. It was beyond my expectations, and I knew I was not making it up. He "followed" me home, not as an unhealthy attachment, but an ancestral contact. I placed his photo upon my ancestral altar and continue to chat with him. He apparently gets along with my relatives who were also musicians, although he does not always agree with their advice. This went a long way to show me that spirits, just because they are dead, are not all wise or all knowing. They can help but, like people, have their own personal quirks and differences of opinions.

When doing necromantic work and mediumship in the context of Witchcraft, various incenses and tools can help. Holding a wand of wood associated with the dead, particularly Yew, Apple, Willow or Elder can help, though many feel there are prohibitions against harvesting Elder. I knew a very successful medium who would hold a wand of Yew wood when communing with the dead. Apple, Willow and Elder also have faery connections, but the Yew is mostly about the spirits of the graveyard, as its bark is toxic. The following incense, thick with smoke and none too pleasant smelling can help conjure spirits and give them enough etheric presence, akin to ectoplasm in some ways, to facilitate communication.

Incense for the Dead
1 Part Myrrh
2 Parts Mugwort
1 Part Wormwood
1 Part Dandelion Root
1 Part Mullein Leaf
1 Part Patchouli Leaf

Many of these techniques can be combined to have a successful necromantic working. I know one Witch who, when in fear of physical violence, visited her local cemetery, far from her hometown, so it didn't have any relatives for her to call upon. She used intuition to find the grave of a Civil War soldier, and communed with his spirit, and he agreed to help. She gathered graveyard dirt and used it in a protection spell, banishing the person threatening to cause harm. She was quite successful, and being in a Civil War area, she was able to find information on her soldier and verify things he told her about himself, deepening the connection. She still visits to bring offerings and thanks.

I have successfully called upon various deceased famous people for aid. Intentions include help with writing (Dion Fortune), help with financial planning (J.D. Rockefeller), help with music (Andrew Wood), and even help with exercise programs and nutrition (Steve Reeves). I would find someone who had a level of success in the area who was deceased, and use their photo upon my altar. I'd use facts about their life to show respect and recite their story to them, calling upon them. I even visited one grave and got dirt when I was in town. Many online websites will help you find graves in general or of celebrities. Offerings would be made and questions asked. Sometimes it was a general support they could give. Other times I got specific advice via psychic communication. I mentioned them more in daily life and among my students, helping keep their memory alive and vibrant.

Some tips in working successfully with the spirits of the dead are ignored or unknown in modern Paganism. Some believe if they don't believe them or know them, these restrictions have no power, but they seem to be pretty fundamental beliefs with an inherent and internal dynamic going beyond belief, that can help or hinder your magickal intention.

Sulfur

While according to some burning sulfur is supposed to attract noxious spirits of harm and evil, at least in a Christian paradigm, most believe sulfur banishes spirits. Some say it only banishes harmful spirits, while others believe it banishes all. I learned to use matches, having sulfur, when doing magick, though the tradition I worked in was not particularly focused upon working with the dead. I have noticed improvements when not using sulfur or giving it time to dissipate.

Salt

Salt is another prohibition. Many who do all sorts of spirit work, from the dead to plant spirit healing, tend to avoid salt in their diet. For some, that simply means avoiding table salt while others observe a strict low-sodium diet. Salt is said to be pure, and absorb energy, cleansing and clearing it. The thought is the salt absorbs the etheric bodies of the spirits, making it harder for them to manifest.

Quicksilver

If you carry mercury, metallic quicksilver, in a vial upon your person, it will keep the spirits away from you personally, though not interfere with the ritual. If you wish to attend something and observe, but not interact with the spirits, carry quicksilver. Others will carry an iron nail; though iron is particularly good for warding spirits of nature and the faeries, it is not always effective with the dead.

Interestingly, three of these deal with the fundamental symbols of alchemy – sulfur, mercury and salt. I'm sure we'd find other substances with similar associations, but they are the primary ones to be careful of when working with the dead.

Head Coverings

In the African diaspora, when the head is covered, it is a signal to the spirits that you do not wish to be possessed or have direct spirit contact. Covering the crown chakra, usually with a white cloth, helps inhibit their connection to you if you wish to avoid a possession experience.

THE DEAD AT UNREST

The less savory aspect of working with the unsanctified dead is dealing with the dead who are not at rest. Those who died violently or with extremely difficult emotions and unusual circumstances, as well as those souls who are forgotten, can cause difficulty for the living, even those not particularly psychically sensitive. Such spirits can create the circumstances of illness, misfortune and the classic "negative" emotions typically associated with a haunting. They can even be the nexus of portals through which other harmful forces can enter our realm. Witches, shamans and magicians are called upon by others to rectify the situation of imbalance, though the solutions are not always easy. Those most likely to not be at rest would include those in the following categories:

Violent or Shocking Deaths
Murder Victims
Suicide
Premature Death
Criminals
Lost Remains (Death at Sea, Unmarked Grave, Dismembered and Scattered)
Lack of a "Good" Death
Unfinished Business in Life

Such circumstances around these types of death leave the consciousness more likely to linger in the world of the living, or feel bound to the Earth plane, rather than moving onto the next level of development. What trauma is "shocking" to one individual and not to another is really quite variable. Not all who experience any of the above states of death necessarily end up as a ghost, but most ghosts have experienced one of these states.

The vast amount of hauntings I've been called to investigate are not truly trapped Earthbound spirits, but are either the result of what I would call "bad Feng Shui" in the sense they are a buildup of harmful or destructive energy, but not conscious souls. Weird things happen with this energy, making people suspect a haunting, but no haunting is present.

Other hauntings are really echoes of past people, but not fully conscious beings. They are akin to recordings of a trauma that repeat over and over again, sometimes triggered by the strong emotions of those who pass through the area where the psychic recording is etched in the ethers. Such hauntings will be the same figure, repeating the same actions, over and over again, with no variation or interaction with anyone, even a psychic who can clearly see them. They appear to be on "autopilot" as they have no true consciousness to interact with, any more than an audio or video recording does. The recording medium in this case just happens to be the etheric plane.

Most ghostly activity that doesn't fall into the "bad energy" or "recording" categories is usually a "noisy ghost" or what is known as a hungry ghost. They are the shells, the astral bodies, or what we learned of as the Middle Self in the three soul model, of an individual. They are not the true soul as most people think of it, but an astral double, tied to identity, ego and the worldly life, but not the immortal essence that carries on. Most pass on, decaying away as the body decays and no longer sustains life force. Funerary practices that mummify the body prolong the retainment of this shell. Funerary practices that destroy the body, such as cremation, quicken this shells destruction, as it's a lynch pin to the soul complex and prevents the Higher Self from moving on quickly to the next incarnation.

Those with strong personalities can leave strong shells behind that believe they are alive. Such shells, if fed, can survive in the world as spirits. "Good" shells or middle souls, fed by appropriate rituals of a culture, can be guardians of a household, shrine or group of people. The shell's power is in the Middle World, so such entities are particularly helpful to make things happen in the physical, Middle World of our lives. They don't have any more wisdom than they did in life, and have a hard time holding onto new learning or memories. Some gain enough power in life that they don't need to be fed regularly, but attach themselves to a particular area they love, and become one with the land, a guardian spirit in nature. They do not dissipate as most do, but evolve into something else. Those strong personalities that do not get fed through rituals who do not become something else, seek out nourishment from others, and fear is the easiest response to evoke from people. Most hauntings that cause fear are the method by which such spirits are fed. They learn to live off the vital life force shed when someone is afraid, and that sustains them. The more life force they gain from this process, the more powerful they can appear. So a ghost, given lots of attention and fear, can manifest more than one that is ignored or ridiculed.

Such dead can be akin to the Roman concept of larvae, known as the hungry dead, restless dead or forgotten dead. Household spirits and guardians in ancient Rome were known as *lares*, where they were honored by families. They can be considered to be a combination of genus loci for the family home, like the Northern traditions' concepts of the "house elf," protective spirits, and ancestral spirits. Their counterpart, the larvae, were those spirits who were forgotten and unloved. In certain rituals, meals of black beans would be made as offerings, and when necessary they would be chased away by banging pots and pans.

On rare occasions, the haunting will be caused by the higher soul, the immortal spark that is for some reason, attached to a location, person or life in general, and will need genuine help to cross over to the next realm for future incarnation. Despite popular movies to the contrary, these hauntings are much rarer than the previously listed ones .

At one point in our history, the idea of hauntings was deeply entwined with what we might call the undead, or the embodied dead. In the ancient traditions across the world, the concept of the dead returning enfleshed was quite common and stood side by side with the disembodied dead of ghosts, specters and phantasms. The remnants of this tradition gave rise to our tales of vampires, zombies, ghouls and revenants. Rituals binding the dead to their graves, staking the body or severing the head were not uncommon, all designed to prevent the dead from returning embodied. With the rise of the church in Europe, and the popularization of the Christian Heaven/Hell/Purgatory model, along with the dismissal of traditional ancestor reverence, the belief in the disembodied dead, intangible ghosts fearing the fires of hell, arose and gained popularity, and the embodied dead became more and more a thing of folklore and fiction.

The remedies of the dead are found in most magickal cultures and are considered a part of life, much like any societal issue that all cultures deal with, from harvest to sanitation. While unpleasant, they are not always cause for great alarm unless they go unchecked. Here are some of the common remedies:

Cleansing a Space

Often all one needs to do is cleanse a space, spiritually and physically. By shifting the energy of a place, you can make it inhospitable to lingering spirits. The most common method is the modern New Age practice of burning sage. From many Native American traditions, burning sage releases both negative ions and a vibration, an energy that lifts the vibration and spirit of the place where it is burned. Lingering ghosts and unwanted spirits are considered to be of a "lower" vibration. When introducing a higher vibration, the lower vibrations must either match it, or remove themselves from the space, as it is no longer conducive to their nature. Harmful spirits will try to create lower vibration conditions, through fear and anger, to help sustain their presence. Practices such as smudging with sage prevent it. Sage is not the only substance for cleansing, and burning is not the only method. Along with sage, incense smoke from frankincense or frankincense and myrrh, copal, pine, lavender, cinnamon, mugwort and dragon's blood can all be used for cleansing. You can also spritz the same substances from a spray bottle by mixing a few drops of essential oil with water, or a 50/50 water/alcohol solution, for a similar effect. Along with these clearing substances, oils of lemon, lemon grass, orange, geranium, and rose can be quite cleansing. Rather than spraying, floor washes can be made from similar substances, used to spiritually and physically clear. Traditionally one must take the water beyond the bounds of your property line and dump it out into the street. Dumping it in the plumbing or upon your own land keeps the energy there. Non herbal forms of cleansing are rituals envisioning clearing light, such as violet light, burning white candles, burning an alcohol flame with an epsom salt base in a small cauldron or saying prayers.

Cleansing Spirit Flame

4 oz. of 90 Proof or higher Rubbing Alcohol

2 Tablespoons of Epson Salt

5 drops of Lavender Oil

5 drops of Lemon Oil

3 drops of Rosemary Oil

Place the mixture in a small cast iron cauldron with a lid. Place it in the center of the room or home to be cleansed. Put something flameproof beneath it, like a trivet or pan. Throw a match in and let it burn. Direct all the harmful energy going into the flame to be transformed. Let it burn out, or cover the cauldron with a lid after a half hour or so. Dispose of any remains off your property.

Appeasing the Spirits

Rather than making the area inhospitable to the unwanted spirits, some take the concept of making friends with the spirit, or at the very least, peace. The spirits are given appropriate offerings to quiet their unwanted behavior. You have this practice in the ancient world, such as the black bean offerings to the larvae in Rome. In the modern Neo-Pagan Druidic revival, as in the organization Ár nDraíocht Féin (ADF, meaning Our Own Druidism), offerings are made to the "outdwellers" regularly as a part of their liturgy. An outdweller is not necessarily one of the dead, but it is defined as any spirit that might be disruptive to the ritual. So before beginning the bulk of the ritual an offering is made, usually away from the ritual space, to occupy those spirits that could disrupt. Some in Neo-Paganism will make offerings to all the spirits unnamed and forgotten in the ritual space, to keep peace with all that is known and unknown. Typical spirit offerings can be given, though alcohol is avoided, unless one wants to get more disruptions.

Banishing Unwanted Spirits

Banishing spirits is a more aggressive form of cleansing magick. Rather than simply making the environment inhospitable to unwanted spirits, it is the forcible ejection of unwanted spirits from the space. Imagine a nightclub or bar. Turning on the lights and shutting down the bar at the end of the night encourages people to leave on their own. That's like cleansing a space. Calling the bouncer over and pointing at someone to be removed is more like banishing. Simple banishing can use the cleansing techniques with the strong intention to banish harmful spirits. A ritual tool, from an incense stick to a wand or blade, can be used to trace banishing symbols, such as the basic banishing pentagram. The practitioner empowers it with energy by visualizing it in a bright and powerful color, such as a blue, white or violet light. The pentagram is then directed toward the unwanted spirits. If the location of the spirit is not known, they can be drawn in the four cardinal directions. Some would also include the directions above, below and in the center of the space. Psychic energy and intention can be directed at a spirit, to bind it from moving, then a suitable environment can be created. Some will move the spirit to another plane of existence (see *Crossing Over,* following). More aggressive forms of banishment use spirit traps, akin to the djinn in the bottle or lamp. Other spirits, including deities, angels and other guides, can be called upon to forcibly eject an unwanted spirit. When the unwanted spirit is not a fully formed and conscious spirit, but a remnant or echo of a lower spiritual body from one who has passed, then banishment can actually discorporate the remnant.

Fig. 6: Banishing Pentagram

Crossing Over

Crossing over is the process of moving a spirit, unwanted or otherwise, from one plane of existence to another. Generally it is the practice of helping those who are Earthbound to continue onward on the journey to the afterlife realms, however the practitioner might envision it. The best crossing over practices are those that involve communication with the spirit and cooperation to cross over. Some spirits are stuck and want help, or can be convinced it is best for them to cross over. Yet many occultists would argue that not all spirits of the dead wandering the Earth should be forced to cross. If they choose to remain, it's their choice. The only time I disagree is when they are causing violence and trauma, and will not relocate to a location where the trauma will not continue. Simple crossing over practices include simply lighting a white candle and creating a pillar of light, an axis mundi or "cosmic elevator" from the highest of the heavens to the deepest underworlds, where the spirit can find its appropriate vibratory level. Others use a symbol, such as a pentagram or hexagram, to open a gate to the realm of the the dead, in the air like a door, or upon the ground. Other spirits can be called to aid the process, while many call upon ancestors who have successfully crossed to guide the process. Others will call upon angelic beings. In the European Witchcraft traditions, particularly the Teutonic and Celtic, the waning half of the year is "haunted" by the spirits of the Wild Hunt, who gather the forgotten and restless dead in the pack before returning to the realms of the underworld. They rise at Samhain and return either at the Winter Solstice or prior to spring. You can call upon the various "masters" of the hunt for help in crossing over restless spirits.

While the restless dead are a very real occurrence, they do not occur so frequently to cause a major problem for modern practitioners of magick. While the world is populated with a wide variety of spirits, ghosts and echoes of the dead, few prove to be harmful to others. Some seek attention and help and occasionally one will act in fear, anger or malice. It's good to know these skills, but not to dwell upon these circumstances. Simply use them as you need them.

THE FORGOTTEN DEAD

While not quite as difficult as the dead who are truly not at rest, there is an intermediary category of the dead who are considered forgotten and unknown. They have not been venerated or honored, but are not particularly haunting any one place or person. They are often looking for the attention from another, and their energy, to help travel to a better level of awareness in the afterlife. They are eager to help out magicians, Witches and those who simply pray for them. In the Christian traditions, they would be akin to the souls in Purgatory, seeking entrance to heaven by good works in the afterlife that they did not commit in life.

One of the most effect methods of working with them is to call upon them for protection, or to help with the restless dead. They are eager to help. They must be thanked and blessed as a part of the process. That will also help prevent them from attaching to you. If you do not provide them with an energy for the working, they will simply feed on your energy unknowingly.

I had a profound experience with the forgotten dead in New York City, after a shooting at the Empire State Building. I felt their presence all morning, and did not realize that there was major violence until much later. We walked together to the scene of the violence, but it was blocked off by the police. I did feel the Forgotten Dead aid the area, helping "clean" it up psychically.

To the Forgotten Dead
Of the long lost places.
To the Unknown Ones
Who left us no traces.
I ask for your help, your blessing, your boon,
And in return, I shall call on the Moon
To open her gates, to take you away.
Once you are done,
In her heart you will play,
Until you move further,
Or until you return.
To the Forgotten Dead
For you a candle shall burn!

Keep a candle in your ancestral workings for the unknown and forgotten dead. Help them as they help you.

Chapter Five
The Well Crafted Soul

What is the dividing line between the illustrious souls of the Mighty Dead and all of the rest of humanity? Why are we not automatically included in their order? What separates us? In the East, it would be described as enlightenment. The term enlightenment is a hard one to explain. It really means a full and complete understanding of a given situation, usually in a spiritual path referring to the human condition in the context and purpose of all of creation seen and unseen. It implies a profound awareness of divinity, and how everything works within creation on a spiritual level.

Enlightenment is colorfully described in terms of "light." Light is a symbol of consciousness and one who carries the light of clear consciousness, clear understanding, can be considered enlightened. Various traditions divide levels of understanding and enlightenment into several different strata, as enlightenment is a somewhat subjective experience, colored by the framework in which you reached it. Buddhists will perceive enlightenment in a different context to a

Christian, though they might be speaking of the same level of consciousness. One characteristic of the so called enlightened is a detachment from dogma or being "right," so such individuals are said to recognize each other and the plurality of paths to reach it, even if it was a radically different life path that brought them both to the same place.

Witches, while also seeking the same level of consciousness, don't use the same terms for it. In fact, due to the relatively recent modern movement of popular Witchcraft, we don't have many maps or models for seeking enlightenment; almost to the point that many don't believe it's a part of our spiritual tradition. To me, through my experiences and communion with the Mighty Dead, the answer to the question of what divides us from them, is a matter of soul crafting.

While Witchcraft does refer to the Craft as the art of magick, the crafting of sigils and potions and ritual tools in our spell work, it ultimately refers to crafting the soul as a vehicle for consciousness. One of the village Witch archetypes is the blacksmith, and the metal shaped is the iron, the star-born metal of the self. Another is the horse whisperer, but the animal one seeks control over is the self, through both training and understanding of the true nature of the world. Both are shaping themselves through the tools of their Craft. We do the same through our spells, rituals, meditations and subtle alterations of the energy field, the container of consciousness.

THE CRAFTED SOUL OF A MASTER

The soul of a master must be made. While we have the belief that we come into the world pure and perfect as children, and it's only once we lose touch with our divine self through language, need, want and trauma in the physical world that we become "imperfect." The truth is we come, as souls, into the world to grow, change, and evolve. It is only in the fields of time where one can change. In the realm of spirit beyond time and space, where we can imagine things are perfect, very little changes on a fundamental level. We have to enter the flesh to change, and we are changing from one evolutionary model to another.

How is the soul made to evolve? From the modern Witch's perspective, what we think of as ourselves is a multitude of souls, or at the very least a multitude of soul parts. Not all of which were connected prior to incarnation. Incarnation, being in the body, provides the lynch pin to bring together a wide range of energies to one nexus point. The body exists in what the shamanic practitioners call the Middle World. It provides a connection to the realms above and below, existing in the sacred between. Without it, the above and below seemingly have difficulty connecting to each other. The world between is both the dividing line and the force for potential connection, and our role is to bridge that gap between worlds.

In the most simple of models, the soul self is divided into three parts, as briefly outlined in Chapter Three. They can generally be thought of as the Higher Self, the Middle Self and the Lower Self. The Higher Self, or Upper Soul, has its origin in the Upper World of the shaman, with a more global, detached and impersonal view. It is described as a bird perched upon the tree of the world. The Higher Self is what people think of in more mainstream traditions as the Soul. It is the individual divine self, with knowledge of the past, present, and future, life's purpose and what magicians call True Will. Occult traditions call it by many names, including the Bornless Self, Holy Guardian Angel and, in the Temple of Witchcraft, the Watcher.

The Middle Self, or Middle Soul, is the human identity. While centered in the body, in the world of time, space, flesh and blood, it is not the instinctive wisdom and knowledge of the body. That bodily gut wisdom is the province of the Lower Soul. The Middle Self is the identity, the face, the ego and personality. It is what most people prior to mystical revelation think of as themselves. It is referred to as the Namer in the Temple of Witchcraft because it is the part of us that likes to divide things by identifying, naming and cataloging them.

The Lower Self, or Lower Soul, is found in the rivers and oceans of ancestry, the primordial pools of genetic wisdom. Scientifically minded witches can think of this self as the energy of genetic memory or the morphogenetic fields of consciousness described by biologist Rupert Sheldrake. The Lower Self is considered the connecting force between the Higher and Middle Selves, acting as a psychopomp or messenger. It is instinctive, animalistic or childlike, and considered pre-verbal. The actions of rituals, not words, engage it. It is sometimes referred to as the Fetch, and associated with a totemic beast. In the Temple of Witchcraft, it is referred to as the Shaper, for it responds to play, like a child shaping clay, to change and shape your life.

Soul	Perspective	Contact Method	Magickal Uses
Upper Soul	Global-Transpersonal	Spiritualism	Information & Perspective
Middle Soul	Daily-Personal	Graveyard Magick	Worldly Power
Lower Soul	Genetic-Interpersonal	Tribal Traditions	Blessings & Healing

Fig. 7: The Three Souls

Upon incarnation, the vortex of conception draws together these three disparate parts. The Higher Soul descends from "heaven" like a bird to oversee the development of the new entity. The Lower Soul is drawn up from the Lower World, through the archetypal "rivers of blood" in the underworld, from both parents' ancestral pools. If they come from very different "tribes" or ethnic groups, then possibly new connections are formed between these groups energetically through this child, forming a new soul with the energies of both sides of the ancestors. The energy of the parents in the Middle World come together to give the energy that will form the Middle Soul, along with the energy of where they are at birth, the astrological and location forces, including country and time period of the new generation. Some traditions believe the more passionate the parents, the more vital life force the child will have. Dispute in all traditions rises regarding when the soul is actually anchored into the body, or in this case, when all three souls are anchored into the body. Some believe it starts right at conception, while others feel it is all nebulous until birth, or even until the child is named and/or blessed ritually.

Upon excarnation, or death, the three souls usually separate. It's a teaching that people don't like to hear, as we get very attached to our individual and distinct sense of self. But just as we shed our body, we shed our souls, and they each have a different fate. The energy of the body, the Middle Soul, stays in the Middle World, becoming one with the land where it is returned. It is strongest at the grave site, or where the ashes were scattered. The Higher Self returns to the heavens awaiting rebirth. The Lower Self descends back into the pools of ancestral wisdom, anchoring these new experiences in the collective clan's wisdom. This accounts for the experience of some having "past life" memories considered genetic memory, while others have very global experiences of past lives, without obvious direct genetic connections. The genetic memories come from the Lower Soul. The global memories come from the Higher Soul. This theory of the soul holds both experiences to be equally valid.

When this separation occurs in the death process is up for debate, and in the process of aiding those in their transition might not matter, but once the transition is final, these three souls provide separate access points to the energy that was once an individual. In a holographic model of reality and spirit, any one part has access to the information of the whole, though the style in which we receive that information differs.

Mediums, necromancers and ancestral worshipers connect to a different part of the soul when they perform their rituals. One can wonder if the television psychic and the voodoo priestess are talking to the same type of dead. The answer is they are not. While each part of the soul upon death contains the essence, the hologram, of the entire being's knowledge and experience, the way they manifest is different, depending on whether you are aiming for the Higher, Lower or Middle Souls, based upon your technique.

Spiritualists performing séances, mediums and the television psychics they have spawned are generally speaking to the Higher Self. Their messages are of love, harmony and not a lot of specific esoteric information. Sometimes they will get information about money or something hidden, but it's very detached. No other emotion than unconditional love comes through, for that is the state of the Upper World.

Tribal traditions that feed the ancestors do so because they receive blessing and healing from the ancestors. The nature of the relationship is reciprocal. They feel that through offerings of high-energy food, they will help the progression of the dead towards their own healing and enlightenment. The more difficult the life, the more that spirit has to atone for by doing good works and balancing out their "karma" or "wyrd." From a Christian concept, the soul is in purgatory or hell, seeking to be redeemed. From a tribal perspective, it is family helping family. But the results are often less sentimental and more practical. The ancestors will help you get a job, a husband or a new car if you need it.

Graveyard necromantic traditions work with the energy of the Middle Self, the echo of their power in the world. The graveyard dirt and spirit of a soldier is great to help protect you. The Middle Self of a doctor is great for aid in healing. The gravesite of a lawyer or judge is great for legal help. The magick corresponds to the earthly power that individual gathered during life. It is returned to the land, but can be "borrowed" by the clever practitioner. But it's all very human.

So what is the consciousness of the masters? The would-be masters enter into the world of flesh, bringing together these three souls for a chance to craft a vessel of consciousness in two ways. They must have alignment and conscious connection between the three selves, to operate simultaneously on all three levels, and craft a container, an energy body, that builds up enough vital life force to sustain this connection and contain the expanding levels of awareness that it brings. If one should die in such a state, they can step out of this cycle of rebirth if they so choose, and become one with the collective consciousness, the body of saints, and begin a new evolutionary cycle. This is the difference between the dead and the Mighty Dead, between the ancestors and the masters. This state of union and expansion is a Witchcraft expression of enlightenment. This is the metamorphosis of the souls. But how does one get to this state of alignment and expansion?

SOUL ALIGNMENT

In most people, the three aspects of the self are not working in harmony. Most people live from the Middle Self, from the personality. Some live from the Lower Self, the primal instinct. Very few live from the Higher Self and must function in the world of space and time. To live from the Higher Self, one must live in alignment. To bring the blessings of the Higher Self into daily life, it must be grounded into the Middle Self, through the connection of the Lower Self. The three selves must be in harmony, in alignment, so their energies flow in constant communion. One who lives in alignment is operating consciously in all three worlds at the same time. Only through this alignment do we have the flow of energy from the highest levels to the deepest. One who operates in the three worlds simultaneously is thrice blessed, and only with that awareness do we approach the consciousness of the Mighty Dead.

Sometimes the three selves are aligned with three major energy centers in the body, or a triple division of the chakras. Generally the Lower Self and lower cauldron is focused upon the three lower chakras, known as the root, belly, and solar plexus. The Middle Self and middle cauldron is aligned in the heart space, the middle chakra of the seven, and the Higher Self and upper cauldron is aligned with the throat, third eye, and crown. Performing energetic and consciousness alignment in either of these systems helps align the three selves through bodily awareness. Various traditions that use the model of Three Souls have techniques to align the three souls as a part of daily practice and prior to any major magickal working.

Exercise: Three Soul Alignment

I Am the Namer.
I Am the Shaper.
I Am the Watcher.
The Three in One,
The One in Three,
As it was,
As it is,
As it always shall be!
Blessed be.

This exercise combines a pranic (energy) breathing technique based upon tree imagery with the three soul alignment principle. Take a moment to relax yourself. Calm your mind and body.

Focus your awareness on your heart. Remember the heart is the center of the Witch's Perfect Love, our key to the sacred space of the magick circle. Imagine planting the seed of a spiritual tree within your heart. Feel the seed germinate and take root. Feel it grow, moving the trunk into alignment with your spine. The branches reach out of your crown and to the stars. The roots come through the base of your spine and soles of your feet into the deep Earth.

Say "I am the Namer." and inhale through the Heart. Exhale.

Say "I am the Shaper." and inhale through your Roots. Exhale.

Say "I am the Watcher." and inhale through your Branches. Exhale.

Say "The Three in One." and inhale through all three parts. Exhale. Feel Perfect Love.

Say "The One in Three." and inhale through all three parts. Exhale. Feel Perfect Love.

Say "As it was, As it is, As it always shall be!" and inhale through all three parts. Exhale. Feel Perfect Love.

Say "Blessed be." Relax and feel the flow of energy and the alignment of your souls.

Continue breathing in alignment and remember that alignment through breath in your daily life.

INITIATION

Some would argue that true initiation is what begins to confer status into the illustrious order of the Mighty Dead. Without initiation, the gate to the mysteries does not open. I would agree, but I think it depends on what you consider initiation. From a more conservative view, it would only be an initiation conferred upon one from another initiate, in a proper, formal and organized manner recognized by that lineage. I do believe such initiations can provide the proper connection to work upon the Soul Alignment of an individual, threading them with a current of energy from an egregore of tradition that, if it is a true and living tradition, is fed by the wisdom of the otherworld world and the ultimate collective consciousness of the masters.

The egregore is the group consciousness of a terrestrial order of initiates. It's like a much larger thoughtform. The Gardnerians have an egregore, as do the Alexandrians, the Golden Dawn and Thelema. If a group is what is considered in old occult circles to be "contacted" or possessing genuine communication and partnership with inner plane adepts, then the egregore is in turn fed not only by the bodily initiates, but by these inner plane adepts. Initiation is described as a current flowing from the egregore, down through the chain of initiates. The current is passed from teacher to student, and if one is aligned, seemingly threads the three souls, helping them stay more cohesive in alignment. Subsequent "elevations" or further degrees of initiation help craft the soul bodies as a vessel of consciousness particular to that tradition's work and teachings. Some of the crafting is common to the human experience, while others might be particular to specific lineages practices.

In the pre-initiation rites, or Dedication Rite, outlined in *A Book of Pagan Rituals,* edited by Herman Slater, you have a specific reference to the Mighty Dead:

"Then you shall be taught to be wise,
That in the fullness of time
You shall count yourself
Amongst those who serve the Gods,
Amongst those who belong to the Craft
Among those who are called the Mighty Dead.
Let thy life, and the life to come
Be in the service
Of our Noble Lady." [1]

Though working under a different initiatory formula, structure and ethos from the British Traditional Wicca influenced lines, the Temple of Witchcraft tradition references the Mighty Dead as the Hidden Company of the Timeless Tradition in our High Priest(ess) fifth degree initiation:

Tonight I join the ranks of the Hidden Company,
the Unnamed Order,
fleshed and upon the Earth,
And upon death I seek to join their Timeless Tradition.
I join the ranks of the witchblood yet again,
as the first to be born,
the last to die and all the lives in between.
I am a witch.
I am blessed in the mysteries of life, death and paradox.
I am a High Priest(ess) of the Mysteries of the Witch.

Beyond the structured and more orthodox ceremonies, we have the experience of initiation directly from the ancestors, gods, spirits and life itself. Initiation can be seen as a process occurring outside of time and space, but affects us while we live and grow in time and space. Initiation is a catalytic process of change. One could say it works through the process of destabilization, alignment, and attunement. One is separated, traumatized, made ill or somehow made "other" in the process of initiation, sometimes in profoundly disturbing ways. Initiates are confronted literally in ritual or metaphysically in vision with death, mortality or vast transpersonal powers. This destabilizes them and their fixed human personality and point of view. They are realigned in the process of the initiate, organized in a new way of being, a new consciousness. And they are attuned to it, to make it not simply a peak experience, but a permanent change. They are literally "tuned" to an initiatory current or frequency, even if it's not passed from one teacher to the next. Such initiates might end up being lineage bearers who pass it on, or a mystical teacher who passes on techniques to have your own direct attunement.

This threefold process speaks to the threefold nature of many Witchcraft traditions and the three orders of many ceremonial and Qabalistic traditions. Initiates are sometimes referred to as Twice Born or Thrice Born. The meaning is multiple. It can refer to either those who remember their previous past lives and being born into this life have a special perspective on death. Often mystical training includes the remembrance and lessons of such lives. In a similar vein, some traditions do not believe in the integrity of the soul without initiation and development. The soul energy, the consciousness of most people returns back to a more primal pool, described as a cauldron, losing its individuation. While the idea of losing individuality is scary for most of us, causing us to reject this idea out of hand almost immediately, the blessing of this point of view is that in the end, we all share in and have shared in the karma or wyrd of all humans, good, bad and everything in between. The burden of our problems is shared and thereby lessened, and the blessings of our triumphs are shared and imprinted upon all.

In these more controversial teachings for some, only those who create a cohesive structure in their soul matrix can be reborn whole. The soul is not given, but must be earned, crafted, through work. An initiate receives the training to do so. Much like other religions, we of the Craft are a chosen special people, destined for a special retreat, but not through grace. We are chosen through our own works. Our retreat is Witchdom, the Grove of the Mighty Dead or, in the East, the Diamond of Shamballa.

In the teachings of the Temple of Witchcraft, the paradox of dissolution and individuality in past life experiences is solved through the three soul model, with the Higher Soul retaining global individual identity, that spark of divinity, while the Lower Soul dissolves back into the ancestral pools, rivers, oceans, or perhaps cosmic cauldrons of blood. But to be among the true chosen, you need to craft the vessel that can contain all three souls and step off the wheel of rebirth.

The Twice and Thrice Born initiate also refers to the three levels of initiation, ritually or through life. We find three initiations in British Traditional Wicca. The general pattern of destabilization, alignment and attunement can occur under many guises, not always in a linear order. The first of British Traditional Wicca is a declaration or making of the Witch. The second degree mysteries are a descent into the underworld and confrontation with the Lord of Death. The third degree is the mysteries of creation embodied in the Great Rite, union of male and female, Goddess and God.

In the styles of magick in the Golden Dawn, the ten levels of initiation have three orders. In the Golden Dawn, initiates from the first through fourth degree were in the first order, considered the outer order of the organization. Technically this outer order was known officially as the Golden Dawn, though all three were referred to collectively as the Golden Dawn. Initiates of the fifth, sixth and seventh degree, corresponding with the Tree of Life's Ethical Triangle, were in the second order, the Order of the Ruby Rose and the Cross of Gold, considered adepts. And the highly developed masters corresponding to the last three degrees were in the third order, almost described as superhuman, as the Secret Chiefs.

In the poetic mysteries of Merlin as detailed in the work of Geoffrey Monmouth, *The Life of Merlin* and *The Prophecies of Merlin*, this archetypal magician-witch initiation undergoes a threefold death of falling, hanging and drowning, though some versions also include stabbing with the act of hanging, like Christ or Odin pierced by a spear. Many of the gods of magick and Witchcraft are trifold in nature, including Hecate of the Three Ways and Hermes Trismegistus. Threefold initiations show we are operating on three levels simultaneously, sometimes detailed as physical, mental and spiritual, or the Middle World, Lower World and Upper World of the shamanic practitioner.

Though modern initiations tend to emphasize the more cosmic gods, traditional initiations place great emphasis on the ancestors and the spirits of tradition to confer the connection and energy to move forward. In his book *The Mist Filled Path*, Frank MacEown, quoting a conversation with fellow author Alberto Villoldo, states the following about initiation in terms of the spirits of tradition:

"In the medicine traditions there is the understanding that you embody a lineage that continues to live through you. Your sense of personal identity begins to merge with the lineage of men and women who have come before you and will come after you. And it is very destabilizing psychologically, or it can be, and this is why you have to be very grounded and connected to the earth to be able to have this merging of souls that happens within you, which increases your individuality but appears to be undermining it at the beginning of your work. A lineage can be interrupted and can even come to an end. Yet even if it is interrupted for hundreds of years, it is like a fire that disappears: you rub two sticks together and the fire is there, intact again, and the same." [2]

So many fascinating points are raised by this quote. It emphasizes the early destabilization, but also how the process can eventually lead to great strength and unity. He also clearly articulates how the chain of ancestry in such a magickal lineage goes both forward and backwards in time paradoxically. And perhaps most importantly to modern Witches, that the lineages can be restored through spirit contacts even when they seemingly have died out, despite popular opinion that the knowledge is lost. We can find our own thread of ancestors and move with them in the future and past. But the rekindling requires a certain friction. With that friction, the light returns, fueled by the same ancient wisdom. Many of us today are using our experiences and abilities to rekindle old lineage traditions and take them into the new age. Working with the Mighty Dead is the key to reviving the old traditions and taking them in the most appropriate direction for our coming age. There is a reason, for good or ill, that they died out and there is a reason why they are coming back in this age. Often a thing, like a person, must die first to grow wise. Sometimes it dies through the deaths of initiation, and sometimes through the deaths of reincarnation.

Exercise: Dedication to Joining the Mighty Dead

Light a candle and create a sacred space in whatever method you choose. This ritual of dedication can be done before a coven, circle or community, and many consider that preferable, giving you a clear obligation and duty to your community to behave and operate in a manner in harmony with the dedication; others feel that doing so before the immaterial body of the Hidden Company is not only more appropriate, but more binding, as it is a private vow between you and the hidden masters.

I (name yourself), dedicate myself to become one with the Hidden Company
The Unnamed Order of the Timeless Tradition
Eternal and Ever Present in All Ways.

By the blood of the Witches
I seek the Wisdom hidden in all things
And choose the Wisest course of action.
By the heart of the Witches
I seek the Love found within all things.
And choose to follow the true heart.
By the power of the Witches
I seek the Will found within myself and therefore the cosmos.
And enact it for all things are possible.
I remember and vow to return to the body that is first, last and all in between.
I become one with the Living Dead, beyond the grave.
I dedicate myself to the service of the Gods,
I dedicate myself to the Earth, Depths and Starry Heavens
I dedicate myself to the Great Work of Transformation
and unite my three souls in union
By life, death and paradox
This I vow.

When done, release the sacred space and let the candle burn out on its own. Know that you have altered your course irrevocably towards union with the Mighty Dead and the mysteries beyond the grave.

This dedication to join the ranks of the Mighty Dead is somewhat akin to the Oath of the Adept in the Golden Dawn tradition or the Bodhisattva Vow found in the story of the Bodhisattva Avalokiteśvara. It is the genuine desire to achieve "Buddhahood" or enlightenment for the good of not only the self, but for all. Specifically and simply it states, "May I attain Buddhahood for the benefit of all sentient beings." The traditional ritual from Mahayana Buddhism is far more complex, but the heart of the rite is this vow. While this rite and the traditions of Witchcraft do not confer that specific vow or responsibility, it is inherent in the understanding of many modern Witches, with the web of life, that to change and heal the self is to change and heal the rest of your ancestors, species and the world. Our entire lives become rituals to attaining our Highest Will with Love and Wisdom, and joining the Mighty Dead for the next round of our journey. Our magickal evolution is not just for the self. It is for yourself, your people and the entire world.

MASTERS UPON THE TREE OF LIFE

Qabalistic tradition has seemingly outlined an object map of consciousness and the various initiations related to each level of consciousness in the most thorough and complex manner. While it's important to realize this is only a map, and not an absolute truth, it still is a powerful tool to use.

Each level represents a degree of spiritual consciousness. While we assume the upper levels are reserved for the highest initiates, perceived by many as incorporeal secret chiefs, it is only through the experience of flesh, space and time that the individual can grow and evolve to enter those higher dimensions of consciousness. So we should not equate non-corporeal as inherently superior to those in a body, while at the same time we should be vigilant against self-proclaimed masters who never exhibit the qualities of mastery and only use such titles to control others.

At each level, initiates of that sphere exhibit certain "virtues." They fulfill certain "obligations" to that sphere. They are able to clear the illusions through the experience of a vision, of a comprehension, either mystically, or a realization in life. Depending on how you define the term "master" these initiates are found higher on the Tree of Life.

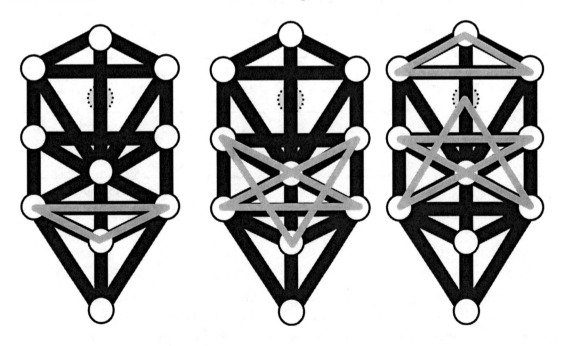

Fig. 8: Tree of Life with Triangles and Initiation Degrees

Sphere	Experience	Obligation	Illusion	Virtue	Vice
Malkuth	Knowledge and Conversation of the Holy Guardian Angel	Discipline	Materialism	Discrimination	Inertia, Laziness
Yesod	Vision of the Machinery of the Universe	Trust	Security	Independence	Dependence, Idleness
Hod	Vision of Splendor	Learning	Order	Truthfulness	Dishonesty, Falsehood
Netzach	Vision of Beauty Triumphant	Responsibility	Projection	Unselfishness	Selfishness, Impurity, Unchastity
Tiphereth	Vision of Harmony	Integrity	Identification	Dedication to the Great Work	False Pride
Geburah	Vision of Power	Courage	Invincibility	Courageous Behavior	Wanton Destruction, Cruelty
Chesed	Vision of Love	Humility	Self-Righteousness	Obedience	Bigotry, Tyranny, Hypocrisy, Gluttony
Da'ath	Vision Across the Abyss	Detachment	Attachment	Self Knowledge, Mastery of Demons	Self Delusion, Ignorance of Self
Binah	Vision of Sorrow, Vision of Compassion	None	Death	Silence	False Enlightenment
Chokmah	Vision of Source	None	Independence	Devotion	None
Kether	Reunion with Source	None	Attainment	Completion of the Great Work	None

Fig. 9: Ranks of Initiation

The bare minimum of mastery is considered to be adepthood, found when one crosses the veil and reaches the level of Tiphereth. In rituals of Tiphereth, one takes the vow to achieve union with the Higher Self, classically called the Holy Guardian Angel. When one is operating at Tiphereth consciousness, it is no longer a vow, but that union is a reality. The next two levels give us greater adepthood with the Advanced Adept, or Adeptus Major of Geburah, and the Perfect

Adept, the Adeptus Exemptus. Prior to these three grades, one is still training in the elemental realm of the previous four spheres at the bottom of the Tree of Life. True mastery is found in the title of the next highest degree, Master of the Temple, or Magister Templi, the rank of Binah. In many traditional Witchcraft circles, the male leader of a group is known as a Magister, but such awareness may or may not be directly linked to this Wiccan degree of spiritual initiation. At this level, one can gather a "garden" of their own initiates they tend and truly teach. The higher ranks perfect the Master, with the Title Magus for Chokmah and Ipsissimus for Kether. These highest ranks are seen by some akin to the living masters of Jesus Christ, Buddha and other truly enlightened or incarnated divinities starting their own world changing movements and religions.

One might look at the ranks of the Qabalistic Tree of Life, used by the Golden Dawn and Thelemic magicians, and not see any of value to the Witch, yet western occultism is filled with imagery that informs the Witch. One needs to only reframe the images of these spiritual principles to see its influence in Witchcraft.

Malkuth

As the material world, Malkuth is called the Kingdom in Qabalistic terms, referring to the Kingdom of God, the universe as we can see and measure objectively. Pagan Qabalists might call it the Garden, both referencing its true nature as the body garden of the Earth Goddess and the body of the Universal Goddess, and the Biblical story of the world prior to the "fall." Witchcraft theology lives in a world of the "fall" but does not necessarily subscribe to it. The only fall comes in our forgetting the true nature and falling out of relationship with the world. When we don't see it as the paradise it is, our level of consciousness, of initiation, perceives only the hardship, difficulty and seeming randomness of it all. There is nothing beyond the senses. It is the Wasteland of Arthurian myth, the poisoned land where true happiness and fulfillment cannot grow for the people and the land is out of balance. It is the Marketplace of the African traditions, where things are exchanged. Materials are bartered. It is the threshing room floor of the goddess Ceridwen, where the wheat is separated from the chaff. It is only those who have knowledge and conversations of a Higher Self, a higher reality, in some instance that can rise beyond the materialistic view.

Yesod

The Sphere of the Moon opens us to patterns and meaning through the gate of the psychic senses. Through the Vision of the Machinery of the Universe, one sees part of the pattern and begins a quest for meaning. The wasteland becomes the labyrinth, the maze pattern that offers danger, potential madness and the promise of something greater. Like those of ancient Greece, the labyrinth walkers must face the Horned God as guardian of the greater mysteries. To others, this is the first manifestation of the Triple Goddess, as Lady of both the Moon and of Fate, spinning the loom of pattern, offering the chance to spin with her.

Hod

Within the consciousness of Mercury, the initiate experiences the Vision of Splendor, a greater understanding of the intricacies of creation. Rather than a mechanical machine or static maze pattern, the world is the game board, and we are all playing the Game of Life. It is a multi-level, multi-player chess game. Or if the binary metaphor of a win-lose game doesn't appeal to the initiate, it's an intricate dance between everyone and everyone else, with the universe.

Netzach

It is here that the initiate of the Venusian sphere of Victory returns to the primal garden of the creation. Here the seed of the material world comes from the flower of fire, from the most ethereal of elements. Here is the pattern of the primordial garden before any fall. Beauty is triumphant for the beautiful pattern is seen, balanced by its splendid dance-game, along with the material reality.

Tiphereth

We step through the portal, cross the veil of unknowing and enter into the realm of the adept. Many images are suggested through the mysteries of harmony and sacrifice. It is the Solar Wheel, where the gods live and the gods die to be reborn. The center of the solar wheel is eternal and timeless, seen as the center of not the Loom of Fate, but a higher wheel, a higher force of Justice or Adjustment. Harmony implies balance. It is the Round Table of Arthurian Myth, for all the Grail Knights in their own way are solar sacrificial gods seeking immortality and redemption through the grail. Here we gain the first glimpses to the path leading to the secret grove of the Hidden Company.

Geburah

Geburah is another level of purification, but it is purification for the adept rather than the novice. It is the realm of the forge and the forge gods, shaping star metal into form with their secrets of nature. It is the gallows and the home of the gallows gods of death and sacrifice. It is the guillotine, severing the head from body, so one can be free of ego and personal identity, and be led by the solar heart of harmony.

Chesed

If Tiphereth is the Round Table of the Sun Warrior's path, then Chesed is the four squared castle of the Grail King. It is a Temple of unconditional love and mercy from the otherworld. It has aspects of the cosmic library, the Akashic Records. It is the last realm of form beneath the abyss, with all the necessary four elements to truly be manifest in the world. Everything above it is supernal and beyond our true understanding at these lower levels of consciousness. Many believe this is the realm of the Ascended Masters, our Mighty Dead, or simply the realm of the Living Dead, those who are as ascended as possible in the flesh, but tradition tells us one must go higher to truly be a master.

Da'ath

Da'ath is the realm that is not a realm, so its false "initiation" does not truly confer a level of consciousness, but an opportunity and a test. Knowledge is readily available in this realm, neither good nor evil, or perhaps both. The unknown of the Abyss is seeking to be known and will share itself with you. It is the true realm of the Two Headed God of the Witches, and one must not mistake his knowledge for the ultimate crown of creation beyond it. One is tested through this dark veil and cosmic Dweller on the Threshold to not fall into the Abyss and never come out, to not seal yourself away for knowledge's sake, mistaking it for divinity. The true aspiring master must then trade knowledge of the world below the Abyss for a true throne of understanding, to sit at the table of the honored ancestors. Without that understanding, you cannot take your place in the realm of Binah, and understanding is far more than knowledge.

Binah

Binah is the true home of the masters. Depicted in many visions, I see it as an eternally burning grove, a phosphorous grove of trees where the ancient Witch masters gather. It is where the eternal sabbat takes place. Others would see it in the diamond city of Shamballa. It is the Temple of the Starry Night, the cosmic ocean. Aleister Crowley envisioned it as the City of Pyramids beneath the Night of Pan. Pyramids are a great teaching of occultism, either in the form of the Wisdom of the Sphinx or the Witch's Pyramid; one has mastered and moved beyond the wisdom to Know, Will, Dare, and keep Silent. When one becomes the Magister Templi, one not only dwells in the Garden of Souls, one becomes a gardener of souls, tending to their own garden through their teachings and work with seekers and initiates. There is understanding in the growth and unfoldment. The ritual of your life becomes clearer. Every action becomes a sympathetic action to fulfill your True Will. If you do active magick in the world while enfleshed, you are said to accrue no karma, for a Master of the Temple is having a relationship not with just individuals, but with the whole of the universe. By their vow, every manifestation is a communication from the universe to them as an individual.

Chokmah

In the consciousness of Chokmah, one has a clear vision of the Source and is illuminated as a full Magus, able to utter a magick word into the world and usher forth a new teaching, current or religion. Chokmah is the realm of the stars from which we come, as we learn in the ancient Orphic mysteries of being a child of the "earth and starry heavens, but my race is of the heavens alone."

Kether

The consciousness of Kether is one of full enlightenment and communion with the source. You become your "very most self," the true meaning of the title of Ipsissimus, but your true self is not the personal self. When you attain this level for a time, the Tree is said to send you back to the sphere that is most like your true nature, so you can operate from that level of consciousness, at least while incarnate. The discarnate master has free reign to climb the tree as desired, but the gathering place of the Masters still appears to be in Binah.

While couched in Qabalistic and Thelemic imagery, the ethos of the occultist and European Witch can be seen in the imagery applicable to the tree, and our quest to reach the Grove of the Mighty Dead where the sabbat is celebrated eternally beyond the bounds of space and time.

SOUL CRAFTING

As many esoteric traditions believed, you do not automatically have a complete and distinct soul, but must "craft" your own soul body through your own esoteric work, making a vessel of consciousness. Various traditions have come up with ways to do this. There is not one road of human evolution and initiation in crafting the soul body. Magick is an art as well as a science. Traditions work in the art of soul alteration, the use of rituals and spiritual allies, to better, or at least differently, craft your soul body vessel for consciousness.

Initiation into any tradition with a current, an egregore, thoughtform, or true contact from the inner planes, begins to shape the soul vessel. If you practice Qabalistic magick, you have the Tree of Life ingrained in your energy body through the repetition of imagery, rituals, words of power and intention. The simple Lesser Banishing Ritual of the Pentagram of the Golden Dawn roots the Tree of Life within your aura, as you envision Kether at your crown and Malkuth at your feet. If you train in the Qabalistic lore of Aleister Crowley's Thelema, you will perform similar practices but envision your feet firmly planted in the Sun of solar consciousness. Moving almost upside down in the "normal" world, a Thelemite operates under different theology. This inversion has led many to misunderstand, and believe Crowley a Satanist, but he was not, in either the stereotypical meaning, or in the modern context of the Church of Satan, which was influenced by his writing, but postdates his own work. Both Golden Dawn and Thelema work well, but differently. The same can be said for the imagery used in various traditions, from Tibet to esoteric Christianity. Each shapes what we call here your soul, even if their particular theology does not recognize the soul as individual, immortal and distinct.

Complex traditions of esoterics go beyond the simple three soul model of alignment, marking several different soul components to humans. Some appear to be dormant, or unformed, in most humans, and only manifest with spiritual effort and work. The Egyptians depict nine souls. While not as theologically complete, gathered sources in Celtic and Norse esoteric writings indicate seven or nine souls. While one can look at each of the ten (or eleven) sephiroth as an aspect of the soul, the oldest sources of Qabalistic lore usually depict three souls. Later, to conform to the fourfold worlds and name of God, YHVH, a four soul model was adopted. By the time of Crowley's Thelema, he was using a fivefold model of the soul.

The overall message in these teachings usually depicts most people as unaware of this complexity, and it is only developed consciously in those seeking adepthood and magickal immortality. Perhaps in more evolved ages in the past, the aeons or yugas described as the Gold or Silver Ages, humans naturally had more soul bodies developed upon birth, but at the low end of the spiraling cycle of evolutionary consciousness, fewer soul bodies are consciously available to the average human.

The spiritual bodies are described as a vehicle, the Hebrew "merkavah" or modern merkaba chariot that can bring you to the source, the creator. One builds the chariot from the energy bodies. Constant attention and challenges to clear, strengthen and grow the energy bodies, unifying them into a vehicle is necessary, much like an athlete or body builder shapes their body as the perfect vehicle for success in their chosen sport. Practices that help craft the soul body include:

Meditation

Meditation can denote a wide range of contemplation practices, but generally exercises that generate a stillness of body, mind, emotions and spirit, focused concentration and a fluidity or flow to life force, preventing blockages, are the best for developing the body of light. These qualities allow all the various "parts" of the soul to align better.

Purification

Rituals to clear and balance unwanted and unbalanced forces, including rituals to purify the self in body and energy, the tools of the Witch and the energy of the temple or place of working. Purification can remove any forces preventing the alignment of the soul from occurring.

Sacred Space

The continual use of ritual to create a space "between" where spirit and matter are equally recognized in paradox, creates the ideal environment outside of time and space where the soul can attune to its natural qualities. Rituals require intention and action, despite being "between," putting to use many of the other developmental skills.

Sacrament

The appropriate use of sacramental rituals, whereby something is consecrated with the blessing and identity of a divine force, and consumption of that object, typically food and drink, thereby confers the divine quality into the person consuming it. This process sanctifies the individual.

Invocation

To bless and expand the energy body through joining it with the energies of other entities, usually identified as deities, to confer divine qualities and insights upon it. Invocations can be done through loving religious devotion, ritual drama or clear intention to magnify those qualities already within you to divine proportion. With repeated invocations, one begins to manifest those qualities permanently in the energy body. It is akin to adding more air to the balloon, but instead of stretching the rubber too thin, eventually it grows stronger and thicker due to the excess air, like building a muscle. This larger, stronger container can now hold a larger portion of your developing soul consciousness.

Spirit Travel

This is the movement upon the spirit, or astral, planes and the exploration of unknown territories. Eventually one seeks to be strong enough to gain entry into the levels that are "protected" from the ordinary human consciousness because the perception must be developed before experiencing it. These advancements prepare the Body of Light to go further and deeper into the mysteries.

Spirit Work

Summoning (evocation) and communication with spirits facilitates the ability to open with otherworlds, strengthening the energy body that holds the portal open and then seals it, as well as developing psychic communication skills. Better skills help the various parts of the self to better communicate with each other in your consciousness.

You find all of these practices in most balanced magickal traditions, including modern Wicca and Witchcraft. Most modern and ancient magickal practices follow these patterns to a certain extent, with various traditions emphasizing one over another, thereby emphasizing that aspect of soul evolution and craft. You will be drawn to the necessary elements for your evolution, but at the same time, it is easy to get stuck with what you know and feel comfortable with, rather than challenging yourself to go deeper into unknown territory.

Other forms of soul alteration involve the union and pacts with various spirits for mutual evolution and advancement. Some esoteric lore suggests that we are not complete human beings until we are bonded with creatures from the various realms, becoming a composite creature reaching to the highest heavens and the deepest depths. Humans in particular are sought for this work by other spirits because our unique triune nature allows us to span a greater metaphysical distance than many other entities.

While there is no one soul alteration spirit partnership that is right for everyone, there is no one model of relationship that is right over all. Every relationship or marriage in the human realm will be different, just as every spiritual partnership will be different. Role and intentions must be communicated and negotiated. This is part of the source of our idea, and fear of, the Witch's Contract with the Devil. While seen as an anathema to Christian society, pacts with spirit allies are a necessary and accepted part of most forms of shamanic practice in indigenous cultures.

While each is unique, and should not be entered into without great consideration by an advanced practitioner with a deep and clear spirit contact, as they can form permanent alterations of the energy body, some general forms of soul alteration include:

Totemic Union

An initiatory bond with a spirit animal beyond the personal power animal or fetch self, but an animal of a tradition, clan or order. It either manifests as a merging with the patron ancestral spirit of a group, or one of the progeny of that ancestral spirit, bonding you to herd, pack, flock or other animal group imagery.

Overshadowing

Considered both a specific technique and when more permanent, a form of soul alteration, overshadowing occurs when a more evolved or expanded consciousness guides another without fully possessing and taking over. There is a blending of wisdom, knowledge, and love, allowing the one being overshadowed deeper experiences and energies. Individual masters from the Mighty Dead will often take this technique or alteration with teachers, channelers and ritualists.

Soul Gate

One can alter their soul to provide an access point in the physical world for an individual entity or group of entities to have greater contact and do greater work in the physical world. The individual agrees to ground their energy through the physical body into the world in return for greater expansion in consciousness to be able to hold their energy safely. It is not possession, nor is the individual harmed in the process. They provide a willing nexus point for the entities in question. The Mighty Dead do this collectively, working with one person as a collective focus for their group consciousness.

Spirit Lover and Marriage

Forming a sexual, sensual, loving or committed bond with a spirit is akin to a romantic relationship or marriage. It can occur in the Faery seership traditions, with the Faery Lover or Faery Marriage. It can also be found in the African diasporic traditions, particularly Voodoo/Voodoun, where one becomes married to a lwa spirit. Matron or Patron deities can take on lover or spouse roles, and shamanic practitioners can refer to their main ally as their spirit wife or spirit husband. Some see the inner alchemical marriage of the self, with its psychological overtones, to be a form of soul alteration as well.

Walk-In

While technically not a true alteration, it is rather an exchange of consciousness. This happens when a "more" evolved entity makes a higher plane agreement with an incarnated human who is going to die, usually through traumatic circumstances, to exchange places on a soul consciousness level. The evolved entity takes on the Middle and Lower Self of the incarnated individual, taking in their persona and family obligations, but has the opportunity to be in a body at this time without going through the birth process. The exiting soul "walks out" and the entering soul "walks in" under mutual agreement. The evolutionary work done by the walking in soul resonates through the soul matrix and effects, for the better, the soul exiting as well.

Soul Braid

A Soul Braid is similar to a Walk-In, but rather than the entire Higher Self exiting, a small portion of energy, often described as one third, moves out and a "strand" of other consciousness weaves itself in and merges with the individual. Soul Braids can be from specific inner plane entities, angels, fey or other spirits.

Why would someone choose to enter into such a contract? While there can be drawbacks because there are limits to the evolutionary path in this lifetime, the benefit is a quantum leap in the crafting of the soul. Alignments can come more easily; the soul body can hold a greater and more developed level of consciousness, and magickal power, love, and wisdom can be heightened. It's a method to bring evolution into overdrive and take a new step in exploring the hidden realms of consciousness, becoming closer to the well-crafted souls of the Mighty Dead.

---

1 Slater, Herman. *A Book of Pagan Rituals.* Samuel Weiser, York Beach, ME: 1978. p. 127

2 MacEowen, Frank. *The Mist Filled Path.* New World Library, Novato, CA: 2002. p. 106

CHAPTER SIX
RANKS OF THE MIGHTY DEAD

Is there any evolution beyond the Masters, or have they reached perfection? While the further evolution of the Mighty Ones is truly beyond our knowing, as they exist in a field of consciousness beyond our understanding, this limitation hasn't prevented modern day teachings from speculating on their further evolution. By studying the patterns of what we do know, and following the wisdom of the Principle of Correspondence, "as above, so below," we can speculate in a more sensible manner. In the end, we'll never truly know until we get there.

A wide range of teachers have advanced these theories in the Theosophical and Ceremonial traditions, most notably Dion Fortune, Madame Blavatsky, Alice Bailey and C.W. Leadbetter. The spiritual hierarchy pioneered in the channeled work of Alice Bailey, particularly *The Rays and the Initiations*, helped create some of the clearest patterns we have to understand, though they are not particularly rooted in the folk traditions of the Pagan past.

In its most simplified form, the teachings of the seven rays define seven paths of light based in an archetypal force, emanating from the divine source of creation and filtering through to the planetary plane of Earth. Like the colors of a painter's kit, today they are divided into the primary colors of Red, Blue and Yellow, and secondary colors of Green, Orange, and Purple (Indigo and Violet). Each archetypal quality associated with a ray is a "path" to initiation and enlightenment, and while we all work with all seven at various times in our evolution, we may take a time to focus on just one. Like other magickal systems, a range of correspondences, key words, entities, gems, herbs, astrological signs, and religious philosophies are associated with each ray. Over the years, with the changing occult society, the key word and correspondences have altered. Bailey's original system of colors was more convoluted than the modern adaptation. This is the form I use in my own work and teachings from a Witch and magician's perspective:

Red	Will and Power	King, Warrior
Blue	Love and Trust	Seer, Prophet
Yellow	Wisdom and Cunning	Priest, Teacher
Green	Art and Nature	Artist, Counselor
Orange	Information and Science	Scientist, Engineer
Indigo	Devotion and Philosophy	Mystic, Missionary
Violet	Ceremony and Magick	Magician, Revolutionary

On the path of initiation, when one attains mastery, one has done the minimum level of mastery over each of these rays. An ascended master then can evolve to the position of a "cohen," a word meaning "priest" in Hebrew, but in these terms a step above the ascended masters. There are seven cohens of Earth, each overseeing the work of one of the seven rays. These seven cohens oversee the seven rays in terms of human and planetary evolution.

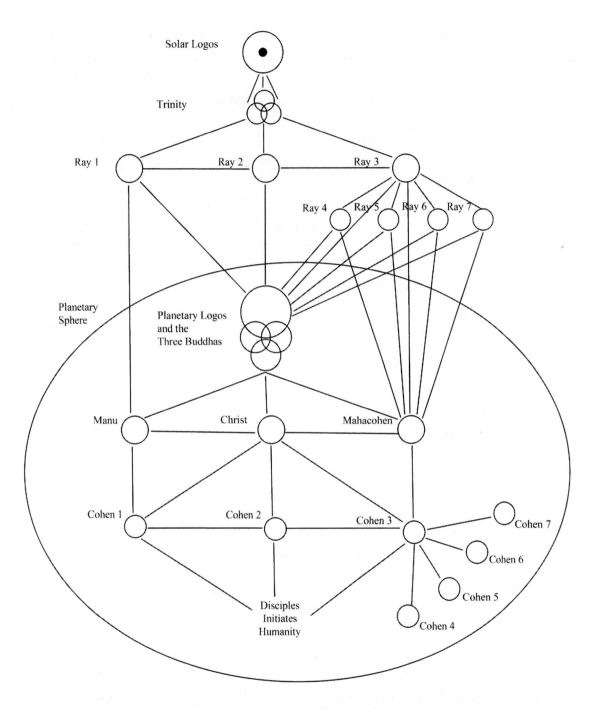

Fig. 10: Theosophical Hierarchy

Beyond the seven cohens are three major masters, who may or may not originate in their cycle of evolution from the Earthly plane. They are known as the Manu, the Planetary Christ and the Maha Cohen. The Manu is chief of the Red Ray and forms the prototype of humanity for a cosmic age, and oversees the formation and movement of planetary land masses. The Planetary Christ is obviously central in Christian teachings, as the teacher of love and healing, and opens a path to the masses of humanity for religious healing and evolution. He is known as the World Teacher. The Maha Cohen, or "much master," is also known as the Lord of Civilization. Technically he is the supervisor of the seven cohens. The four secondary rays (green, orange, indigo, and violet) counterintuitively emanate from this Yellow Third Ray.

Beyond these three are various entities given the titles Buddha or Kumara, and the Planetary Logos. It is then implied that this pattern continues on beyond the planetary scale, with higher solar, galactic and cosmic scales above it.

Taking some of these Theosophical and Neo-Theosophical concepts into Ceremonial Magick, particularly *The Cosmic Doctrine* by Dion Fortune, the Lords are considered to be somewhat cosmic masters, and divided into four main divisions. These divisions are less Theosophical and more in harmony with four fold Qabalistic teaching based upon the tetragrammaton YHVH, even though the correspondence is not explicitly stated. Each of the letters is associated with an element – fire, water, air and earth – and four cosmic elemental realms – Atziluth, Briah, Yetzirah, and Assiah. While given the titles of various Lords in this cosmology, in traditional Qabalistic lore, the entities associated with each of the worlds are the Hebrew divine names of God for Atziluth/fire, the archangels for Briah/water, the various orders of angels for Yetzirah/air and humans, elementals, spirits, demons and nature spirits of Assiah/earth.

Lords of Flame

The Lords of Flame are considered the creative lords who build the structures and laws that direct the cosmos. In scientific terms, their creative work includes gravity, electromagnetism, strong and weak nuclear force, and centrifugal force. Through this structure comes the physical and metaphysical cosmos, visible to us as the suns, stars, and planets. Our cosmos is simply a result of their work. From our perspective, they are born from the "big bang" or any first creative principle. Their work deals in the realm we understand as physics, but goes beyond our simple understanding of Newtonian and even Quantum physics, into realms the structure of which we are only now glimpsing. They are sometimes known as the Lords of Vibration, for vibration is the fundamental structure of all the energies of the universe, or the Regents of the Elements, in their most fundamental states. These are not the elementals of gnomes, undines, sylphs, and salamanders familiar to Earthly alchemists, but their cosmic equivalents. In physics, we see the four fundamental forces of the elements expressed as electromagnetism, strong nuclear force, weak nuclear force, and gravity. The Lords of Flame are impersonal and unconcerned with humanity and individuality. They are cosmic in scope and consciousness, though some Neo-Theosophical lore equates the Planetary Logos, Sanat Kumara, with a Lord of Flame, descending from Venus to initiate life upon Earth. They claim that misunderstandings of this myth and his function led to the exoteric Christian understanding of Lucifer, not the esoteric occult understanding of the light bringer.

Lords of Form

The Lords of Form follow the Lords of Flame. They encourage form to develop upon a chemical level, for chemistry is their realm. They encourage life in their forms, but it is not always the biological and terrestrial life with which we are familiar. One might say the form they create, at its most basic level, is the form of consciousness. From a metaphysical perspective, consciousness must precede a physical entity. One of the most misunderstood components to Theosophical or occult theory is not a disbelief in evolution as a scientific fact, but the understanding that consciousness shapes form, and creates the vehicle for consciousness to operate in the world. Biology rose up to meet consciousness through ever evolving complexity, and consciousness "descended" from higher planes to integrate with it. Due to their association with life and the entrance and exiting of consciousness into form and structure, the Lords of Form are also known as the Regents of Death and Birth. Due to the cycles of life, starting with the cycles and pace of simple chemical reactions, they are also known as the Lords of Rhythm.

Lords of Mind

While the Lords of Form deal with the form of consciousness, the Lords of Mind deal with the true structure of the individual mind. Their realm of science as we understand it is the biological processes. They are the Regents of Life. They oversee and are the guardians of biological life. They take over from the Lords of Form once consciousness has entered a biological vehicle, from the simplest of planktons to the most complex species of humans, whales, dolphins and elephants. The Lords of Mind are the teachers of biological creatures, guiding instinct and impulse all the way to various modes of civilization. In the occult sense, they are the spirit teachers of humanity, but spirit teachers who have not and never will be human, or so occult tradition holds.

Lords of Humanity

The Lords of Humanity is somewhat of a misnomer, implying a distinct separation from humanity and many conspiracy theorists have used this title to imply alien overloads or evil entities from another dimension, but in truth, the Lords of Humanity are what we consider the Mighty Dead. They are the Justified Ones, the Ascended Masters, working in harmony with the Lords of Mind. They have been incarnate, and some say they can choose again to be incarnate if it serves their purpose. They are the leaders of human evolution and their realm of "science" is in the social sciences, in philosophy, religion and understanding. They guide not pure processes, but the impulses to evolve in humanity specifically. They can help build bridges to other realms, incarnate and discarnate, and have great respect and understanding for the realm of spirit and nature, but their origin comes from humanity.

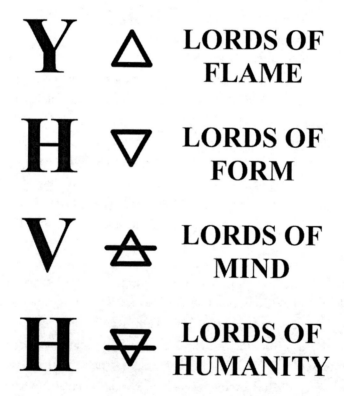

Fig. 11: Qabalistic Hierarchy

When you look at these four sets of Lords, it becomes clear that with our current understanding, it is not technically an evolutionary path, but four distinct categories of being. There does seem to be some evolution implied, as each group works with the one "above" it and "below" it. Humans aspire to know the Lords of Humanity. The Lords of Humanity are linked with the Lords of Mind. The Lords of Mind take over from the Lords of Form. The Lords of Form guide the universe after the Lords of Flame establish the rules.

In some ways, you can also see how the three non-human Lord groups seem akin to the primal alchemical associations, which when combined, help establish the terrestrial world and humanity. In many ways the Lords of Flame are akin to the sulfur principles, to fire, light and the Higher Self. They are the least personal and truly are involved in the bigger cosmic picture. The Lords of Form, despite the name, are more fluid, and are associated with shape and flow of consciousness, akin to Mercury and the Lower Self. The Lords of Mind are the biological or physical component. They are the salt, the body itself that links these two principles in a meaningful way. From the combination of Flame, Form and Mind, or Sulfur, Mercury and Salt, we have the Lords of Humanity and general humanity itself.

In addition to these four categories of Lords are the Regents, or rulers, of the planets. They can be somewhat akin to the planetary spirits of old grimoires and magickal traditions. But these regents appear to be masters whose work has stepped beyond the work of planet Earth and into the solar system. Each planet is said to have a regent, making them masters in the solar sphere, who have ascended beyond the planetary sphere in their evolution. The Regents are said to be more accessible than the cosmic Lords, but less accessible than the ascended masters and justified ones of Earth.

Various teachings have other entities with the title of Lord, such as the Lords of Karma (sometimes equated with the Lords of Opposition), the Lords of Liberation and the Lords of Story. Out of them all, the Lords of Story are most akin to an ascended master group, as they are considered to be evolved or talented human souls conveying ideas to humanity through story, art, and other forms of media. They are the chroniclers and bards, and figures such as W.B. Yeats, Rudyard Kipling and H.G. Wells are considered among them.

Rather than scales of evolution, advancing from one rung to the next, one can look to the paradox of unity and separation among the Mighty Dead, and realize while all are one in consciousness, they manifest in different groups, orders, or even tribes. Looking at it as a hierarchy is typical of the previous Piscean Age. For the Age of Aquarius, the new models are lateral and cooperative. While everyone has a role to play, each is part of a larger whole, with none more or less important, even if their scope is more cosmic. With an analogy of the human body, the brain, a "higher" organ, cannot function if the various cells, a "lower" or more simple structure, within the body do not function.

While we think of the ceremonial title of Secret Chiefs, most tend to think of a more corporate image, like editor-in-chief, commander-in-chief or police chief, but the concept of chief can go back to a more tribal and primal definition. The chief is the leader of a family, clan or tribe.

The Secret Chiefs of the Golden Dawn or Thelema in the world of ceremonial magicians are the clan leaders of those specific traditions. The masters of Theosophy are the spiritual leaders of that particular spiritual movement. The Mighty Dead are the ancestral leaders of the modern Witchcraft movement. While they share a collective consciousness at a level of awareness we cannot understand, putting aside their differences, they express themselves as different individuals, from different traditions, with different backgrounds, to those in their own clan, tradition or organization. Perhaps the only difference is the filter of the human consciousness interacting with them, but the difference is perceivable. Those with a more global filter see a realm of masters from multiple traditions. Those with a lineage specific filter see only the images that conform to their expectations of that lineage. The practical difference would be in purpose or mission in working with incarnated humans.

As the Lords of Story have a specific purpose to work with humanity through story, song and art, it is not unlike those who have taken the name Taliesin in the Celtic bardic tradition. Many believe that the various figures from myth associated with British occultism, particularly those figures from Arthurian lore, were not individuals, but a title associated with a function in the world, and the incarnated human carrying the title was supported by the ancestral order of all those who had previously, or would hold in the future, that title, for the masters exist beyond space and time. Figures such as Merlin, Arthur, Guinevere and Taliesin were really a chain of beings over a longer span of time, mythologized into a single figure in literature. British occultists, particularly those in the line of Dion Fortune's traditions, theorized they were roles from an Atlantean religion. It is a less popular occult theory today among serious occultists, but Atlantis is simply one expression of the idea of an ancient motherland culture, and most mythologies have it. The Egyptians have their paradise of Zep Tepi, and Judeo-Christian-Islamic culture has the Garden of Eden, both with potential historic roots in garden paradises of the ancient Middle East. Gareth Knight, in his book, *The Secret Tradition in Arthurian Legend,* divides the three roles into three ranks or grades.

The Order of Kings

According to some, King Arthur was not a single specific historic figure, but a title, associated with the current Pole Star Polaris, in Ursa Minor, the Little Dipper or more appropriately, the Little Bear. The proposed meaning of Arthur is bear. Arthur's father Uther Pendragon has a last name meaning Head of the Dragon. The previous pole star was Thuban, the alpha star of Draco, the Dragon. Thuban's name means snake in Arabic. The sacred kings, in truth or in occult myth, have been associated with the health of the land, and of the ley lines, also known as Dragon Lines, running through the land. The myth eventually turned into the knights slaying the dragons, but in occult tradition they were dragon kings, manifesting the will of the heavens upon Earth for harmony and balance. In Gareth Knight's work, the Grade of Arthur involves the fellowship of the Round Table, seen as an allegory for the circle of the Zodiac. The tool of the Grade of Arthur is the sword.

The Order of Merlins

Merlin, or Myrrdin, is the popular wizard of Camelot, and sometimes seen as a half-faery or half-demon, but in occult circles, his father is a higher dimensional spirit, and Merlin's function is more akin to a Western mystery version of the Theosophical Manu, or template of a human for his cosmic age. The concept of the Order of Merlins comes up in the psychic investigative work of Bligh Bonds, in *The Gates of Remembrance*. A simple reference in vision to past Merlins, plural, was made. Merlin could be considered the title of high priest of Albion, England, responsible for maintaining the lineage of Dragon (Pendragon) Kings for the benefit of the land, and through the network of energy (ley) lines running through the sacred Stone Age sites such as Stonehenge, the good of the world. In *The Secret Tradition in Arthurian Legend*, the Grade of Merlin is the second rank, associated with the staff. He is the intermediary between humanity and the "faery women" of Avalon.

The Order of Queens

The role of women in Arthurian occult myth is hotly debated, with the demonization of the sacred feminine as the story is reinterpreted and told. The Queen figure of Guinevere becomes the adulteress, and the otherworldly priestess Morgan becomes the scheming lover Morgana Le Fey. In occult tradition the Sacred Queen is the representative of the Earth Goddess, her priestess. The relationship between the King and the Queen indicates the health of the relationship between the people and the land itself. In the three degree system of Gareth Knight, the Grade of

Guinevere is the third and final rank, associated with the Cup and the forces of love and polarity. Beyond the realm of Guinevere is the mystery of the grail itself.

The Order of Taliesin

Often equated with the role of Merlin, as Merlin was a prophet and bardic figure before becoming the more popular wizard, the purpose of Taliesin is more inspired. Taliesin is the transformed "son" of a goddess figure called Ceridwen. After his birth, Ceridwen was later known as Mother of All Bards. We have a wide body of lore attributed to Taliesin, but most likely written by a wide variety of authors, either choosing the name for its role in history and myth, inspired by the spirit of Taliesin, or members of an order, terrestrial or supernatural, where Taliesin is a title. Taliesin shows up with Merlin in various stories. Just as Merlin is the title for the high priest of Albion, Taliesin is the title for the chief bard of Albion.

> *Who owns this grave? This grave?*
> *And this?*
> *Ask me. I know it –*
> – Taliesin (The Stanzas of the Graves, *The Black Book of Carmarthen XIX*)

In other traditions, the advanced spirit allies can be similarly categorized by function or role, in a broader range than the Arthurian orders. In the controversial teachings of the modern Munay-Ki system of author and teacher Alberto Villoldo—where the process of Incan initiatory shamanism is stripped of its cultural context and provided in a framework accessible to most modern people regardless of background—four of the higher "initiation" rites are known as lineage rites as they connect you with these "tribes" of allies, with specific purposes.

Daykeepers

These spirits evolved from the human realm and connect us to a lineage of master healers from the Earth's past. They are the spirits of the indigenous shamans and healers who honored the cycles of time, particularly the cycles of the day – sunrise, noon, sunset and midnight, to bring the Sun and Earth into harmony. They are the herbalists, the wise women and men and, dare I say, the Witches by vocation if not name. In Central and South America they would be known as the *curanderas* and *curanderos*, the healers. In Europe, they would be the cunning women and men, and later the "white" Witches. They are the healers who work with nature, ceremony and the directions. They are the altar keepers, and their nature is more feminine. In Mayan traditions, incarnate daykeepers are the sacred calendar keepers, performing rituals and divinations in alignment with the calendars. Daykeepers could be considered "ascended" masters in the sense they are ancestors by magickal and healing vocation, though the teaching does not necessarily imply that all Daykeepers are enlightened.

Wisdomkeepers

Wisdomkeeper spirits are those in the lineage both past and present who hold divine knowledge. While the Daykeepers are about holding ceremony to heal and to create change, the Wisdomkeepers hold and share the knowledge and memory of our ancestors regarding the mysteries. Based upon knowledge, the Wisdomkeepers can be considered more masculine than the Daykeepers, who are more intuitive and cyclical. The realm associated with the Wisdomkeeper is the high mountain, and our archetype of the wise ones, are those who retreat to their mountain caves and hidden mountain cities to contemplate the nature of the cosmos and infinity. While incarnate, the Wisdomkeepers are associated with the ancient mystery schools and priesthoods, educating people in the evolution of the soul. Like the Daykeepers, the Wisdomkeepers can be considered ascended masters as those passed who hold a specific purpose; though again, the teaching does not necessarily imply all Wisdomkeepers are enlightened beings.

Earthkeepers

Earthkeepers specifically refer to non-human entities charged as stewards of life upon Earth. They are compared to the devas, angels and archangels in their "charge" of maintaining life. Despite the name Earthkeepers, they are not terrestrial, but described in more cosmic imagery. Yet, despite their non-human angelic nature, initiation into the Earthkeepers lineage through the tradition of Munay-Ki is said to charge you with also being an Earthkeeper, a steward, of life upon planet Earth. The original Earthkeepers, like the angels of Qabalistic tradition, are not considered human ancestors or truly ascended masters, even though they have an "ascended" nature.

Starkeepers

The Starkeeper rite is not considered a lineage rite, but one of consciousness. Initiation into the Starkeeper Rite, despite the name, does not align you with the stars as the Earthkeeper rite does, but aligns you with the currents of time. You can let go of the past, both personal past and the past of our planet, and step into a time beyond, associated with the future golden ages. Starkeepers can be said to be creatures of a future, or beyond time. As Starkeepers include the future humans, they can be considered a form of ascended master, our future selves visiting with us.

By looking at Theosophical, Qabalistic, occult, and even neo-tribal models dividing the tribes and nations of evolved spirits, we can come to some simple and practical divisions for the modern Witch for the more terrestrial masters and "lords." They can roughly be divided into the secret kings, queens, priestesses, and priests of the inner planes.

Order of Kings
Fire, Energy

The Order of Kings or the Lords of the World are the spiritual leaders maintaining the world's balance. They lead, but they do not lead by command or edict, rather by example. It is said an enlightened king spends much time in meditation, mediating the cosmic forces for his people, and these priest-kings, much in the tradition of the Arthurian Dragon Kings, draw down the heavenly energy, including solar and stellar fire, to the Earth for its revivification. Like the Tzaddikim, without these secret kings, the world would not continue on its proper path. The secret master of the hidden city of Shamballa, Shangri-La or Agartha, the World King, is of this order. The Qtub, the Brahatma, the Matrieya, the Lord of the World, and Theosophical Planetary Logos Sanat Kumara are all manifestations of this order's energy. One could see the priests of the Temple of the Sun, and beyond the Temple of the Sun, to the Order of the Stars that started all inner and outer orders upon Earth.

Order of Priests
Air, Time

The Order of Priests are the keepers of sacred knowledge, the Wisdomkeepers of the mysteries. From the Arthurian perspective, they could be considered to be the Order of Merlins, the High Priests of Albion hailing from the ancient mystery land of the sunken western cities. Their job is to align the Earth with the vast cycles of time. So in that sense, they are also calendar keepers, Daykeepers of the cosmic cycles and the procession of the equinoxes. They harmonize the alignment of the Earth's pole with the pole star cycles. They bring the new Kings, whose office is harmonized with the Pole Star in the case of Swan Kings (Cygnus), Dragon Kings (Draco) and Bear Kings (Ursa Minor). While the Kings draw the blessings down, the Priests raise up the energy of the Earth to the heavens in the sacred patterns of cosmic time. They are the

Gwynwyddigion and Awenyddion. They can also be considered to be linked with the Order of Melchizedek, the Priests of the "God Most High" named after the ancient King of Salem, for they serve the king, but are not the king. Many believe they are the foundation of all the withdrawn orders upon the Earth. Within their order are the record keepers, the Lords of Story, akin to the Order of Taliesin, the bards who hold the lineages, history and myths.

Order of Priestesses
Water, Space

The Order of Priestesses are the healers who hold sacred space and open the portals between worlds. They are the Ladies and Lords of Harmony and Compassion. They are the Principled Ones of Maria Sabina, sharing the knowledge not of the world, but of the heart, of healing the connection of body, mind, emotions and spirit by putting one back into sacred space, first in the body, then everywhere in the earth. They are the masters intimately linked with the faeries and otherworldly beings who open us to parallel perceptions of reality where change is possible. In Arthurian myth, this would be the Sisterhood of the Morgans, the ladies of the Isle of Avalon. These are the priestesses of the Sea Temples and the Sacred Lake. These are also the wise women and cunning men of all traditions open to sacred space, simple ceremony, healing and nature.

Order of Queens
Earth, Matter

The Order of Queens holds the principles of sovereignty, the divine reign of the material world and of those who are in harmony with it. While the sacred kings mediate energy from the heavens to revitalize the Earth, the Queens disseminate the energy to the land itself, to the plants, animals and people. These are the orders of the Shakti, and of the Earth and Dark Goddess. Just as the sacred queen is the representative of the Goddess, the Order of Queens mediates the blessing from spirit to the terrestrial, in many ways overseeing the opposite flow of the Order of Priestesses, who align the flow of the terrestrial into the spiritual world.

ORDER OF QUEENS

ORDER
OF
PRIESTESSES

ORDER
OF
KINGS

ORDER OF PRIESTS

Fig. 12: Mandala of the Ladies and Lords

Exercise: *Meeting the Orders*

Prepare yourself for a visionary working. Ritually clear and set your space in a manner that is appropriate to your own traditions. If unsure, a simple censing with sacred smoke in the four directions, as well as above, below and between works well. Music, candles and incense would all be appropriate. Get into a comfortable position where you can both relax and focus. Close your eyes. Breathe deep and relax. Perform your Three Soul Alignment. Think back to your Dedication to the Mighty Dead. They are our foundation stones for this work: Prepared Space, Comfortable Body Posture, Soul Alignment and Dedication Vow. If you use a self-hypnotic technique, such as a countdown or visualization to enter a trance state, do so now. I favor a visualized countdown from twelve to one, "seeing" each number on a screen or veil in my mind, and then a non-visual countdown from thirteen to one, as outlined in the *Temple of Witchcraft* series of teachings.

Envision yourself in the center of your sacred place, with the four directions embodied as four lights. Look to the East, or whichever direction you associate with fire. See a red or red-orange light, the color of a bright flame. Feel the point of light expanding larger, until it grows to the size of a doorway. Moving through the frame of this portal comes a master from the Order of the Kings, the keepers of the energetic principle, of Light, from the Temples of the Sun and the further Temples of the Stars. He is crowned in light. Who or what comes through the gate to commune with you? Your exchange might be in words, feelings, pictures or beyond normal categorization, for their providence is pure energy. Ask to understand the Order of Kings and their work in our world.

When the experience is complete, the master will step back, and his light will diminish, yet he will still hold the space of the gateway until your entire vision is complete.

Turn now to the South, or whichever direction you associate with air. See a yellow or sky blue light in that direction. Feel the point of light expanding larger, until it grows to the size of a doorway. Moving through the frame of this portal comes a master from the Order of Priests, the keepers of the principle of time, of the shifts of cycles and seasons and the cosmic clocks of the planets and stars. He is robed in light, emanating like a radiant aura. Which color is the light and what does that mean to you? As the vision grows clearer, who or what comes through the gate to commune with you? Your exchange might be in visions or words, as the Order of Priests corresponds with air and communication, but could also come in other forms. Ask to understand the Order of Priests and their work in our world.

When the experience is complete, you might find the master from the Order of Priests energetically connect with the master of Order of Kings as he withdraws to the gateway frame. Both will hold the perimeter until your vision is complete.

Turn now to the West, or whichever direction you associate with water. See a blue or sea green light in that direction. Feel the point of light expand larger, until it grows to the size of a doorway. Moving through the frame of this portal comes a master from the Order of Priestesses, the keepers of the principle of space. They are healers and the maintainers of sacred space and the boundaries of the liminal. Her heart emanates with light. Who or what comes through the gateway to commune with you? Your exchange may be in feelings, rather than direct information of words or visions. Ask to understand the Order of Priestesses and their work in the world.

When the experience is complete, you might find the master from the Order of Priestesses reaches out to energetically connect with the two other masters from the Order of Priests and Kings. All three will hold the perimeter until your vision is complete.

Bring your attention to the North, or whatever direction is remaining, associated with earth. See a point of green, brown, or black-colored light in that direction. Feel the point of light expand larger, until it grows to the size of a doorway. Moving through the frame of this portal is a master from the Order of Queens, the keepers of the principles of matter, that which manifests in the world, and the matter of the universe. Her hands and feet appear to glow, radiating blessing to all whom she touches and wherever she walks. Who or what comes through the gateway to commune with you? Your exchange might be purely in sensations, though can also include words, feelings and visions. Ask to understand the Order of Queens and their work in the world.

When the experience is complete, you might find the master of the Order of Queens reaches out energetically to the other three masters, of Priestesses, Priests and Kings, forming both a complete circle and a cross within the circle.

In the center, where the four beams of energy meet, a new gateway of white light opens. The white flame grows brighter and larger, like a pillar of flame, a pillar of lightning. The four hold the space around it. There you begin to perceive the collective consciousness of the Mighty Dead, the Eternal Sabbat, the Convocation, the light of Shamballa. Every flame is like an eye of a master peering at you. Every crackle of the flame is like a voice whispering to you. You see the consciousness of Queens, Kings, Priestesses and Priests within the flame, with many more roles and masters, defying description. You learn how the King, Priest and Priestess, or Sovereign, Sorcerer and Seer, all ultimately serve the Queen to maintain the holy order of the world.

When your experience with all five points is truly complete, your perception of the flame will start to diminish. The lines of light connecting the five points will begin to fade. The masters will say farewell and step through their gateways, leaving you, and the portals themselves will shrink and diminish, until becoming nothing at all.

Return your awareness from this trance state using whatever method is appropriate for you. Bring your awareness to flesh and blood, breath and bone. Ground yourself as necessary and release or clear your space as necessary.

As we look to the evolution of human consciousness as an expression of the Mighty Dead, we should not be biased and forget that many realms undergo their evolution, and all the gardens of creation have their spirit teachers to aid us, but also to aid their own kind. One might wonder is there an equivalent of the Hidden Company in the realms of animals, plants, and minerals. As so many magickal cultures revere the eagle, the whale, the lion, and seemingly mythical creatures such as the unicorn, could these not be the evolution of animal consciousness? In my own understanding of the plant world, my green allies have told me that the trees are the teachers, the High Priestesses and High Priests of the plant world. Many of the world's entheogens are considered holy teachers of humanity. Would they not be a specific evolution of plant consciousness? Peyote, Mandrake, Ayahuasca are all very wise plant spirits, with specific roles in the evolution of the entire world. To the alchemist, gold is considered the wisest and most regal of all metals. In their theories, the seeds of metals, untouched by the light of day, are evolving from base lead through a spectrum to gold, and the alchemist's own enlightenment is mimicking the process of becoming more like gold, more conductive, beautiful and incorruptible. As we walk our own path of evolution, we should realize that through our spiritual allies as Witches, through the animal, plant and mineral realm, our magick helps spirits from these realms advance, evolve and understand. We should not look at our own evolution in terms of a human vacuum, but understand the whole system of life upon Earth is evolving not only physically, but spiritually, and we all do so much better if we are all consciously aiding one another.

CHAPTER SEVEN
PURPOSE OF THE
HIDDEN COMPANY

What is the purpose of the Mighty Dead? Why do the Hidden Company gather at the edge of our circle? What could we possibly be doing that interests them? Haven't they done everything we can possible do and more?

Yes and no. They have done much of what we do now, in different ways, in different lands and in different times. Who better to teach us? And like any good teacher, they learn and grow with their own students, from this new perspective of mastery. Their own evolution, as demonstrated in the Ranks of the Mighty Dead, does not end. Through service to those on both sides, both links of the great chain of being, often perceived as above, the stellar masters, and below, us, they evolve.

Many believe the masters are like the Tzaddikim of Jewish myth, or like the Greek titan Atlas, holding up the world, preventing it from collapse. Some see them as omniscient and all powerful. That was certainly the view of the Theosophical Masters and the Secret Chiefs in early modern occultism. All the issues of the world, from the Industrial Revolution to even the World Wars, were a part of the unfolding of their master plan for our evolution, incomprehensible to us at this point in our consciousness. They resided in some eastern or underground enlightened kingdom, led by the "King of the World" waiting to rise up and show humanity the way of peace. Some saw them in conflict with a dark, evil hierarchy of anti-masters, like the Jedi Knights fighting the Sith of the fictional *Star Wars* universe, while others simply believe their greatest enemy is the ignorance and inertia of general human consciousness, and all they do is inspire us. It's up to us to act, and not wait to be rescued by disembodied masters. But without our inner world spiritual hierarchy, or tribal units, something would be greatly amiss with the world. Many think the problems we have with the world today are because we have not been in communion with this secret network of masters, and have not heeded their wisdom, regardless of the religion we practice. When we all do, then balance and evolution will be restored to the world, and usher in a new golden era, at least according to the myths surrounding these enlightened beings.

Benefits of Working with the Mighty Dead

While inspiration, what the Welsh teachings call awen, or at least the impetus to seek awen, might be their biggest blessing to us, working with the Mighty Dead directly, or simply even acknowledging their subtle presence in our lives confers many benefits to the working Witch.

On the most basic level, the work grants us seven basic freedoms that most people do not have. The freedoms are not automatic, but come over time and a deepening realization of their nature.

Freedom From Loneliness

With an understanding of the presence of the Hidden Company, one realizes the truth of the old wisdom teaching, "A Witch is never alone." Originally the concept started in the times of the persecutions, believing if one Witch is found in the community, there must be others to punish, as Witches did not work alone, but in groups. Yet we know the truth of the matter is many Witches prefer solitude. But even in physical solitude, the spiritual support of the tradition is always present. We learn through our arts and practices to commune with spirits unseen beyond the veil, and seen in nature, the spirits of trees, stones, and animals. We have allies and friends wherever we go, at any time, day or night. We simply need to reach out, but we never fear loneliness again when we truly integrate this reality. With the Hidden Ones, not only are we never alone, but we have the advice and guidance of inner plane teachers, those who have walked the path before us, and can guide us now.

Freedom from Grief

While we are human and suffer the trials of life as any other, including grief, those not walking the spirit path are often faced with overwhelming or consuming grief, for they simply do not know the realities beyond death. While we might not know the form, and as mystics, realize however we interpret these experiences now are just that, interpretations, we do realize the reality of consciousness surviving death in some fashion we might not yet fathom, but know that our loved ones can be reached even when beyond the veil of life, and will be met again in our own death. Others simply have fears, beliefs and programming. We seek direct experience with the dead and in the mysteries, understand a reality of rebirth and resurrection in another world.

Freedom from Fear of Suffering

Many are programmed by orthodox religious education to fear death in general, and the possibility of suffering in the afterlife, as punishment for living such a life outside the control of the religion. Many are taught to fear the fires of hell and torment, but those who commune with the dead rarely ever encounter that motif, even if they expect it. Contact from beyond is generally beneficent, and even when not, does not seem to conform to Christian standards of damnation. While we might have physical suffering and pain in life due to illness and injury, and emotional suffering due to the thoughts and feelings we put ourselves through even long after a wrong has been done to us, we do not fear the continuation of that suffering in the afterlife.

Freedom from Control

The previous freedoms from fear help us break the controls and conditioning from orthodox society and religion. When we realize that much has been created, particularly in the form of religious dogma, to control us through our fears and beliefs, and the truth is so much bigger, we are more likely to act in the context of a greater understanding of our life and consciousness. Understanding our current situations and choices now are affected by the past, whether you call that mechanism karma, wyrd, or some other name, helps us choose wisely and with responsibility for this life and the lives beyond. One of the reasons many Witches are seen as rebellious against Christianity, and even purposefully doing "blasphemous" or what we might consider disrespectful actions toward Christianity, to test that conditioning. Many Witches follow a practice first advocated by author Paul Huson in his book *Mastering Witchcraft.* Say the Lord's Prayer backwards. If you can't, examine why you can't. Is there an underlying fear? Can you move through it? If not, perhaps this is not the path for you. It's not about disrespecting Christianity as much as it is about testing our fears.

Freedom from Death

Relationship with the Mighty Dead gives us two understandings regarding immortality. We have the general concept of life after death through ancestral understanding, though some believe such ancestral survival is not the survival of the individual consciousness. If that is true, the Mighty Dead teach us how to craft the immortal soul body, to step out of the current human cycle and become something greater through magickal technique. Rather than go back into the underworld realm of Annwn, we craft something that allows us safe passage into the next "ring" of spirit worlds, Gwynvyd.

Freedom from Fate

Part of the very practice of the Craft of the Witch, beyond the aspect of Pagan fertility religions, is the development of the Will as a magician or sorcerer. Part of crafting the immortal body is to craft and implement our True Will in the world. Part of the initiatory secrets of the Witch is how one can become "free from fate" as Traditional Witch Robert Cochrane puts it, and we take part in weaving our own fate with the Goddess, rather than perceiving it as being spun for us. Truly everyone has this ability to create their own life in conjunction with the Goddess of Fate, by choosing their very actions and working with the consequences of those actions clearly and with awareness, but most do not know it until opening to the mysteries of magick.

Freedom from a Single Identity

The experience of various past selves through regression meditations, and the experience of embodying or merging with various spirits, ancestors and the Mighty Dead themselves help us move beyond our sense of single, individual identity into something larger and more communal. We understand our place in the web of life, and realize that we are not something existing in the web of life, but a single expression of the web itself. Our identity begins to shift into something more transpersonal, the web, and we take our action from this place. We are freed from the confines, limits, and pressures of doing it all ourselves, and enter into the paradox of mystery where we can be both an individual and part of the collective at the same time. Ironically from the perspective of the ceremonial Qabalist, one must become their "very most self" before becoming a true part of the greater whole, embracing the paradox of individuality and unity.

With part of these seven freedoms comes the deeper healing, knowledge and the evolution that comes with the spiritual practice.

Healing and Empowerment

Fellowship with the Hidden Company grants us the opportunity to heal others and heal ourselves. Spirit contact in general helps us develop our mind to its fullest capabilities. Exploring psychic ability, perceptions beyond normal time and space activates portions of the brain unused in most people. Intuition, perception, imagination and inspiration can flow from developing this side of the self. Meditation yields biochemical changes in the body, producing greater health and less stress. Often the techniques of magick and psychic work are healing. Being "beyond space and time" in a ritual sacred space is said to keep one young, aiding the mythic stories of the immortal sages. I know in my own experience dedicated Witches either remain very young looking, or get very old, very quickly, depending on how they apply their power, and what their intentions are.

Those who go beyond simple contact and receive a direct initiation from the spirit in some way are said to evolve, to spiritually mutate, and take a quantum leap forward in self-development and aiding the development and evolution of others. Life becomes clearer. Secrets open to them. An understanding of the hidden meaning occurs and the power to implement their ideas, and compassion, to be inclusive to others occurs. Those initiated radiate an energy that affects others. Healing can be a by-product, not the goal of spiritual evolution, but the healing occurs nonetheless. Through this contact, we become more complete human beings. At first it might not even appear that we need healing, until we reach this new plateau. Once we do, we then realize how much we were missing.

In any ancestral tradition, the healing is said to work both ways. As we heal ourselves, we heal our ancestors seven generations back, according to some popularized Native American belief, and heal this issue seven generations forward. In the work with the Mighty Dead, these ancestors are already redeemed, already sanctified. Are they not? Does our work heal them in any way? How can it, if they are already perfected?

Enlightened and perfected they might be, but in their new sphere of development, they have their own evolution. A necessary part of their evolution is the communion and contact with us, in the human sphere of karma and fate. While they might not need to heal in the same ways we do, they need relationships in order to evolve, or there would not be the same level of communication between us, found in all of these different traditions of sanctified dead. Even if they do it for purely altruistic motives, as the framework of the bodhisattva or saints, our engagement helps fulfill their altruism.

When we look specifically at the manifestation of the Mighty Dead, and the concept of Witchcraft, we see a lot that collectively needs to be healed. While I have no doubt that much of our tarnished image comes from the fact of demonization of the ancient Pagan religions by both Christian and pre-Christian communities, as the Greeks, Romans and Jews all had prohibitions against what we call Witchcraft today, I'm also certain that the call to power by many of these Witches created abuses of power that initially raised some of the fears about Witches in the first place. Any of us who have gained any magickal power have come into positions when we have wanted to, or indeed have, abused it. We have acted with less than impeccable motives. An insult, a loss of something we wanted, an argument can all lead us to directing our power in little, and big ways, against those we perceive are our enemies. The more personally affronted by their actions and the need for retaliation, the less justified we are in taking that action. I have no problem with defensive, or even offensive, magick when necessary, but like the honorable martial artist, I believe you use only the necessary force to neutralize the situation. But with psychic power and spellcraft, it is easy to let passions carry us and go overboard, with far more than what is necessary in the situation.

When we align ourselves with the word Witch and the tradition of Witchcraft, we are aligning with all these forces – the wisdom and mystery, the persecutions and the abuses of powers. We claim the word Witch to redeem it, which is powerful. We seek to restore the wisdom of the ancient traditions to the world table of religions and practices, and have it be a viable option available to those who seek it. In that process, many modern Witches and Pagans go through a persecution complex. Some have difficulty getting past it. Some of us go through power trips. Many too, have difficulty letting them go. But as we work through these issues, we find the true mystery of wisdom, love and power at the heart of the tradition. We find our Craft as a vocation, a calling to our purpose in life.

The Mighty Dead are on that side of healing, and perhaps many originate from a time prior to these power trips and persecutions culturally. Their devotion to the tradition as a whole to support us, and our devotion in turn is what helps heal and empower us all.

Exercise: Healing with the Ladder of Light

Ready yourself for a magickal working. Clear and set your ritual space using a method that is correct for you and your own tradition. Set the tone of healing with appropriate music, light, and scent. For this working, ideally lay down in a comfortable position. Relax your body, starting at the top of your head, and moving down to the tips of your toes, letting all tension drain away through your feet. Close your eyes. Breathe deeply and perform your Three Soul Alignment. Remember your Dedication Vow. Be centered in your foundation stones for this work: Prepared Space, Comfortable Body Posture, Soul Alignment, and Dedication Vow.

Use an appropriate technique, such as a relaxation countdown or breathing exercise, to get into a meditative state. You might perceive the representatives of the four Orders of Masters in each of the four directions, attending and watching over your work. Envision your double, your astral form, becoming increasingly smaller and denser, until you become microscopic. You enter into your own body, into your own cells. You move through the bloodstream of your body, entering the blood of the heart. Your microscopic self enters into the cells of your heart.

Center yourself in a cell. Imagine the spherical shape with a membrane, a fluid, and a nucleus, not unlike the crust of the Earth, the mantle, and the core. Focus upon the core and as you gaze at the center, you see the winding spiral of DNA, the double helix, the twisted serpent of our genetic makeup. As you gaze, you imagine that the DNA spiral extends outwards, upward towards the heavens, the stars, the future. It goes to the center of our universe. As it does, it mutates and changes, becoming the helix of all the ancestors of not only your genetic line, but the future of all of humanity. As you gaze at the center, imagine the spirals extending downward, towards the Earth, to the heart of the underworld, the darkness, the past. As it does, it mutates and changes, and regresses, becoming the DNA of all your past ancestors, and then all the creatures in the chain of ancestry that lead to the evolution of Homo sapiens. This ladder of light, this twisted spiral stair, is the spirit rope, the spirit vine or world axis that magicians and shamans all across the world have seen in their vision. This is the Serpent of Life that leads to the past, present and future of life.

Feel yourself connected to heaven and earth, future and past, but in the present. As you do, you realize that all the cells in your body repeat this process, spiraling upward to the heavens and downward to the underworld. Your entire being is connected.

In the chain, you feel the presence of the ancestors and future kin of the Mighty Dead, and know that the center of the universe and the heart of the underworld lead to the same place, creating a loop, a continuous ring of DNA, a double-helix ring of light. As you are aware of the

DNA of the Mighty Dead, it lights up in the ladder, and the light flows up and down through this ring. The light reaches you, your own personal DNA and begins to heal you. As the light flows through your links in the chain, it fills your cells, healing your cells. It fills your tissues and organs, healing your organs. It flows through the blood and bile, the phlegm and lymph. It flows with the secretions of your glands. It extends outward, radiating with the fibers of your aura. You are transforming. You are healing. You are becoming whole, perfected, en-*light*-ened with this power of the ancestors. If you have a specific illness or issue in need of healing, ask the Masters' light to heal it now.

When you feel this healing radiance is complete, it begins to diminish, returning to the spirals of DNA. Soon you feel the future DNA fade away, as well as the past DNA fade away. You are focused upon your own cells and the cells within your heart. The microscopic sense of self begins to expand as you breathe and return, rejoining your body at full size.

Return your awareness from this trance state using whatever method you feel is appropriate. Bring your awareness to flesh and blood, breath and bone. Ground yourself as necessary and release or clear your space as necessary.

Knowledge

What has been the most important to me in my work with the Mighty Dead is the receipt of knowledge from otherworldly teachers. The importance of connecting with, and receiving clear communication from, your inner Master-Teacher was stressed by my own terrestrial teachers. They suggested, and I teach as well, that one of the best things a human teacher can give you is the tools, techniques, and context in which to commune with the inner world teachers. Human teachers provide an excellent check and balance to make sure we don't go off into delusion, but for the main, the inner plane teachers provide the direction and guidance for each step upon the path once basic training is complete.

Through this given knowledge, we are able to regenerate our traditions. Many modern Witches lament over what has been lost through time and persecutions, and I have done so as well. But I have had a few amazing experiences where I followed the inspiration and advice of inner world teachers, to later speak to more experienced or differently trained Witches of more folkloric persuasions, and be blessed with these elders sharing a technique with me, only to find it is something that the Mighty Dead had already taught me, perhaps with different words, but the same basic concept, purpose, and result. This has given me a great confidence that we can not only reclaim and regenerate the traditions lost, but set them into a practice appropriate for modern Witches.

The regeneration of our tradition comes through what I perceive as three strands of knowledge. The first strand, as categorized in my previous book, *The Three Rays of Witchcraft*, is known as the red thread. The red thread is ancestral teachings given from living blood to living blood. It is knowledge passed on from human to human. These are the first teachings we receive from a teacher, or even a book, that start us on the path and give us context.

The second source is the white thread. The white thread is sometimes given by the Hidden Company, for it is knowledge freely given. It is the direct spirit contact of inner plane contacts. For some it is detailed dictation of channeled messages. For others it is subtle clues given in vision or indirect intuition. Most of our spirit knowledge comes from this path. It is important to realize that this knowledge is not wisdom. Information alone does not confer enlightenment or wisdom. Knowledge must be put to use. Here is where we differ from many modern channelers who feel reception of the message is enough.

Lastly is the black thread, the information earned through an ordeal or trial. While it can be the deepest, it is the most abstract, when compared to the other two threads. You must experience it to know it, and words can be hard to associate with it. This knowledge is the closest we have to wisdom, as the experience that confers it hopefully brings wisdom along with any technical knowledge. Those who manage to share their white or black threads with others transform this knowledge into red threads to be passed on in a tradition.

As most of the knowledge from the Mighty Dead is from the white thread path, the color white is also associated with the bones. While the Mighty Dead might not be Ancestors of Bone in terms of us living in the same physical location, one can think of the entire Earth as the graveyard of the Mighty Dead. The bones of these ancient dead are at one spiritually, if not physically, with the sacred sites of the planet, and the bones of the very Earth herself. Some Traditional Craft Witches, such as author Peter Paddon, call the technique of reclaiming ancestral information as "Tapping the Bone." [1]

Others, myself included, believe that the masters of the ancient traditions have left us hidden treasure troves of knowledge and energy, caches of wisdom in objects and sacred sites. Sometimes they are linked to terrestrial objects, such as stones or statues. Others believe when the time is right, a mysterious relic will appear out of thin air for the recipient, while most believe these objects are strictly of an etheric nature. In the Tibetan Buddhist and Bön traditions, such hidden teachings are known as *terma*. Terma means "hidden treasure." An ancient master is said to have hidden the teaching, as the ages shifted into periods of greater darkness and ignorance, as the world was no longer able to handle it. As the ages shift again and it's time for wisdom to be restored, the terma will be found and understood by a special adept of the tradition. The adept who is "destined" to retrieve the teaching and restore it to the body of the tradition is known as a *terton*. In Tibet these teaching treasures are associated with lakes, caves, rocks, trees and specific ritual and temple objects. They have connections with the four elements of fire, water, earth and air. Sometimes a written script would be found, while others envision a "spirit script" giving information beyond any terrestrial language. The teaching, via oral or written lesson, will eventually be restored into the greater body of the tradition. Today we can associate them with stones and crystals, particularly "record keeper" crystals, those with small triangular formations on the sides of these stone, most common in quartz, ruby and sapphire. One cannot necessarily plan to find and unlock such a teaching. It is either guided to happen or it isn't.

In the controversial Toltec traditions described by Carlos Castaneda, one goes through a process of recapitulation, or clearing and retrieving the energy from past memories of this life time. With greater experience, one continues through the process, but the recapitulation gradually moves towards the memories beyond your personal experience, into the elder sorcerers who have come before you, and you not only help clear, but can gain useful techniques and energies from this process. Carlos receives this advice from the sorceress Florinda:

"You must allow the thoughts, the feelings, the ideas of the shamans of ancient Mexico come to you." [2]

In the same text, but taking quotations from a previous work, *The Power of Silence*, we have another hint to the importance of the lineage ancestors. "Their past" refers to the collective past of the shaman-sorcerers, not any one individual.

"Shamans are vitally concerned with their past, but not their personal past. For shamans, their past is what other shamans in bygone days have accomplished. They consult their past in order to obtain a point of reference. Only shamans genuinely seek a point of reference in their past. For them, establishing a point of reference means a chance to examine intent." [3]

We too can gain a point of reference to truly examine intent by letting the knowledge of the past Witches come to us.

Exercise: Tapping the Golden Bones

Prepare yourself and your space for a visionary working with the Mighty Dead. Use ritual to clear and set yourself and space. Assume a comfortable body position for trance work. Perform the Three Soul Alignment. Remember your Dedication Vow. Feel all four foundation stones in place and use whatever technique that is appropriate for you to enter into a meditative trance state. You might perceive the representatives of the four Orders of Masters in each of the four directions, attending and watching over your work.

Envision the Three Rays of Witchcraft descending downward from the stars to your crown. The First Ray, the Straight Line, the Red Ray of Will and Power descends down and enters the crown. It flows straight down from the crown into the heart, turning to gold. It then flows down into the belly, turning to the color white. The Second Ray, the Bent Line, the Blue Ray of Love and Trust descends spiraling down and enters the crown. It flows around to the heart, turning to green. It then flows down into the belly, turning to the color black. The Third Ray, the Crooked Line, the Yellow Ray of Wisdom and Cunning descends down like lightning and enters the crown. It crashes down into the heart with a thunderclap, turning red. It then descends down into the belly, turning to deep scarlet. The three rays, white, black and scarlet red braid together, and as one, descend from the bottom of the spine, the root, into the bones of Mother Earth.

The trifold braid of light seeks out a deposit of ore, or metal. One of the deep bones of the earth will resonate with the masters you want and need. As your line of light touches the metal ore, you feel an alchemical transformation occurring. The dark metal shifts from the gray-black of lead to a lighter, shiny, brittle tin. From tin it becomes hard like iron. The iron lightens to the rose color of copper. The copper becomes fluid and shiny, like quicksilver. The quicksilver hardens to pure silver, and the silver turns to gold. This gold stone, this gold bone, has the mysteries of those who have died in a state of golden enlightenment. It has always been gold and always will be, but remembers its time deep within the earth as lead, tin, iron, copper, quicksilver, and silver, rungs on its journey of enlightenment, as the masters it corresponds with went through their own seven stages.

The knowledge of the golden bone is tapped by your cord, in both senses of the word. It is tapping, striking the deposit of wisdom in the deep ethers of the Earth, and the vibration responds like pulses of Morse code along the energetic strand you have descended into the depths. And it is tapping it like a well, drawing out the rich energetic "marrow" of the wisdom, which flows along the three cords of red, white and black. As the wisdom flows upward to you, you begin to digest it in your belly.

As your belly cauldron fills, you begin to feel the digested wisdom rise up. It is still unconscious, but now you begin to feel it. It resonates with your heart space. You feel its power and significance. As your heart beats, the marrow of your bones beats with the rising golden light. Your bones become like gold, gilded and fine with the wisdom of the deep ones, the wisdom left by the Mighty Dead. Your bones vibrate and buzz with your heartbeat and the vibration and tapping of the braided cord of light. They come into resonance. You might feel as if the ancient forge gods are striking them, beating them in cosmic rhythm, tempering them in fire and water. They could be etching golden symbols on your bones.

Then this energy rises up like a fine mist into the cauldron of your head, and you begin to decipher the specific message, from your body to your heart to your head. Receive the wisdom, potential knowledge, and instructions from the deep well of wisdom.

When you feel this experience is complete, the flow, the vibration slows and then stops. The braided cord of light dissolves away. The golden etheric bone of the Earth fades away from your awareness. You affirm to remember all you learned on all levels—body, heart and head.

Return your awareness from this trance state using whatever method is appropriate for you. Bring your awareness to flesh and blood, breath and bone. Feel the difference in your bones now, in harmony with the remaining bones of the Mighty Dead. Ground yourself as necessary and release or clear your space as necessary.

This work regenerating a tradition and taking it into the next era is vital, and separates groups into what traditional occultists call "Contacted" and "Non-Contacted" groups. There are those magickal groups, covens and lodges that gather together with common purpose, shared insights and like mind, but are not working with their elders and peers in spirits. The work begins and often ends in the human realm. They are doing personal work, becoming better people, celebrating the seasons and often doing very successful spellcraft, but they are not bringing anything new in, or partnering with the ancestors of spirit in the same way contacted groups are. Contacted groups have communion with inner plane adepts, and these inner plane adepts guide the teachings and work of the tradition, providing a critical "voltage" of spiritual current, allowing deeper teachings to occur. These spirits act as guardians to the tradition, and if someone approaches the group who is not in harmony with the group mind, they will actively discourage that participant from joining the group. Sometimes the applicant will feel unwelcome by the spirits themselves. If the living members of the group do not heed these intuitions and advice, then either the contact diminishes, or things go awry until balance is integrated. Sometimes the one who pressed forward appears to be driven mad, as all imbalances are magnified. Other times, the voltage of the tradition's current is too great, and the individual is not prepared for it, so when initiation is received, the psychic vessel is "cracked" and will not function in a balanced manner again, if at all, until removed from the group and massive psychic healing is performed or a long period of time passes where natural healing can occur.

Those who are contacted will experience several aids in their magickal work:

Mind Touch

To be mind touched is simply to receive clear mental contact from one of the Mighty Dead, to hear their voice or words and be able to absorb them and share them with others. Sometimes it occurs only through deep meditation and elaborate ritual, but those who lead a contacted group will experience mind touch in the most subtle of circumstances, allowing them to guide the group in the most appropriate manners and share teachings as the need arises in daily life. A declaration of being mind touched should never be used to get your own way or behave poorly.

Overshadowing

Overshadowing is a stage beyond simple mind touch. While mind touch is akin to someone whispering in your ear as needed, overshadowing is having someone guarding your back, guiding you every step of the way. While you are not out of control, it is a more cooperative effort. Words and energies might flow through you unexpectedly, but not unpleasantly so. Those with psychic sight might feel a presence all around you and over you, and many who encounter you as a Witch, healer or teacher might perceive the energy of the overshadowing entities before they see the more personal self beneath it. Many sages and healers are said to be overshadowed by a greater entity that is providing the power or wisdom through a vessel at the time. Some who do channeling work in the New Age are overshadowed, though many are simply mind touched with a gift for elaboration.

Indwelling

As overshadowing is a step beyond mind touch, indwelling is a step beyond overshadowing. To have an indwelling spirit is to have a much deeper partnership and blending that is continual, though not necessarily permanent. The perceptual difference to psychics is that rather than coming from a presence around the individual, it is coming through the individual, as the entity appears to be dwelling within, or reaching through a portal of consciousness within the individual's consciousness. While the thoughts, words and actions of an overshadowing spirit are perceived as separate, even though partnered, those of an indwelling spirits are harder to distinguish from the personal thoughts of the initiate. Founders of orders and temples can have a permanent indwelling spirit.

Why would such mighty entities need to perform actions such as mind touch, overshadowing and indwelling? You can look at the mythic symbolism of the Arthurian Quest. An analogy can be made between the king of the castle, who is like the Master. They have made their quest in the world and now are retired to the central point of the kingdom, the castle. They cannot leave that point or it would lose its center. They are the anchor, the rock upon which all else revolves. Yet their work is not complete until all the land is healed. So the king sends forth a new knight into the world to fulfill the quest again. Some equate the King to the Mighty Dead, the ascended masters who need vassals in the world of shape and form, but guide them from beyond. You can also look at the King as the soul, the perfected self that will take his rank among the Mighty Ones, but lives beyond the world of form. The knights are each incarnation of the soul, seeking to fulfill the quest. If we are all moving towards the realm of the Mighty Dead at some point, seeking to perfect the soul, then the difference is inconsequential.

Many practitioners feel it is important to discern the identity and quality of inner plane contact without necessarily taking everything they have to say as truth. Spirits, even masters, are like people, and everyone has an opinion on everything. Just because their opinion is right for them, does not mean you have to follow it without question. Don't perpetuate dogma in any form. Many times a group leader who is less than honorable will use this technique to gain unswerving loyalty from a group. "I'm not asking you to do this, but the invisible masters are ordering it," is the line used.

Some have specific code words and symbols to their tradition. A vision, sound or word is induced by the spirit in the inner world senses of the magician-witch to prove their identity. Some have Qabalistically inspired tests, believing the complex formulas associating letters with numbers and value will correspond. If a spirit says it is here to teach you about the virtues of Mercury, then the letters in its name better add up to a number associated with Mercury, eight. Other words with the same numeric value will have similar qualities to the spirit's nature. Magicians might perform a simple banishment of harmful spirits, and if the spirit remains, assume their benign nature. But with spirits, as with people, use your intuition and discernment, and never stop thinking for yourself.

One way to start building contact for your group is to follow the advice of Alex Sander's spirit in *A Voice in the Forest*. Place a chair out for the masters in circle or ritual. Invite them to be a part of your group. Seek them in vision and spirit contact, and see who comes to your table.

EVOLUTION

The ultimate gift the Hidden Company can give us is an understanding of our own evolution. From this theology, where they are is where we seek to go consciously. They teach the art of the well-crafted soul. They teach us that when we operate on all three worlds at once, we are transformed. If we can see the higher purpose of the Watcher, the play of the Shaper and the real world action or grounding of the Namer, all at the same time, we are transformed. If we can hold our true purpose, in divine love, and embody wisdom, we are transformed. We craft a new vessel of consciousness and join them in their eternally illuminated grove beyond our understanding. Love, power and wisdom in all three realms are necessary. Those who gather power without love and wisdom can be seduced by it. Our history and myth is ripe with that tale. If we don't cultivate those blessings, we go awry, like the tales of the ancient Witches Medea and Circe. Those who have love, but no power or wisdom are ineffective. And those who seek wisdom without the heart or the power to enact it simply have knowledge, which is admirable, but not an end to itself. Knowledge must be enacted to be wisdom.

I've noticed a transformation among Witches who hold the ideal of the Mighty Dead. Good Witches are made great by this aspiration of transformation. I see the qualities of the Witch, divided by elements, transformed and purified. Good qualities become refined.

Good Witches are determined, and can't be deterred from the course they have set themselves on. The will is strong. A wise Witch seeks to know purpose, and will be deterred if they realize they are on the wrong path. They seek the True Will, which often conflicts with the ego's desire.

A good Witch is opened-hearted and generally kind. A wise Witch has found the Holy Grail, which is divine love and forgiveness. It is the eternal and overflowing cup of the heart.

Most Witches, by our nature, seek to be practical. Even those who study high arts and philosophies seek to put them to use. We live in the world around us. A great Witch is a secret King or Queen, sovereign in their own life, and encourages others to be rulers of their own life. We each seek the kingdom of one subject, ourselves.

Witches must know their Craft and their world around them. They must be knowledgeable in the arts and sciences. They must apply their knowledge. But a wise Witch is constantly seeking the truth in its greatest scale. While book knowledge and facts lead us, they must turn on the flow of inspiration, so we can receive knowledge from the patterns of nature and energy that most do not see. They have ears that hear the truth and eyes that see the truth, and cannot be deceived, because in their quest for the truth, they stopped deceiving themselves.

Witches are a proud people. It is said that a Witch bows before no one but the gods. Yet in many of our initiation ceremonies, the teacher kneels before the student, for the wise one is humble, and sees the gods in all. We are each evolving into our own god selves, and the wise know this truth and live humbly because of it.

Seek to transform on these five points, uniting Power, Love and Wisdom in all that you do, and you are well on your way of evolution towards the realm of the Hidden Company.

Element	Power	Quality	Ideal
Fire	Light	Determined	Purposeful
Water	Love	Open-Hearted	Compassionate
Earth	Law	Practical	Sovereign
Air	Life	Knowledgeable	Truthful
Spirit	Liberty	Proud	Humble

1 Paddon, Peter. "Cosmic Soup and the Mighty Dead". *The Crooked Path*, Issue I: Spring 2008. Pendraig Publishing, CA: 2008.

2 Castaneda, Carlos. *The Wheel of Time.* Washington Square Press. New York, NY: 1998. p. 253.

3 Castaneda, Carlos. *The Wheel of Time.* Washington Square Press. New York, NY: 1998. p. 259.

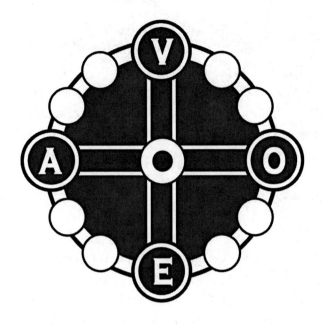

CHAPTER EIGHT
WORKING WITH THE
ANCESTORS OF THE WITCHES

Unlike ghosts who haunt us without invitation or permission, those of the assembly of Mighty Ones come uninvited only to observe. They gather around our circles and by our candle light, making their presence known, waiting for an invitation. But they will not participate unless directly asked. Because so few of us have learned to ask, at least from the Witchcraft perspective of training, so few of us get direct help. We do feel their love and support, but to work with them we must actively engage in our relationship. Through this active engagement, we can become more like them on our own path of evolution.

Communion with the Mighty Dead occurs in several ways. No one way is better than another, but one way might be more effective for a particular practitioner.

Ritual Invitation

Ritual invitation can occur formally or informally. Informally, every Witch circle is an invitation to the Mighty Dead. Most people's first experience is unknowingly and unconscious. They become the company of shadows gathered at the edge of the circle. Sometimes the perception is aid, help and support. Sometimes it's simply witnessing. Other times it might be judgment and evaluation. But their invisible presence is perceived. When I speak of this manifestation to others who are never formally taught about the Mighty Dead, they nod in agreement in having this experience and a light goes on, from those trained in formal traditions, to those with circle casting techniques from the simplest Wicca books. It's universal to those with eyes to see.

Formal ritual invitation is to know about the presence of the Hidden Company consciously, and to consciously invite them to participate and gather at your circle. While you can ask for their help in any number of things, the formal declaration of intent and invitation opens a gate to stronger communion. While they might be ever present in our magick, we need to open the door and invite contact if we seek deeper communion. Many don't, and are simply satisfied with the dead staying at the edge of the boundary as they will, and we work our magick in our own way, but I have found my magick deepening and becoming richer with their aid.

A simple link to add to your circle work, after the evocation of the quarters and the calling of the gods and spirits typical to your tradition would be:

We call forth the spirits of the Mighty Dead,
the Hidden Company of our Timeless Tradition.
Be here now with your kin.
Aid us in our magick,
So we may go deeper on the spiral of evolution.
Hail and welcome.

Evocation & Appearance

Evocation usually means summoning a spirit to manifest its appearance, be it a visible apparition, or a tangible manifestation in smoke, the flickering of candle flame or the gust of wind. While I'm not sure if we can summon the Mighty Dead, Witch Masters in their own right, as we could an elemental or goetic demon, they usually willingly accept our invitation. So evocation is really the possibility and condition to manifest in some tangible way. For some, they can appear as shades, particularly visible as shadows and blurs, particularly to those of psychic sensitivity. Like other spirits of the dead, they can manifest in the tangible and psychic phenomenon of modern spiritualism – phantom scents such as roses, flickering of lights, ringing of phones and fluctuations of other energies and electronics.

One of the methods of visible appearance of spirits in the goetic traditions found in the *Lesser Key of Solomon* is the use of incense within the triangle of evocation. The incense allows the spirits to form a "body" of smoke, to ground their presence more tangibly in the world. The key incense of Malkuth is most often used, Dittany of Crete, as Malkuth is the sephira of the material world and its scented smoke creates a physical body. While we don't seek to "capture" the Mighty Dead in a Triangle of Art, we can aid their presence to our senses by providing heavy incense for them to manifest. While the manifestations are not full bodied, detailed apparitions, the heavy magickal smoke in the air does lend solidity to the Company of Shadows that gathers. With the greater solidity, we find the communication becomes clearer.

Mighty Dead Incense (Complex)

3 Parts Myrrh

3 Parts Opopanax

2 Parts Dragon's Blood

1 Part Gum Arabic

1 Part Wormwood

1 Part Mullein Leaf

½ Part Tobacco

½ Part Juniper Berries

½ Part Elder Flower

½ Part Thyme

¼ Part Solomon Seal Root

¼ Part Bloodroot

¼ Part Unicorn Root

¼ Part Black Cohosh Leaf

$1/8$ Part Poppy seed

7 Parts Red Wine

5 Parts Brandy

1 Part Honey

Mighty Dead Incense (Simple)

3 Parts Myrrh

2 Parts Dragon's Blood

1 Part Wormwood

1 Part Mullein Leaf

½ Part Tobacco

½ Part Thyme

3 Parts Red Wine

1 Part Brandy

1/2 Part Honey

All of these ingredients can help produce a powerful smoke, as well as have associations with the dead, spirit summoning, dreams and spiritual protection and evolution. I particularly like to use brandy along with wine, as wine is considered blood in many traditions, while brandy, distilled spirit of wine, is the evolution of wine, as the Mighty Dead is of the evolution of the ancestors.

Grind all the ingredients. If you want a "popping" sound when burned, leave the poppy seeds whole, otherwise grind them. Mix the dry ingredients thoroughly. Gently warm the wine and add the honey and brandy. Then add it to the incense and mix thoroughly. Spread the incense out upon wax paper or a glass tray to dry in small chunks. Then use on charcoal discs.

Visionary Meditation

One can commune with the Mighty Dead much like any other spirit guide, by seeking them in vision and meditation, be it as a part of a larger ritual, which is ideal, or through simple trance. Guided visualization, pathworking and shamanic journeywork are all methods of seeking the masters in visionary experience.

Guided visualizations can take place from your own Inner Temple or Soul Shrine, your own safe place psychically, where you open a gate of consciousness with your will, a gate of guidance, and ask the most perfect and appropriate ally from the Mighty Dead to step through and commune with you.

Pathworkings in a Qabalistic framework can be an excellent method to commune with the masters, though one must know which aspect of the masters to seek. While they are associated with the "angels" of Malkuth, the Ishim (or Aishim), I have found it most productive to seek them in the sephira of Binah, the sphere of Saturn.

The shamanic experience of the masters can be found through simple shamanic ritual, but in the context of Witchcraft, the meeting of the eternal Sabbat, the focus of the next chapter, can be the most powerful method of contact.

Invocation and Mediumship

Invocation usually refers to bodily possession, and while not as common in the Witchcraft traditions, as that experience is usually reserved for the deities, as in the Drawing Down the Moon and the aspecting of godforms; bodily invocation, or what is known as trance channeling, is more common in Spiritualist and Theosophically inspired traditions. While some will simply perform conscious channeling, or repeating back the message of the spirit consciously, others will invoke the spirit into the body, giving the spirit a greater degree of control. Those considered mediums, channelers or "death walkers" are most likely to commune with the dead, and some with the masters, though it's good to have a healthy dose of skepticism of any who channel the masters and then seek to command your actions or gain your loyalty. Mind Touch, Overshadowing and Indwelling are forms of invocatory communion with the Mighty Dead, and often precede experiences with full possession and mediumship.

Dreams

Dreams are one of the most common ways our deceased loves ones speak to us, and also one of the most common ways the Mighty Dead can commune with us. In the ancient Greek times, one could seek out the aid of the Heroic Dead as intermediaries with the gods. Anyone could seek out the Heroic Dead. Usually one would perform an act of sleeping and dream ritual at the site of the dead's grave, or another sacred site associated with them. Today, we might use a picture, a writing or poem associated with them under the pillow or on the nightstand. The trick is having enough dream memory and discipline upon waking to write and record our dreams before forgetting them. Practice with conscious dreaming prior to dreaming with the Hidden Company as suggested, but in the Sabbatic experiences of the next chapter are often described "oneiric" or dreaming trance. Certain herbs can help us with our dream work.

Dreaming with the Dead Tea

1 Part Mugwort
1 Part Jasmine Flowers
1 Part Hops
½ Part Mullein Leaf

¼ Part Dandelion Root

¼ Part Valerian Root

$^1/_8$ Part Poppy Seeds

$^1/_{16}$ Part Celery Seeds

Take 1 Tablespoon of the dry mixture of herbs, with one cup of boiling water and steep for at least twenty minutes. Add honey to taste and drink an hour or so before bed time, with the intention of visiting with the Hidden Company in your dreams. Make sure you have a notebook or recorder by your night stand.

Oracles and Omens

You can ask the Hidden Ones to guide you through some form of established oracular device, from the classic spirit board, or Ouija board, to pendulums, tarot or runes. They will guide your work to the most appropriate answer. While I've found working with spirit boards for entertainment less than fruitful, when you find a true ally willing to commune through this method, it can be quite powerful.

Fig. 13: Spirit Board

And just as you can work through manmade devices, you can also ask the masters to give you a sign, and omen or portent in nature. The dead can get your attention and give you a message through such synchronicity. One particular type of omen might indicate the ancestors in general, or a specific ancestor or member of the Mighty Dead. Such omens can manifest as music, particularly specific songs on the radio, animals, unusual weather, strange coincidences or other seemingly random phenomenon, particularly when requested. They can be more difficult to read, but for those who find guidance through such omens clear, it can be a powerful sign when requested in response to a specific issue, question or problem.

Interface with Holy Sites or Relics

Objects and places play a role in our communion with the Mighty Ones. Various traditions use relics to commune with their saints, typically material from the physical remains of the enlightened one. The basic concept is that one who was so divinely touched in life leaves a remnant of that divinity or connection, in their bodily remains. Bones, teeth, hair and even clothing or ritual tools can be considered relics. The Catholics are most famous for this, with the concept of a Church needing some form of saintly relic in the altar of the Church. This was proclaimed as Church Law in the Second Council of Nicaea, and indicates it was most likely standard practice at that time, and the council simply approved and codified it. The early Christian Church had no use for relics. In the ancient Pagan traditions, particularly in the cults of heroes, the remnants were not so much divine touchstones as protective and blessed talismans. You find the use of relics in Buddhism—often as a stuppa, or shrine, which is said to contain some article associated with the Buddha—as well as in Hinduism, Tibetan Bön, and forms of shamanism.

Skulls, bones, and other human remains, along with graveyard symbolism appear gruesome to the casual observer, but they serve a purpose. They help us get over the fear of death by making its inevitability more familiar and comfortable. Bones are the human made "stones" that last beyond our death, the closest thing we create physically that lasts beyond our life. People thousands of years from our lifetime can learn about us by looking at our bones and fossils. Bone plays an important role in alchemical fire traditions. To calcinate a remedy is to "burn to bone" as we turn our black ash to gray and then pure white, three stages of spiritual evolution. Crematory traditions speed up the incarnation cycle by purifying the earthly remains, making it harder for a lost ghost to remain on the physical plane. Skulls hold a mystery, as so many cultures have venerated them. The skull has become cup or chalice in the east, vessel for the mystery sacrament. Bones become wands and trumpets.

In modern Witchcraft, the use of bones, skulls and various ritual tools take on the role of relic, even if their origin is not in the earthly remains of a Witch. While a few traditions actually use human skulls, they most often are not communing with the previous "owner" of the skull, but using it as a vessel for the traditions' ancestral connections, preferring bone to other substances for the vessel. Others will use skulls and bones of carved wood, resin, metal or crystal. Crystal skulls associated with the Ascended Masters and ancient advanced civilizations have grown more popular today. While there are many theories on the origin and myths of twelve ancient crystal skulls, many reproductions prove to be effective ritual tools. The Temple of Witchcraft uses a human size crystal skull to commune with our Mighty Dead. The crystalline nature of the skull implies the manifestation of the diamond of consciousness, as the light body of ascension or enlightenment is referred to as the perfected diamond body in the Eastern traditions. For the three souls to become one, the perfect diamond vessel or diamond vehicle must be formed.

Relics lend way to the idea of sacred sites, as most are interred permanently in a sacred spot, a temple or shrine. The place then becomes a location of pilgrimage. For others, the attunement to the spirits of the tradition is not so much relic specific, but geographical, to where the ancestors of the traditions lived and died. Those following an Irish Celtic path feel a kinship with the land of Ireland itself, in total, though those devoted to a specific deity might feel power in a place literally associated with that deity. Wiccan and Witchcraft traditions associated in their origin story with a particular place, such as the New Forest for Gardnerian Wicca, have access to those spirits when doing magick in such a place. The Cabot Witchcraft tradition claims Kent as its home, as those sacred sites in the county of Kent bring connection. When following an Avalonian path, the land of Glastonbury makes connections to the Watchers of Avalon. And those worshipping Diana in a Strega tradition will find power in a visit to Lake Nemi in Italy. In the Ascended Master teachings, powerful masters have etheric "ashrams" or schools linked to various global sacred sites, from Mount Shasta, Luxor Egypt and even the Statue of Liberty in America. Holy Sites can initiate contact as much as any holy relic. They become interface sites between the etheric reality of our holy inner plane orders with the outer physical world.

Initiation into Lineage Traditions

Gaining initiation into specific lineages of magickal or spiritual tradition links you to the continuous flow of consciousness that the past practitioners, and masters, are a part of still.

Through the ritual initiations, the magickal current that is passed from teacher to student, and the similar practices and beliefs, a resonance of similarity is created, attracting those who reached their enlightenment with similar methods to you. Through initiation or sacramental joining, the flow of this body of saints comes to you, and you can benefit from their wisdom and guidance.

The current can connect you with the greater archetypal flow of wisdom from a tradition, or to those of the specific denomination and lineage line, depending upon your intention and experience. For example, initiation into a Gardnerian Wiccan coven can gain you connection to the greater Mighty Dead of the British Witches, or specifically to the dead who are in your direct line, all the way back to Gerald Gardner, or to Gardnerian style Witches and those in similar practices across the lines, which in that case, would include all the Alexandrian Witches as well. Mythically it connects you to all of the New Forest Witches before Gerald Gardner.

While self-dedication and self-initiation can confer a resonance with Witches in general, it is the passing of a current that forges such a strong link to the ancestors of the past. This is one of the benefits, but also one of the drawbacks of lineage initiation. Lineage initiation connects you to all in your lineage, both good and bad. So you reap the wisdom, but by joining a group, you are said to take on some of its karma and the karma of its founders if the founders were not enlightened beings.

You might not feel inclined to explore all eight of these techniques, but use the ones that seem most appropriate for you.

Magickal Rite to Work with the Company

The following ritual guideline can be adapted in many ways to suit your own work and goals. Use all or part of it, as you see fit. It incorporates many aspects of the contact ideas in the previous section.

Create Sacred Space

Create sacred space in any manner you feel is appropriate for the working or your own tradition. For most Witches, this would include some form of the Magick Circle.

Ritual Evocation

Strike a bell reserved for ancestral work nine times to gain their attentions and summon forth the Mighty Dead of the Hidden Company. Then perform a ritual evocation, a poetic invitation to your rite and your life. This poem was used at a Temple of Witchcraft Samhain ritual to call forth those of the Timeless Tradition. Its imagery is based upon our own rituals and liturgy, and can be adapted with imagery pertinent to your own working.

By Stone and Stang and Cauldron Well
By the darkest of Earths
By the deepest of Hells
By the light of the Watcher Stars
Who shine through the night
By Law and by Love
By Life and by Light
By the truths found between the Horns
By the Child who is never born
By the Skull and Crown
By the Root and Cord
By the Web of the Lady
By the Song of the Lord
We call you to come and be with us still
By the Sovereignty of the Stone
The Compassion of the Cup
The Sword of Truth
And the Wand of Will
Come one, come many, come one, come all
Come by the Stone and Stang and the Cauldron call.
Hail and welcome.

Consecration of the Relic

Obtain a relic to be the focus point of contact between you and the Mighty Dead. I prefer a crystal skull, both for the overt symbolism, and the natural magickal qualities of quartz crystal. Today many different types of mineral skulls are available. I have a larger one of quartz for the community and a smaller one, of aqua aura quartz, for my personal work. Skull bottles are also available, and could be filled with herbal powders or magickal potions appropriate to the Mighty Dead.

Consecrate the future relic tool for your work. Pass it through the cleansing smoke of your working. Anoint it with simple oils. I suggest a few drops of Myrrh in olive oil, like a funerary oil. Others prefer a tincture of diviner's sage. Other washes from the Witch's garden would also be appropriate. Hold and speak these words or something similar:

By the oils of the dead,
By the knocks upon the door,
By the light of the fire,
I stand upon the shore.
I consecrate you as my vessel,
I consecrate you as my charm,
I ask the gate be opened now,
With love and without harm.
Be with me now.
Speak so I can hear.
From the edge into the center,
Now be here!

Place the object in a prominent spot on your altar for the working, where you can gaze upon it when raising energy and communing with the spirits. Illuminate it with candle light if possible, and many would suggest covering it when not in use.

Before raising energy, or whenever you wish to use it, gently tap on it with your wand or the hilt of your blade. I prefer to knock nine times or thirteen times. Others in Thelema would knock eleven times, opening with a rhythmic pattern of 1-3-3-3-1 and closing with eleven taps in the 3-5-3 pattern.

For those not inclined to use a large central relic, an amulet can be created, or another piece of jewelry can be consecrated for this purpose, and only worn for communion with the Mighty Dead.

Fig. 14: Amulet Design

Raising of Energy

The raising of energy facilitates the communion with the Mighty Dead. I've found circle dance and chant to be the most effective. This particular chant came out spontaneously in a Mighty Dead working, and seems to be attuned to the enlightened ones I personally work with in our Craft. The chant is: *Obrimos, Abrados, Verados, Eximos.*

Obrimos	East	Fire
Abrados	West	Water
Verados	North	Earth
Eximos	South	Air

Each word of the chant is associated with one of the elements and directions as we call them. If you focus your attention when chanting each word with its corresponding direction and element, you create a powerful transformative cycle, not around the circle, but through it, creating a lemniscate or infinity loop building power alchemically through the union of opposite elements. We have used this chant repeatedly to great effect.

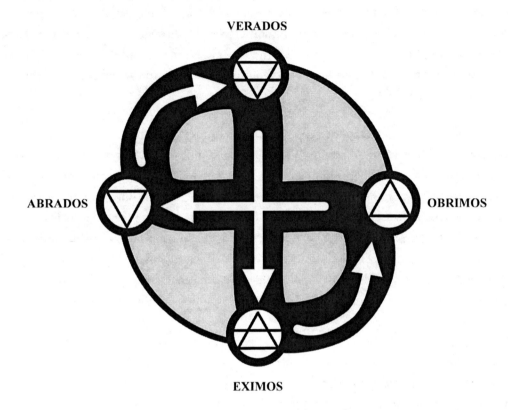

Fig. 15: Elemental Lemniscate

Another word of power gathered from a participant in a Mighty Dead working that has been used to help attune to them is less clear in the symbolism, but has still been repeatedly effective: *Arunastart Foh-ill.* Experiment with both and see if these words of power aid your communion with the dead.

Oracular Transmission

Oracular transmission simply means communing with the Mighty Dead. You can start by gazing at your relic as a focus, and then use the method you find most appropriate for working with the dead. You can speak to them directly, and listen psychically. It helps to do this with another, or in a small group, as the dynamics of one becomes the receiver and the other both the anchor and the "battery" in classical spiritualism. The polarity is not unlike that between High Priestess and High Priest, using dynamic tension to improve the quality of communication. The energy raised should fuel the transmission process, making the communication clearer.

You can also use oracle devices, asking the spirits to speak through the device of the cards, runes, or sticks, and have the interpretation of the symbols be considered the message. The Mighty Dead will subtly guide your hands and your interpretation to the right answers when the communication is clear.

Initiation into the Mighty Dead

Similar to the Dedication to Joining the Mighty Dead in Chapter Five, this is not simply a dedication to their ideals and becoming one with them in the future, but a conscious request to receive a current of initiation, from them to you. It need only be done once, not in every ritual of this type, but forms a link between you and the Mighty Dead directly. Like other forms of initiation, it can be transforming, and potentially destructive in your day-to-day life. Initiation can bring up issues of health, past relationships, and emotional clarity. All need to be purified for the initiation seeds to go deep and bear fruit in this life. But the process often requires support from teachers, peers and family. If you don't have that support, don't ask for this initiation.

By the Golden Chain,
And the Silver Hooks,
I see the flow of Power, Love and Wisdom,
Not found in the pages of any book.
I seek initiation into the Timeless Tradition
Of the Nameless Art,
The Unnamed Order
Of the Perfected Heart.
Teach me the Ways of Power.
Teach me the Ways of the Wise.
Teach me the Ways of Love.
And the Secrets of Those Who Never Die
In Service to the Lady
In the Service to the Lord
Flow with lightning through my blood

Flow through me the sacred cord.
Join me to you and join you to me.
Join me to the Three In One
And to the One in Three Forever More.
So mote it be.

WESAK, THE FULL MOON IN SCORPIO

In many of the Buddhist traditions, *Wesak*, or more appropriately *Vesākha*, is usually the full Moon in May, the Full Moon when the Sun is in Taurus and the Moon itself is in Scorpio, though some interpretations of the lunar calendar puts it in June depending on the lunar year. It is considered Buddha's birthday, and it is the celebration of his life, enlightenment and death.

In the interpretation of many of the Theosophical traditions of the ascended masters, Wesak is considered an important alignment and gathering of the planetary masters. While by their very nature they are in continual group consciousness beyond the bounds of space and time, at this time of year, their union is particularly powerful and working for communing with them, as well as working for the healing and evolution of all of humanity and the entire planet is powerful. It is like a lunar esbat for the Mighty Dead of all traditions, coming together in love and blessings. I generally find this time of year and Full Moon powerful, and this understanding helped me know why, beyond the obvious astrological associations to my personal natal chart.

I find this a powerful time to commune with the masters in what is considered to be "Spirit Council." The spirit council phenomenon has occurred to many practitioners in a variety of traditions and world-views, but it appears when someone has taken on a leadership role in their community in some fashion, even if it's simply leading by example. The leadership work usually involves not just exoteric leadership, but inner spiritual leadership recognized by the masters. During meditations, dreams or other vision work, you find yourself sitting in or speaking up at a "meeting" of various powerful entities in council together. Sometimes they are a gathering of masters and you are part of the proceedings. Sometimes the gathering is a mix of deities, animal spirits and other powerful entities, but not all human.

The purpose of the council can be personal. They gather to guide you in your work. Or the purpose of the council can be more far reaching and global, and you are a member of it, but not necessarily the focus of it. Sometimes you are present only to observe and lend energetic support, or to be informed of decisions being made. Other times you are an active participant on the council.

The council is the mode of operation for the Aquarian Age. Decisions are made jointly in community consciousness. Participating in spirit councils allows us to learn the skills inwardly to bring these modes of being out to our daily life and physical communities.

Exercise: Joining the Spirit Council

Prepare your own self and the space you are in for a visionary working with the council of the Mighty Dead. While you can do this in ritual, you can also do it in simple meditation, or as you go to sleep, mentally, to commune with the council in your dreams.

Use ritual techniques to clear and prepare. Assume a comfortable body position for trance work. Perform the Three Soul Alignment. Remember your Dedication Vow. Feel all four foundation stones in place and use whatever technique that is appropriate to you to enter into a meditative trance state. Be aware of the representatives of the four Orders of Masters in each of the four directions, attending and watching over your work.

From the four directions and the guardians of the four Orders open four spirit gates, one in each direction. From each of these gates comes three beings of light and shadow, creating a ring of twelve figures, with you as the thirteenth in the center of the circle space. They may enter all at once, or slowly, one at a time. Sometimes they all come out of the same gate, and if that is what occurs, take note as to which gate they came, as it might be important later in your practice. That particular order might want to work with you.

Observe them. Do they have any distinguishing features? Often the masters are nondescript and collective, rather than individual and colorful personalities. Sometimes they manifest as the great prophets and teachers of the ages from outside the traditions of Witchcraft and sorcery. Other times they appear as familiar gods and goddesses, and perhaps they are. No one can predict how the council will appear to you, but generally they come from the Phosphorous Grove, the City of Pyramids beyond the Abyss.

Commune with this spirit council of masters. What do they say to you? Are you the focus? Are you there to observe silently? Are you simply a participant in the proceedings? Each of our experiences will be unique, so work with your unique relationship to the Hidden Company.

Continue until you feel the experience is complete, and you are given leave by the council to depart. Return your awareness from this state of trance using whatever method is appropriate for you. Bring your awareness to flesh and blood, breath and bone. Ground yourself as necessary and release or clear your space as necessary.

As you progress through the stages of initiation, your perception of the council might become more of your daily perception, as you enter into a greater collective union with the hidden ones. While unnerving at first, this can be a normal part of our evolutionary process.

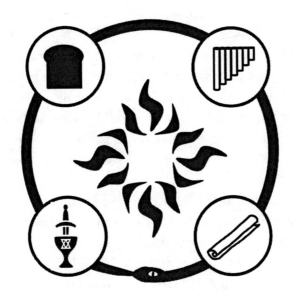

CHAPTER NINE
THE GATHERING OF
THE AKELARRE

The mysterious Witches of Basque Spain, notorious in their reputations for their ability to actually drive off the feared Witch hunters due to their sheer numbers, gathered at a magickal place known as the *Akelarre*. A Basque term for the meeting place or meadow "of the he-goat," it appeared to be a code for the Horned God, or for the Christian Witch-hunters, the Devil. There the Witches, or Saorginak, would gather for their celebrations. Along with the meadow, the Akelarre also become associated with the caves and hills. It referred to a place where the Witches could gather safely for their secret rites.

Akelarre later became synonymous with the meeting place for Witches, not only in northern Spain, but everywhere, at least in the romance of the modern Witchcraft revival. Today Akelarre is used by some to refer to not only the place of the Sabbat, but the Sabbat itself. Not simply the rituals of the solar and agrarian calendar, but for the Sabbat behind all such rituals, the eternal gathering of our ancestral Witches in spirit, who continue to dance in celebration and communion of our gods and nature.

While most Pagans today use the term sabbat for seasonal celebrations, it could relate to a wide range of meanings beyond the yearly cycle. While most believe the word entered English indirectly through the Hebrew word Shabbath, for the seventh day of "rest" in the creation cycle, and the use applied to Witches was either in reference to the belief the Witches inverted Judeo-Christian beliefs or was possibly a comparison or equation between the Pagans and the Jews by the Christians, the term could come from Zabbat, a lunar ritual to Inanna, at least in the work of occultist Kenneth Grant.

Today most Witches usually choose to ignore the post-Christian era medieval depictions of the Witch's Sabbat found in woodcuts and in Witch-hunters' manuals; some Witches have embraced those images and find empowerment, giving rise to a branch of Witchcraft focused upon the reality of the eternal sabbat. Termed "Sabbatic Witchcraft," it is seen as a living and regenerative current of Witchcraft, if not a direct linear transmission of wisdom from incarnated teacher to student. It can be found in the work of Austin Osman Spare, Rosaleen Norton, Kenneth Grant, and Andrew Chumbley, giving rise to Chumbley's tradition the Cultus Sabbati. All are particularly known for their creative and visionary art as inspired by this spirit congress. This is the true gathering of Witch power, and through it we can deepen our experience of the Mighty Dead.

The sabbat, in all its forms, depicts the paradox we find in Witches in all times to this day. We are generally individuals, rebellious, and prefer to do things our own way. We have a strong solitary nature. Likewise we have a desire to gather, to find kinship and community. Sometimes we find that community in the flesh. Other times we find it in the spirit world. We seek a communal consciousness. Sometimes we try it out through covens and traditions, but what we are truly seeking is the communal consciousness of a higher order of evolution, where in paradox we can hold our individuality and our unity without sacrifice to either.

Fig. 16: *Witches' Sabbath* **by Francisco Goya (1798)**

THE MANY GROVES OF THE MIGHTY DEAD

As we have experienced a variety of ranks within the "hierarchy" of the dead, it is possible that the Akelarre is simply another expression of a particular "rank" linked with the eternal sabbat. Those of the Akelarre do seem particularly associated with lives upon Earth instead of the more cosmic masters. Yet as one who always looks for the cross-cultural strands in occultism, it appears that many cultures have a concept of a meeting place for the "enlightened" and those who aspire to be. Today many of us perform vision workings to experience our own personal Inner Temple or Soul Shrine. I think of the sabbat meeting place in the spirit world as the Inner Temple of the collective consciousness of Earth's masters. Each culture expresses their idea and understanding of it differently. Each name, image and myth provides an entry point into something that is beyond our understanding while entirely linked to the terrestrial world. To those who dwell in this timeless consciousness, the name and form matter little, but if a particular name and form provide the setting that helps us make contact, then by all means they will use it.

Other mystics would disagree entirely, seeing each group of "masters" separate and distinct, and each inner world sacred space as being wholly separate. Each realm is "built" or discovered by specific entities, for a specific group of "The People" rather than looking at it as a universally welcoming term. They become refuges for those souls bonded together in tribe that will not break down into the cauldron, having their essential aspects, or three souls, separated. One realm cannot be equated with another. They are part of a pact or covenant between the entities that created them, the ancestors and/or gods of that tradition, specifically for the members of the tradition, rather than open to the public at large, or at least those who can find them. To make sure only those for whom it is appropriate to enter get there, tests, codes, and passwords are given to the worthy in the form of symbols, words, and images. Those who do not know the codes cannot pass.

My own experience and worldview has shown me similarities and connections, and that higher consciousness by its own nature is connected, and the lines that separate it are needed only in the human realm for us to access it. The masters are the masters are the masters, and once they are beyond form, in true Theosophical spirit, there are no differences. They all come from the mystic core of the One Tradition that has many faces and facets. When I observe those whom I think of as spiritual masters, they have a commonality to them, even if different practices and theologies got them to their own mastery.

Perhaps both views are true, and there is one central domain shared by all masters of all spiritual traditions, but smaller "satellite" realms that are independent to a tradition, governed by a specific covenant. In that way, realms such as Shamballa and Avalon are as different as the real life realms associated with them, the Himalayas and Glastonbury, but these realms are nexuses to the central spiritual core, the anima mundi or holy spirit of the world, where the masters eventually gather.

But if you believe all of these realms to be leading to the same center, or all of these realms to be entirely different, choose to work with the ones that resonate the most with the spirit contacts you have made.

Abbey

A term used for a gathering place of inner plane contacts by Gareth Knight, as outlined in his work, *The Abbey Papers: Inner Teachings Mediated*.

Academy

A general term for the inner world gathering emphasizing the educational aspect of the masters towards their seekers. In New Age and Theosophical lore, it is believed the seven mighty masters, or cohens, each has an individual inner plane "ashram" that is dedicated to their teachings. These ashrams are visited in dream and vision by those whose path aligns with that master, and often the ashram is linked with a physical location or sacred site upon the Earth.

Adytum

The term adytum refers to an inner sacred shrine within a Temple, a place where the profane are not to enter, and the term can be applied to the inner world gathering of masters, where only the true seekers who have done the work and received the keys may enter to meet with the masters and experience the Holy of Holies.

Agartha

The hidden city theorized to be in the hollow Earth, where the King of the World resides to guide humanity. Most often considered synonymous of Shamballa (following), Agartha is depicted as accessible from the North Pole, with a theory that the world is actually hollow and contains a whole new realm beneath the crust. Others see that it was a vast complex of underground tunnels with their nexus in Tibet. Today we scoff at such an idea, but the truth was not literal, and that is the key misunderstanding. The city in the Hollow Earth was really perceived in the underworld, the magickal interior of the Earth where miracles do occur. Most of our information of Agartha is said to come from those who have "attunements" to it psychically.

Aryavartha

Literally translating into the "abode of the noble ones." In traditional geography it is used to refer to the northern portion of India, and the home of the "aryans" in its most literal sense. Noble ones is seen by some as an aspect of the masters or justified ones, believing a community closest to Aryavartha existed, similar to those of Shamballa. It is said to be the origin point of the holy texts known as the Vedas, and is equated to Shamballa for that reason, as many see Shamballa as the source of all Eastern wisdom.

Avalon

A Celtic term for the otherworld, found in the lore of King Arthur. Associated with faeries, gods and immortalized humans such as Merlin and Morgana. It was first depicted in the writings of Geoffrey of Monmouth, with Morgan and her eight sisters. First they are depicted as healers and sorceresses, and later in the lore as faery women. Avalon is considered to be an Island of Apples or an Isle of Glass, strongly linked with the village of Glastonbury and its sacred Tor. Many consider Avalon a crossroads or meeting place between the masters of human consciousness and the faery realm.

Bali Hai

While a show tune from the musical *South Pacific*, some consider Bali Hai the paradisal island of the Samoan culture, where perfected masters live in peace and harmony. The Island of Manono was said to be the inspiration of the song Bali Hai. It plays a role in the spiritual traditions of the Pacific, such as Huna, when introduced to westerners. Bali Hai is said to be a volcano island covered with lush emerald green vegetation. If the term predates the musical, it is unclear since most documented spiritual references to it come after the popular song.

Belovodia

Belovodia is considered to be the Russian Siberian or Mongolian version of Shamballa, but rather than in the Himalayas, it is associated with the Altai mountain range. It is part of the ancient shamanic faiths of Siberia. In one version of the myths, Belovodia is a lost Christian Orthodox city. More often it is thought of as a hidden mystical city on par with Shamballa.

Cibola

A term for the legendary cities of gold in the folklore of Mexico, along with Quivira, El Dorado and even Akator, in the movie *Indiana Jones and the Kingdom of the Crystal Skull*. Location is usually considered north of Mexico, from the South Western tribe areas to Kansas, Nebraska or Missouri. It's an allegory for not just a lost civilization with vast amounts of metallic gold, but an alchemical symbolism for a lost and mysterious civilization of adepts.

City of Pyramids

The City of Pyramids is a Thelemic reference to the resting place of Binah. One who crosses the Abyss reaches the Understanding of the sephira of Binah. Their "hoods and robes become like pyramids" according to Crowley in *The Vision and the Voice*. It is also an obvious reference to the mysticism and mastery found in the images of Egypt.

Coelestial University

A term for the gathering of masters in Christian Theosophy. There teachers with "clarified bodies" are said to teach the New Science of Angelic Philosophy. [1]

College of the Holy Spirit

Not to be confused with any terrestrial educational organization of the same name, the College of the Holy Spirit is a term used in the Rosicrucian mythos for the gathering place of education established in secret by Christian Rosenkreutz, and many consider it to have an equivalent in the inner world planes, speculating that perhaps it only existed on the inner planes. Also known as the *Collegium ad Spiritum Sanctum*, it can sometimes be equated with the House of the Holy Spirit or Laboratory of the Holy Spirit, but that truly references the reserve of feminine planetary life force, or planetary kundalini, in the shamanic world axis.

Conclave

While the technical definition of a conclave is a secret assembly or gathering, and is most often associated with the Conclave of Cardinals of the Catholic Church, when electing a new pope, the term has also been applied to assemblies of spirits, particularly faeries and angels, but can be associated with gatherings of the masters.

Great Lodge

A generic name used in Theosophical circles, along with the Great White Lodge. While most associate it with a lodge or fraternity in a Rosicrucian or Masonic sense, today many in American New Age communities automatically assume it has a Native American connotation.

Grove of the Hidden Company

A term given to me in meditation to describe the gathering of the Witches' Eternal Sabbat as used in the Temple of Witchcraft. The Grove of the Hidden Company or Mighty Dead, or the Phosphorous Grove that burns eternally but is never consumed.

House of Israel

A reference to the inner world sanctum of masters, adepts and prophets in Qabalistically inspired traditions, looking at the heavenly ideal of Israel as the inner world spiritual nation for those perfected and justified men and women.

House that Jack Built

In the myths of Traditional Craft, particularly those of the Clan of Tubal Cain style craft, a term for the otherworldly gathering of Witch souls with the Pale Faced Goddess in the otherworld, considered to be "built" or crafted by the God of Witches, reference here as "Jack," also equated with various "castles" in the otherworld.

House With Wings

A reference to the Invisible Academy found in the work of Grant Morrison's comic, *The Invisibles.*

Hurqalya

A Sufi term referring to the otherworld, specifically the heavenly otherworlds. Hurqalya also references the city, country or land of spirit where things are unexpected, time flows differently and both past and future can be changed. Particularly in the teachings of Gurdjieff, Hurqalya is considered a synonym of Belovodia.

Inner City of Light

The gathering place of the Perpetual Assembly in the works of R.J. Stewart.

Inner Convocation

The gathering of the masters and allies of the Inner Convocation teachings of William Gray and R.J. Stewart.

Invisible College

Both the historic informal gathering of intellectuals and the psychic gathering place of masters and members of The Invisibles.

Island of the Sun

A sacred Incan site in Bolivia written about by Alberto Villoldo in *Island of the Sun*, considered to be the cradle of civilization, but also a spiritual allegory for the mythical isle of masters where seekers can be initiated in a journey in flesh to the site, or in spirit psychically.

Janaidar

The mysterious hidden city at the top of Mustagh Ata, translating as the City of Eternal White. The Shamballa equivalent of the Kyrgyz people of Kyrgyzstan.

Olmolungring

Olmolungring, also known as Tagzig Olmo Lung Ring, is the cognate of Shamballa from the Tibetan Bön religion and some might argue the original vision of Shamballa. It is a realm of perfection beyond any duality, associated with Mount Kailash, though explicitly not considered a physical realm, but a spiritual one that can only be visited through spiritual discipline and purification. You can climb Kailash all you want, but if you are not in the proper state of spiritual perfection, you will not find any city. The "city" is established in a mandala pattern, associated with the image of a lotus and central to it is a pyramid mountain in the center, aligned to the cardinal directions, and four rivers flowing from the "cross quarter" points. Animal images are associated with each river.

Pali Uli

The Hawaiian equivalent of Bali Hai. A mythic volcanic isle where healing and enlightenment can take place, in the westernized Huna traditions. The name is said to mean "dark green cliffs of rock" referring to the vegetation.

Sanctum

A general term for the sanctuary of the masters, an inner temple space where they gather and where we can meet them in peace and healing.

School of Shadows

A term for the Invisible College found in Grant Morrison's work, *The Invisibles*. Not to be confused with a BDSM club of the same name.

Shamballa

The most famous incarnation of the hidden city of masters secretly guiding and ruling the world. Factoring most strongly in Tibetan Buddhism, it is traditionally believed to exist in the Himalayan mountains, atop the world's spiritual axis, a third axis around which our planet's etheric realms rotate, different from the rotational axis and magnetic axis. At one time in the golden age, all three were said to be in alignment and now shift. As the spiritual axis shifts, so does the location. Some believe it is, or was, located in the Gobi desert, etherically. Still others now believe in this age the axis has dramatically shifted, with one point moving from Tibet to Peru, indicating the Peruvian traditions will hold a level of importance in the spiritual hierarchy that Tibet has held. Believed to be a community of masters who withdrew from the world, to help guide the spiritual evolution of humanity and offer refuge to those who reach this level of attainment. Shamballa is the name adopted by Blavatsky for the realm of her masters, but most considered to be a tangible realm, these days most in the New Age community who inherit the Theosophical lore see it strictly as a spiritual reality. Along with the Great White Lodge, they are most popularly known as the Lords of Shamballa. Rather than the image of a true city, a diamond image is suggested, where the masters dwell in a collective consciousness, joined, but each facet is an expression of an individual master. The diamond etherically rotates with the spiritual axis, and its uppermost point is in the dimension closest to the divine source and its lowermost point is the densest expression of form, stretching through all dimensions of reality upon Earth. In these teachings, the diamond, or octahedron, and other Platonic solids, form the basis of the soul body or merkaba vehicle that allows enlightenment and ascension. A form of Theosophical Reiki, stressing contact with the Ascended Masters is known as Shamballa Reiki and later Shamballa Multidimensional Healing uses the diamond imagery for the ascended masters of Shamballa.

Shangri-La

A corruption of the term Shamballa, used more commonly in accounts not directly linked with wisdom traditions.

Sodality

Sodality is a term used most often in Christian theology to denote a task oriented group within the Church, also known as confraternities, rather than a modality, or the diocesan expression of the church. In occultism, the term is used in the work of William Gray, and his Sangreal Sodality organization and tradition. On an esoteric level, a sodality is a manifestation of the universal church, or body of initiates dedicated to a particular task. One could look at the Lords of Shamballa as a sodality, or perhaps *The Sodality*, dedicated to the enlightenment, healing and leadership of humanity on planet Earth.

Solomon's House

Another term used as a synonym for Invisible Academy of Grant Morrison's, *The Invisibles*.

Tara

Both a physical location in Ireland and the home or realm of the Irish gods. Seen as a metaphysical ideal, the center. Along with Avalon, it is called upon specifically in the creation of sacred space in the Cabot Tradition.

Valhalla

The Norse realm for the Einherjar, or chosen dead. It is the hall of Odin in Asgard for these noble warriors who feast, drink and fight awaiting Ragnarok. A similar realm is held by Freya called Sessrúmnir.

Valley of Josaphat

The gathering place for the Good Walkers or *Benandanti* of northern Italy. Technically it is a valley mentioned in The Bible, as the Good Walkers perceived themselves as Christian. Josaphat is said to mean "Yahweh's judgment." The Good Walkers would gather here to battle the Bad Walkers on the ember days. The valley implies a mountain, which would be seen as the World Mountain, or comic axis of the shamanic journey.

Witchdom

The term used in the psychic communications of John Brakespeare to Doreen Valiente, specifically to refer to the psychic realm inhabited by past Witches, with its own beautiful lands, streams and temples. Within Witchdom, according to Doreen Valiente's spirit contact, can be found a wide range of spells, charms and knowledge used by Witches of the past, ready to be reclaimed by the Witches of today. Unlike some Traditional Craft realms of spirit described to the exclusion of others, including other Witches not of that particular clan, Witchdom appears to be inviting to all those who walk the way of the Witch, a Summerland or happy hunting ground where our wisdom thrives. Today, Witchdom can also mean the points of personal sovereignty found in each Witch, adding up to a hidden, or secret, nation within the world of land and the world of spirit.

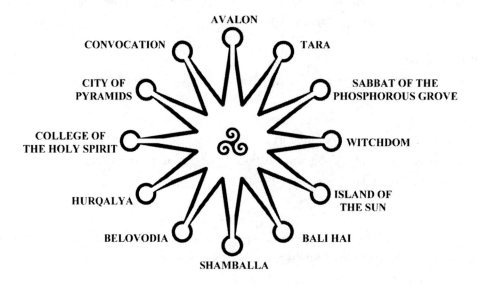

Fig. 17: Realms Leading to the Center

My own visions provided by the Hidden Company seem to show their realm within the central energy point of the Earth, much like the central column of the chakra system within our own bodies. I most often refer to it as the Grove of the Hidden Company, using the forest imagery of the European Sabbat. Particular images are like points on the body, leading to that main channel of energy.

Practitioners can perceive this gathering place in any of the three worlds, but in truth, it exists in all three, in the entire central column of our experience, in the very "wood" of the shaman's World Tree. Some perceive them down below, in the underworld, as they focus their own work on the land and the ancestors. They are focusing in more ways upon the ancestral souls of these dead. Most Witches perceive them below. Others focus upon the heavens. Most Christians couldn't dream of a "saint" being anywhere else. They are set up on the higher planes. In truth when we look at the spirit flight visions of the European Witch's Sabbat, they journey forth and meet in the dark places between, not just up or down.

Realize that your own perceptions are just that, perceptions. Making contact with these enlightened ones is more important than how you perceive it. Do the work with them. Make any necessary connections and receive your pass codes to go deeper. Then the work to join them will truly begin.

THE LAYERS OF THE SABBAT

There are many layers to the mystery of the Witch's Sabbat. Some are helpful and enlightening. Some are less so. Based upon wisdom I received from an honored elder, I realized that while there is much spiritual truth in the Medieval sabbat, so much fear and misunderstanding has been heaped upon it psychically, you have to peel through the layers to get to what is true and helpful. But the same process can be said to occur in any healing work. Healers describe the process of becoming whole and returning to our original imprint and purpose as peeling back the layers of the onions. Lots of tears, some difficulty, but what lies in the center is a pearl beyond price. When we work with sabbatic imagery and the Mighty Dead, we are peeling back the layers of fear, hate and mistrust around the traditions of Witchcraft with our honored ancestors, helping heal not only ourselves, not only the tradition of Witchcraft and all of Witchdom, but the collective psyche of the world and all who have been, are, or ever will be, upon it.

The traditional lore of the medieval sabbat, as depicted by the Christian Witch hunters is lurid and heretical in their own belief system, but still wildly titillating for men of a repressed culture. Modern Witches either reject it wholeheartedly as pure fantasy, lacking any worthy spiritual dimension, or seek to decode what potential mysteries are enshrouded within its abominations. While we have no hard evidence, many modern Witches speculate those seeking practices other than Christianity might have practiced inverted forms of Christianity, emulating the sabbat, not in organized cults as once suggested, but as individuals and small groups, in flesh or in spirit vision, for they knew the mysteries were not found in the Church. The heretical teachings of the Christians melded with the Pagan folklore and remnants of the ancient mystery teachings and found a new expression. I personally don't find the heretical nature of much of the sabbat appealing, but I find what lies underneath to be pure gold.

In the Medieval sabbat, we have the image of the Witches gathering in some haunted and dark wood, or other isolated place. They might go in procession, depicted as flying on brooms, stangs, pitchforks, goats and demons. Some testimonies have unearthly numbers of Witches reported attending, which leads more sober minded modern magicians to think the gatherings were truly in the spirit world, not in the flesh, for how else could they never be caught in the act.

At this gathering, they would partake in all of the Christian sins. They would not only feast wildly and drink alcohol, but would eat the flesh of babies. They would experience a "black mass" or inversion of the Christian mass, taking a desecrated host. They would get naked and dance "back to back" with wild abandon. These medieval Witches would not only have sex, but have all manner of wild sexual encounters with humans and beasts in the sabbatic orgy. They meet with the Devil or his representative at the height of the sabbat who would charge them to do his unholy work in the world. They were responsible for cursing people, animals and the land, for causing bad weather and bringing illness. They would send forth spirits to cause havoc and make mischief. In fact, they were said to be responsible for the opposite of everything the traditional wise woman or cunning man as healer was responsible for doing.

New Witches would have to sign a pact in blood, and receive a familiar spirit as tutor and informant, and even teacher of their malicious magicks. To seal the pact, the new Witch would have to perform some even more heinous act, such as kissing the Devil's ass, having sex with the Devil, get a mark such as a cut, brand, tattoo or physical deformity to mark the Witch or desecrate a Christian symbol, such as trampling a crucifix or the communion host wafer. This act would prove they crossed the threshold from "decency" into the world of the sinful Witch.

While so much of the sabbat came from the repressed minds of those Christian Witch hunters, the lore itself points its way to deeper layers of meaning. Beyond the Christian heretical imagery, what do we see buried in these images. The Devil is usually a reference to the Horned God, be it a stag horned god of northern territories, or a goat horned god of the south. A popular image of the horned "Devil" is found in occultist Eliphas Levi's work, with his image of Baphomet as a goat horned hermaphrodite. The named Baphomet comes from the Knights Templar, a Christian organization accused of devil worship, Witchcraft and homosexuality. Baphomet has been speculatively linked to Gnostic gods such as Abraxas and Aion. And the image is often equated with the Egyptian Goat of Mendes. The Greeks equated the goat with Pan, Priapus and satyrs, and reported that the goat was so honored in Mendes that women openly had sex with the goat.

Fig. 18: Baphomet from Eliphas Levi

The procession in flight is a spirit journey, a shamanic vision. Sometimes it takes form as a battle march, with angelic warriors in the later Christian era, off to fight demons. Other times a funeral procession of mourning, visiting homes or even a church. A procession upon the ground could be found in the ceremonies of the ancient mystery cults of Greece, particularly those of Eleusinian Mysteries of Demeter and Persephone. Similar processions and secret meetings in secluded places can be found in the cults of Orpheus, Dionysus, and Sabazius. Processions are found in the worship of many goddesses, from Isis up to the Roman era to the Teutonic Nerthus. Mystery religions had a sacrament, usually around the grain, beer or wine, made from items sacred to the gods of fertility and regeneration, as grains and grapes grow back year after year, showing the eternal mystery of life and the soul. Reports of eating babies, along with desecrating graves, have dogged any people who are marginalized and dehumanized by the dominant culture. Modern Witches would like to think that only the Christians did this, but the late Greeks said it about the Witches, and the Romans continued the tradition. Likewise both the Jews and the early Christians were charged with similar crimes and conspiracies.

Sexuality in the human world was in harmony with the sexuality of the animal and plant world. To act in one realm is to cause a sympathetic reaction in the other. Initiation ceremonies to preserve the mysteries and swear secrecy, some act that connects all members and separates them from the rest of society in secrecy, ensuring the oath be maintained, is not uncommon. We know of the Eleusinian mysteries, but to this day, we are not certain exactly what happened in them, as the inner mysteries were still kept secret.

So in observing the layers of history, beyond the medieval, we have folk practices of rural European Pagans in the Christian era mixed with the orthodox Pagan religions of Rome, Greece and most likely the Celts and the Teutons, along with parts of their inner mystery teachings. Due to the writing of the philosophers, we even have some influence from Egypt, directly or indirectly. If we go far enough back to those we might think of as our Stone Age Witch ancestors, the tribal celebration around the fire, with dance, feasting, drumming, sex and spiritual contact is not a far cry from the Medieval Witch's sabbat, minus the overt Christian heresy.

If we look at the Sabbat as an extended ritual formula, or the convergence of several different types of rituals in one, we see a number of themes and steps in the ritual.

The Sabbat itself can be divided in to four main themes – dance, sex, feast and battle – which can be seen as four different rituals or progressive stages in a larger play. Each encodes a particular mystery to the modern Witch. They are initiatory in the evolution of the Witch's soul. These four parts are enclosed by the procession and test aspects of the ritual before, and the dawning of the light as the ritual ends.

Procession

The procession, or getting to the Sabbat, is the first test. We start on the path of the Witch, described as a Winding Way or Crooked Road, because it appears we are wandering alone and without purpose. Many of us feel that way before the road is shown to us. But to get to the Sabbat, we either have to find others of like mind, and follow their ways, or through direct spirit contact, take flight on the back of the spirits of animals or the spirits of woods and plants within the broom or pitchfork. Through the use of the ointment of psychoactive plants, we can get there, or through strong will and imagination. Some believe we must be "invited" by one of the spirits already gathered – another Witch in the flesh, an ancestor, an imp, faery, or deity. The leader of the Wild Hunt, gathers us up, along with the spirits lost in the wilds from the year, and we process to the otherworld. The master or mistress of the hunt issues our invitation, joining the pack. Without this invitation, we do not find the way. The night flight is but one test to make our way.

Fig. 19: *Witches Flying to the Sabbat* (Ulrich Molitor's De Lamiis, 1489)

Test

The test can come in many forms. Sometimes it is in the form of a guardian or gatekeeper. You must know the way. Others feel if you can find it, none can bar your admittance, but the true test is in the first level of the Medieval sabbat. All the supposedly "inverted" behavior, going against the norms of society. Can you witness it and participate in it? Can you break your fears and cultural conditioning? Then you have passed the test. A test for many modern Witches, and one that many fail, is the ability to say the Lord's Prayer backwards, popularized by author Paul

Huson in his book, *Mastering Witchcraft*. It's not done because it confers any special power or magick, but if you feel you can't simply say something that you are told by a dominant power is wrong, but in reality hurts no one, and in the privacy of your own space, offends none, then perhaps you have more conditioning than you realize, and if you are not willing to get over it, then Witchcraft is not the path for you. A deeper spiritual teaching in the abominations of the sabbat is finding the beauty in any situation and accepting any situation. All is divine. All serves a purpose, and to expose ourselves to horror and still see the divine, then we are truly blessed.

Initiation

Initiation into the cult comes from the intentions and vows given in the pact. Imagery is sometimes associated with the funeral in the sabbat, as the dead, or ancestors, come to life. Some macabre woodcuts show the skeletons and cadavers dancing in hell. Funerary images come to initiations, for in many ways, initiation is death to the old self, and rebirth to the second self, the one who has already died and experienced the mystery. The first time going to the sabbat, to what might be perceived as Hell by a good Christian, can seem like death, but upon return, the classic idea of damnation from the Church would have no power. In the pact with vows and marks made and tests and familiars given, the true teaching begins with the familiar spirit, guide, confident, helper and mentor. It becomes the intermediary for communication.

Dance

The dance is animalistic in its scope, and many believe the "familiar" spirit given to the medieval Witch is a corruption of the shamanic nature of Witchcraft. The familiar, or fetch spirit, is more akin to a totemic animal guardian and teacher. The wild dancing puts us in touch with this spiritual ally. The horned god of the sabbat who gives us this familiar spirit is considered the master of animals, or nature, in Pagan traditions. The first initiation can be considered a part of the animal dance, reflected today in rituals of animal masks and "shapeshifting" dances where we seek to become one with this spirit.

Orgy

For those in more traditional spiritual models, the orgy of the sabbat can be the hardest part to understand as spiritual. But in some ways, it is one of the most important aspects of the sabbat experience. While it involves sex, the secret it also realizes that it is much more than the carnal sex depicted. If the sabbat is performed in spirit, out of body, then it is much more of a merging of consciousness with others. While that happens with physical sex, the sabbat orgy indicates an initiation into group consciousness, a multiple perspective consciousness, rather than simply a resolution of the dual consciousness of more traditional two partner tantra. The wildness of the sabbat orgy indicates a fusion of male and female, human and animal and human and spirit. The initiated Witch is united through sexual union with the fetch, who now manifests as lover. When you look at the artwork of Austin Osman Spare, regarding the Witch's Sabbat, you see a flow of one entity merging into another, sexual and somewhat grotesque, but revealing a truth beyond simple carnal sex to a mercurial merger and shapeshifting that has an obvious mystical significance.

The Sacrament & Sacrifice

Part of the orgy of the senses is the feast itself. The feast either of fine foods denied in the flesh, or later, of abominations as depicted by Christian inquisitors, indicated celebration and revelry in life. It is sacramental feasting. Even in its abominable forms, it is as barbaric as the Eucharist celebration of Catholics who state they are eating flesh and blood of a crucified man themselves. In that light, it is easier to see greater potential misunderstanding, and greater potential for sacredness hidden beneath the misunderstanding. The sacrament as celebration can be considered a celebration of the initiation of any new Witches present, and a deepening of those initiates. As the other self, the fetch, moves from animal to lover and then lover to spouse in the spirit world, conferring a new level of partnership. After this stage, the fetch as teacher moves into more abstract and symbolic representations, beyond the animal and human realms.

Battle

The last aspect of the sabbat is akin to the first, with the procession. The battle aspect of the otherworldly sabbat is a ritualized procession of the spirit throughout the land, to protect the land and people from harm, as in the Wild Hunt, though the appearance of the Wild Hunt often preceded disaster. The true battle motif is most popularized by the Benandanti, the Good Walkers, of Northern Italy, as documented in Carlo Ginzburg's *The Night Battles: Witchcraft and Agrarian Cults in the Sixteenth and Seventeenth Centuries*. Interestingly enough, it appears that the Benandanti men would fight the "Bad Walkers" in shamanic battle, while the Benandanti women gathered at the Sabbat to dance and feast.

In fact, these different stages exhibit the characteristics of some classic soul crafting with the fetch or flygia self. In the initial states, the fetch, or Lower Self aspect is considered to be beast -

like, a totemic animal. We first encounter the master of animals as the Horned God and "receive" or perhaps "realized" our fetch. If we already have it, it's revealed, or for those traditions that feel the Witch must be made, the fetch beast is "given" making the individual something more than your typical human in terms of soul construction. Some traditions add an animal spirit from the tradition to the soul complex as well as help you realize your own innate beast self.

In the sabbatic orgy, the tantra is with the fetch, who in the second stage assumed the form of a lover, usually of the opposite gender. This accounts for the modern psychological associations of the spirit with the anima/animus concept. The feast sacrament can be seen as a wedding celebration with the fetch, helping clearly unite us with the Higher Self, and in that mystery of the divine marriage, it takes on this third and final form, something abstract and beyond definition, but closer to its true shape and form. Lastly the battle is the work the two united must do in the world, for themselves, their people and the rest of the world. Being a Witch is a duty, and you can't just enjoy the world of flesh without contributing to it. And when solely in the world of spirit as one of the Mighty Dead, you must aid those who come after you, for they are simply parts of the one body of the First Witch, one part of the entirety of Witchdom.

THE DANCE OF THE DEAD

After the processional journey to reach the Sabbat, you find the most common first experience of modern Witches seeking the Eternal Sabbat is that of the dance. Despite the medieval images of initiation and oaths, I've found the realm of Witchdom, the Grove of the Hidden Company, quite welcoming to one and to all, as they all dance in a perpetual state of union and ecstasy with the mystery of the Goddess.

Many of us encounter the sabbat in dreams and visions. Looking back, I've found that I've had many dreams of ecstatic dance, spinning and rotation, but did not have a context for it. Yet this eternal dance is a common point of communion, a nexus zone where we can meet and commune with the Mighty Dead, with our Master Teachers, or even our future selves, often without words, just energy and ecstasy. It is from this place they simultaneously dance, and reach out to gather at the edges of our circles.

Elements of the sabbatic dance can range from a formless intuitive tribal dance, to more formal circle dances and the often described "back to back" folk dancing vilified by the Christians who received forced confessions of the sabbat. In today's Craft, a shapeshifting dance of your animal ally is not uncommon, and those creating flesh and blood sabbatic rituals would do well utilizing animal masked dances. Similar animal dances can occur in the vision of the Sabbat, taking the "dance your animal" to another level.

Central to the dance will be a focus, a large bonfire, or a pillar of magickal flame that is the central divine mystery of the gathering. This is the Secret Fire we all serve. If not flame, then a tree or mountain becomes the axis around which all dance and spin. Gathered with us are all manner of spirits the ancestral dead, the Mighty Dead, faeries, nature spirits, satyrs, fauns, and other beings from classic mythology. All may come to commune in this place of ecstasy.

Dance is a metaphor for life to many. Just as in life, we need to keep moving. We might trip, we might fall, but the dance goes on, with us or without us. When we are in the grove of our True Will, it is as if we have the dance steps of life down. Will there still be mistakes? Sure, but there is a flow and rhythm that was not there before. Through enjoyment of the dance we feel the love of ourselves, the love of life and the love and support of those dancers around us. Then we gain enough knowledge turned to wisdom to aid others in finding their own steps to the dance.

Fig. 20: Sabbatic Dance (15th Century Woodcut)

The sabbat dance of the Akelarre can be accessed by many different forms of trance meditation, visioning and journey work, but it is particularly effective when performed with the use of a central fire, be it a candle, wood fire, or alcohol flame. I tend to prefer a high grade alcohol in a small cauldron as my focus point, as it is easy and effective both indoors and out, and various herbs and oils can be added to it for specific intentions and meditation. The fire acts as a spiritual touchstone, a pillar or light representative of the Secret Fire, that Holy Formless Flame that is the central mystery with which we unite.

Many mysteries can be glimpsed at the Akelarre dance for those with eyes to see. The gathering includes not only the Mighty Dead and our gods, but the realm of faery, as well as the first teachers, the ancient ones of stone and tree. Those who take the time to look up might see a company of angels gathered at the dance, circling around us from above, unseen by most visitors. The dancers can all appear at times to be skeletons themselves other times naked and most of the time in ritual or "holy" vestments. While in many forms of the Craft, skyclad, the removal of clothing, is the great equalizer of class and status, in the spirit world, the removal of flesh is the great equalizer. We all have the same basic underlying structure, and the bones are the last part of our physical identity to leave the world.

Fig. 21: Dance of the Dead (*Liber Chronicarum*, 1493)

When in vestment, practitioners notice the wide range of clothing from the Witches of the past, present, and future, and a few notice quite a few of clerical garb in the mix – priests, nuns, monks and even the occasional Bishop, whose true allegiance was to the old ways in life, or the wisdom of the path was illuminated upon death, moving beyond religious differences into spiritual truth. Otherwise we range from simple peasant clothes, to robes and cloaks, to the ancient garb of priestesses, priests, wizards, yogis, and lamas.

The fire itself, around which the dance moves, provides a deeper level of the mystery when we enter it. The fire is equated with the most celestial form of the Witch Goddess, Hecate, as portrayed in the Chaldean Oracles. Within it she is the Voice of Lightning and Light. She is the voice within the fire. While in many Craft teachings of polarities, the Goddess is considered to be the matter of the planet and the Universe, as the Goddess of the Earth and of the Starry Heavens, and the God is manifested as energy and pure vibration, the Binah and Chokmah of the Tree of Life, or the Nuit and Hadit of Crowley's Thelema, they do have a point where they switch manifestation. The Goddess becomes the fire and light and voice, the vibration within the fire, and the God is the matter of the universe, the Lord of the World.

Exercise: Dance with the Hidden Company

To dance with the Hidden Company is to flow with the powers of our tradition in harmony and sympathy. Rather than ask them to come to you directly, or to an intermediary point, you now go to them. Truly they are everywhere and nowhere, but this act of "going to them" helps raise your consciousness, your own vibration, to theirs, rather than the masters attuning to a more human level of awareness.

This act of ritual envisioning attunes us to the Mighty Dead of the tradition, and becomes a potential fifth point in our preparatory foundations, at least in terms of our work here in the Akelarre gathering. Practice this dance regularly before deepening your connection with the subsequent workings of this chapter. The dance itself can become a core practice for your meditative work, always bringing you back to the collective sacred space of the sanctified ones.

Focus upon the four foundations for our work: Prepare yourself and your space. Assume a comfortable body position to facilitate trance. Perform the Three Soul Alignment. Remember your Dedication Vow. If you cast a form of sacred space, you might sense the presence of the Four Orders guarding the boundaries of your space, but such formal ritual is not always necessary. Simply envisioning the space set after cleansing and preparation can be adequate, though more ritual for the initial contact and experience certainly facilitates the process, as does the use of incense, candles, oils and your ritual relic tools. In fact, a candle flame can be a powerful focus, as the dark arch found within the center of all candle flames can be focused upon as a gateway, an archway to the Phosphorous Grove of the Hidden Company.

> *By the voice of light and lightning*
> *Who guides us on the way*
> *By the Secret Fire in the heart of all*
> *Whom we still do serve*
> *By the powers of life and love*
> *And those of death and decay*
> *By the Mysteries of the Old Ones*
> *Which we all preserve.*
> *I open the gate*
> *I open the way*
> *I walk the path to the Phosphorous Grove*
> *I will not wait*
> *To the Akelarre*
> *I enter the land of Witchdom*
> *The nation our Lord and Lady wove.*
> *So mote it be.*

Envision yourself entering through an arched gate, perhaps of stone, perhaps of boughs of tree branches forming a natural gate. Enter into the darkness beyond the gate and walk the processional road. Some walk alone. Some are joined by the spirits of the dead and the good neighbors, the spirits of shades and shadows, creatures of flesh and blood and creatures of sap and bark. As you walk, divest yourself of all that does not serve. Leave it upon the path. Let all your worries and cares fall away. Clothes can fall away, leaving you skyclad, or revealing truer vestments of spirit. With each step you become more ghost-like, more of a shadow, more of a shade. Process upon the shadow's path, knowing you are entering into a new understanding of your own way.

You reach the gate, and perhaps there is a gatekeeper there, guarding access. The secret passwords are different for different Witches. What will they be for you? Often Perfect Love and Perfect Trust are the keys, as well as the Five Fold Kiss, your own magickal name, or the correct answer to a riddle asked by the gatekeeper. Some find no guardian at all. Some have a key to open the gate themselves.

If you pass the test, enter a dark temple with a central pillar of flame. At times it manifests as a castle or tower. Other times it is a grove of trees forming a dark temple, as wood and night become its walls. The starry sky and branches become its ceiling, there are standing stones and trees like columns, and other archways, other gates at the edges of your temple. The layout and geometry of the trees and gates is perfect and symmetrical, instilling a sense of perfect harmony and precision not found in the temples of the forest or the temples of man. Many find there are twelve points, be they pillars, stones, or trees, at the edge of this sacred space. The trees are illuminated from within, an inner fire radiating outward. They may be illuminated by fountains or fiery fountains with water that burns, the fire that flows, the same substances filling the central pillar of light.

As your eyes adjust to the dichotomy of darkness and light, you now see the wise ones, the adepts and masters from many cultures and times, dancing around the fire in spirals and circles. Some are dressed like classic Witches and wizards. Some wear exoteric Eastern garb, or even modern day street clothes. They move clockwise and counterclockwise in a perfected harmony, adoring the pillar of fire, the column of liquid lightning which is the spirit of the Queen of all the Wise. None bump or jostle another. Each is like a star dancing in the orbits of the universe.

You are bidden to enter the dance and room is made for you. Jump in! These are our sisters and brothers in the Timeless Tradition. These are the priestesses and priests of the Hidden Company, the enlightened ancestors of the Mighty Dead. They might speak to you as you dance. They might also touch you, and in the touch, feel a transfer of energy.

As you dance, you might see other entities and creatures within the dance, and around it, that you did not see before. Hosts of faeries, flying angels and archangels, and the wandering gods and goddesses walk within this sacred grove.

Notice how your own image and shape can change as you dance the perfected dance of the dead. You might find your own clothing and self-image match something truer to your soul and that might surprise your rational mind. Look down at yourself. What are you wearing? What do you look like? It can change every time, with each image teaching you something new about your timeless nature.

As you dance, you might even feel your skin slip away, and suddenly, for a time, the entire dance is the dance of skeletons, the true dance of the dead where everyone is one by their bones, no different from the next.

Spiral inward and soon you will be led by a sister or brother into the Holy Formless Fire. Enter into the fire that is found at the heart of creation. This is the fire of the Queen of Witches and the King of Witches in their most pure form. Become one with the divine souls of the universe, burning brightly in heaven, earth and hell. It is the true axis mundi. Be at one with the divine fire that burns within the heart of all things, all places and all people. Feel your sense of self dissolve into the fire. Merge with it.

Listen to the voice within the fire.

Watch the images that come to you.

Feel deeply and truly as you become one with the flame.

Soon you will be intuitively guided to reconstruct yourself. Feel the fire aligning into three souls, in perfect balance, acting as one unit. Feel the three cauldrons of life, heart and head within you. Feel the various chakra points and the etheric templates come into awareness. Perfect yourself beyond any illness, injury or blockage on any level. You are divine perfection.

When you have reconstructed yourself, step back out of the fire. Join the dance again. Dance your way around the spiral, eventually coming back to the edge.

When you make your way out of the dance, one of the Mighty Dead might also speak to you as a guide, as a teacher, to help you understand your experience in the fire and give you a chance to ask questions and receive clarification. As you return, such allies can take you through the various gateways to explore its edges, filled with libraries, classrooms, elemental kingdoms, healing chambers and the void itself, for the fire is the axis mundi.

Know that when you pass from this life, as a dedicant of the vow and keeper of the three souls, you will be given an opportunity to serve here if you so choose, as a part of you always resides here, and eventually we all serve here before we move from the realms of Earth.

When you feel your experience is complete, say farewell to any guides and follow your path back out. If you opened any gates, close them. Return through the path, and while you might find yourself becoming more solid, you do not re-gather your worries and problems, and you retain your perfected health. You enter into flesh and blood, breath and bone with this revitalized self. Return from trance. Ground yourself as necessary and release or clear your space as necessary.

With repeated practice of this dance, and entering the fire, we can go deeper and deeper. Staying within the fire, and its later silence, will help you go to the deepest level of brain wave activities, delta, no thought, and reach a pure communion with the deep where you can become all that was, is, and ever will be.

THE PACT OF THE WITCHES

The initiation of the Witch into the cult is a powerful theme for the Sabbat. One might say the whole ordeal and celebration revolves around various aspects of the pact. The essence of shamanism is agreement. One could say all of reality is an agreement you make with yourself and consciousness. Consensus reality is a joint agreement between us in a society, and our personal reality is made up of wide varieties of agreements we make with ourselves and others. They carry weight in society and in our psyche, because we deem them to have value. Just as transitory concepts like money, valuing slips of paper and coins for time, energy, and goods, are societal agreements we have set into motion. Toltec mystic Don Miguel Ruiz has made a mission of teaching the use of agreements to the general public in his books, particularly *The Four Agreements*. In shamanic lore, a shaman gains power and benefit by making agreements with the spirits and gods, and modern practitioners find the same thing.

While we'd like to think the entire world of spirit as altruistic and there solely for our own personal benefit, until the modern self-help mystical movement of the West, that idea was very foreign to a magickal practitioner. Just like people, there are certainly a wide range of spirits who seek to help and aid for altruistic reasons. And just like people, there are ranges of spirits who seek to do harm. And probably the most like our society, the average person, like the average spirit, doesn't care that much about you either way. They have their own business to attend.

In terms of spiritual evolution and advancement, our religions are filled with compacts, contracts and covenants. This particular aspect of Witchcraft tends to upset those from a strong Christian background, wondering if the whole thing is really about selling your soul to the "Devil" but the foundation of Judaism is based upon a covenant of Yahweh, with his "chosen" people. After the Biblical flood, with parallels in many different cultures, there is a covenant between Yahweh and the people, to never undergo that ordeal again. Mainstream Christianity is based upon a covenant between Jesus Christ and the world. He agrees to die for all people's "sin." All you must do is agree to believe in him and follow his ways (as outlined by your particular denomination of Christianity) and your sins are forgiven and you gain entrance into the heavenly kingdom. Islam is a covenant where one surrenders to the "one true God" Allah.

Many mystical traditions, on the other hand, particularly the teachings attributed to Buddha and Krishna seek a focus upon the individual and direct relationship with consciousness, pure spirit. In those teachings, many of the gods and spirits, while quite real as entities, are also allegorical, in the sense that one moves "through" them to a purer, less personal consciousness. All entities, including gods and spirits, are on their own path of evolution just as we are, and we should not get fixated on any one without realizing what lies behind it, the field of universal consciousness supporting us all.

One could argue the initiations of the Sabbat, while a shamanic contract, are also a means of breaking Christian conditioning from the spiritual reward/punishment mode to enter into a more direct and balanced relationship with the spirits of nature and super nature, as embodied by the various creatures of the sabbat, from animals and animal-people perceived as demons, but would-be magickal creatures like the satyrs and fauns of Greek myth, and the various faery beings.

The Devil, equated with our God of Witches, a horned god, appears. Horned Pagan gods take all forms, most popularly the goat horned god Pan from the Greeks, who has become an archetypal father of all nature upon the planet, to the stag horned god of the Celtic traditions, known to us today as Cernunnos or Herne. Ram headed gods, such as the Egyptian Amon-Ra and bull horned gods, such as Dionysus, are also possibilities, but less likely in Medieval sabbat imagery. The horned figure is equated by occultists with the Goat of Mendes, the Egyptian goat-god figure worshipped and celebrated as the life force of nature, who, in turn is equated with the later Baphomet of the Knights Templar through the depictions of Eliphas Levi. What are unusual are the other forms the "Devil" takes at the sabbat. Along with a goat form, the Devil can take the shape of a black cat, toad, frog, or wolf. In my own visions, he has also been a three legged hare.

There appears to be a deeper mystery to the order of animal lord entities, relating to the primal reptilian/amphibian. In Christian lore, the "Devil" of the Garden of Eden is the snake, and many "demonic" forces appear as dragons, though to the average Pagan, the dragon is seen as a beneficent, or at least natural, force. The "pawed" animals, ones that we are a little more familiar with and consider generally benign, the dog, cat and hare, have strong magickal associations with the Craft. The dog and cat are almost certainly black, associated with the dark or Black Goddess. While the hare, the chosen form of animal to shape shift into by the accounts of Isabel Gowdie's trial, is associated with the White Goddess or faery queen. The wolf is the most dangerous of the four, related to some myths linking the Witch and the werewolf. The hoofed animal lords have a fearsome presence, as their horns indicate a certain level of danger, particularly when placed upon the scale of a god figure. Each category represents a spectrum of animal wisdom a Witch would need to be in tune with to effectively work with natural, animalistic forces in the flesh and in the spirit.

As part of the initiation, the new Witch had to renounce Christianity, as a part of the pact. Their renouncement is the first step in breaking this conditioning. Can I step out of the framework and ask for something different? An interesting and unusual account, if all confessions were simply forced based upon propaganda, is found in *A Brief History of Witchcraft.* The Devil, in his conversations with those seeking his help, indicates he is tired when people come to him for help, but then once they have the help, they go back to Christ and forget about him.[2] That doesn't seem like the response from the ultimate source of evil, as Christians would suspect, but a spirit contact in a shamanic context, asking for fidelity and consistency in their work. Shamanic work considers honoring the agreement paramount, and develops strong relationships between the spirit world and the human world. As the spirits operate in the unseen world for us, helping manifest change, we must be their advocate in the world of flesh, for there are some jobs better done by those who have eyes, ears, legs, hands and tongues.

The contracts of the sabbat are traditionally signed in blood. If they are occurring in spirit vision, then what is blood? Is it life force? The contract is a vow of life force, of personal power. It is not uncommon for a compact to require an offering or sacrifice, and in tribal traditions, before modern day squeamishness, the idea of a blood offering would not be out of the question. The agreement outlines what is expected of the Witch and what the spirit is offering. In the case of the sabbat, the offer is to join the cult of the Witch, and to be given a familiar spirit.

The familiar spirit, an imp that will act as teacher, helper, scout, and intermediary, was critical in the working of this Witch magick, beyond the simple folk charms and remedies common to the population. The imp would teach the ways of magick, of charms and knots and poppets, and would be the force to deliver the spell itself. While serving the Witch, the familiar would report back to the Devil figure on the Witch's progress and work.

With the sinister connotations of the transaction peeled away, one can see the Lord of Animals, awakening the lower soul, the fetch as the familiar spirit in the Witch. The lower soul is the intermediary and connection between the personal consciousness, and the Higher Self. This conscious relationship would only serve to deepen the magick and understanding, and deepen the connection to deity. It could be seen that the lower soul is missing in common medieval humanity, feeling so disconnected from deity directly and living in the dark ages, the darkest point of the Kali Yuga according to the interpretation of Swami Sri Yukteswar, a time when humanity is the least developed spiritually and least conscious and requires the most help. Perhaps the Animal Lord is creating a soul alteration, giving them a spirit from the underworld to fill that place of the lower soul, or to bond with whatever remnant of the lower soul is there and aid it in proper functioning.

Part of the pact is performing an unspeakable or heinous act, setting one apart from normal society, if attendance at the sabbat was not enough. Initiation rituals of all sorts involve fear, and facing boundaries and limits, pushing past them to be something "other." Usually when of a sacrilegious nature from the point of view of mainstream society, it helps break that mode of consciousness and conditioning. If you grow up believing you will be sent to hell immediately by the wrath of God for such an unspeakable act, even for considering it, and nothing happens, then you begin to wonder what else were you told that is untrue? Common acts described either involve the feast meal where either desecrated communion wafers or human flesh is consumed, the unspeakable kiss of the Devil's ass or penis or trampling upon the crucifix. The Knights Templar was accused of trampling upon the crucifix as part of their secret initiation rites. Please keep in mind, for those unspeakable acts that go against good legal and ethical judgment, to the best of our knowledge, these acts were only carried out in vision. One can look at it akin to the rituals of certain Eastern practitioners, such as the Tibetan Chöd, where the practitioners are imagined as devoured by demon goddesses. Those rituals, in flesh, not vision, use cups made from real human skulls and trumpets from thigh bones. The mystics known as the aghori regularly seek out the macabre and unspeakable, doing rituals in graveyards, haunted temples, crematoriums and in the presence of cadavers. They, like Witches, are considered "unclean" by most, though the aghori are recognized as holy people on a difficult path. The shocking images of the sabbat serve much the same purpose, though muddled and mixed in its Christianized form. Medieval Europeans certainly didn't see them as holy.

Upon completion of the initiatory ritual, the Witch was given a new name, marked with a sign of initiation, a spot, tattoo, scar or birthmark created, and the name was recorded in the "Devil's" record book, to make them a part of the Witch cult. A familiar spirit would be given and bonded to the Witch, and instructions on how to work with, or summon the spirit to do magick.

In the light of modern mysticism, the sabbatic initiation is not different in function to our many agreements, deals, and help given and taken in our relationships with various gods, elementals, and ancestors. Many describe in the New Age context of "doing work" with various entities, indicating mutual benefit for both. Perhaps the conditions that brought about the partnership were not so forceful and confrontational, but the result is the same. In this age, perhaps they don't need to be in order to establish contact and form a bond.

Modern Witches need to look at these images of the sabbat to help them resolve any last vestiges of birth religions that do not serve. If there are aspects that do serve your highest good, by all means keep them, but make sure in keeping them you are not also keeping fear, guilt, and pain. Use the imagery to reconnect to the animal world, the lower amphibian, the middle clawed creatures and the higher horned deities. All are necessary to have a clear connection with your three selves. Be clear in your communications and agreements with your contacts and allies. Form reciprocal relationships. Treat the spirits like people, fairly, and like people, maintain healthy boundaries. Just because they are spirits, don't feel they always know what is best, even if they think they know what is best. Use your own discernment and inner wisdom. Evaluate the current agreements and relationships you have, and how they shape your life. Renegotiate as necessary. Make agreements with others, and with yourself that serve your highest good and evolution, leading you on the path of the Hidden Company, and ultimately through them, to pure consciousness rooted beyond.

Exercise: The Lord of Three Faces

Perform the start of the Dance with the Hidden Company, as it should be a core practice before attempting this rite. Focus upon the four foundations for our work: Prepare yourself and your space, assume a comfortable body position to facilitate trance, perform the Three Soul Alignment, and remember your Dedication Vow. Use this evocation to enter into the grove:

> *By the Phosphorus Light*
> *In the Grove of the Dead,*
> *By the River of Tears*
> *Where we find weavers of thread,*
> *I seek to make agreement*
> *With the Lord of Three Faces*
> *By scale, claw and hoof*
> *And the love of the Graces*
> *I seek baptism by light and life*
> *In the doorway of dread*
> *I seek the Mark of the Witch*
> *By the tears that I have cried*
> *And the blood that I have shed.*
> *So mote it be.*

Rather than entering the central pillar of light through the dance, circle around behind the pillar, into the darkness of the grove. Follow a path illuminated by small balls of light, often yellow or white, like floating will o' wisps guiding you along in the dark.

One burns higher in the distance, with a diamond-like brilliance. As you approach it, is the light floating above the crown of the Lord of Witches? What form does he take?

Does the Lord manifest to you this time as the Lord of the Primordial Waters? Is he the toad father, the frog faced lord? Is he the serpent, the dragon, the wyrm?

Does the Lord manifest to you this time as the Lord of the Claw? Is he black furred? Is he the cat father? Is he the black dog of the night? Is he the three legged hare of black or white? Is he the dreaded wolf man of the forest?

Does the Lord manifest to you this time as the Lord of the Hoof? Is he the goat foot god, Lord of Mendes? Is he the stag headed father? Is he the Bull of Heaven? Is he the ram horned one?

How does the God of Witches make himself known to you?

In any form, his crown is illuminated, as if lit with the candle of knowledge, like the god Baphomet, who is Aion, who is Abraxas. That light illuminates you as well while in his presence.

Greet the Lord of Witches and he shall greet you in kind.

Commune with this Master of the Craft. What does he want from you? What do you want from him? Do you seek to go deeper into the mysteries of the Mighty Dead? He is the father, guardian and guide to the Hidden Company. Through our communion with them, they help release his power into the world as the Wheel of the Year turns, and he helps empower these Watchers who in turn can aid us. Going to him directly helps us build our connection to not just work with the Mighty Dead, but to join their ranks.

The Lord may make an agreement with you. What does he offer and what does he ask for in exchange? Is this acceptable to you? This is no sentimental agreement, but a binding and lasting pact. Negotiate your terms if he is open to listening. Sometimes he simply offers, and his offer can be accepted or rejected, so think wisely. Make sure both your obligations and benefits are crystal clear before agreeing to this contract.

Often the agreement will require something on your part to show your freedom from fear or restriction. Nothing that would harm you or another, but something that will challenge you, to clearly demonstrate that the pact will not be easy. In return, as part of the agreement, either a spirit ally in the form of a new familiar and guide, or some secret knowledge will be given to you. Traditionally the agreement is written in blood. While in spirit vision, you might have an experience of something similar, depending on how influenced your inner vision is by the Medieval sabbat. But in truth, it's an offering and exchange of life force, of vital energy.

To seal the pact, the Lord will usually consecrate you, indicating a baptism into a new level of the Craft, or a confirmation into a deeper level. The ritual consists of a mark being made up on your flesh, in this case, the flesh of your spirit body, or upon the aura, typically near the third eye. You might find the mark is made with the light of the Lord's crown candle. A new name might be given, or a reaffirmation of an old spirit name and such a name is recorded in his black or red book, adding you to the ranks of those consecrated by the Lord of Witches.

When you feel your experience is complete, say goodbye to the Lord of Witches and return the way you came. Affirm you will remember the pact perfectly and when you awaken and enter into flesh and blood, breath and bone, write down all the details. Fulfill the contract as requested, and watch for his end of the bargain to come through for you, whatever it may be.

You can ritualize the formalization of the contract. Write it up as a contract, record it in your own records, but ritually burn a copy. Mix the ashes with oil and consecrate yourself with the mixture where you were marked in spirit vision, to anchor the initiatory experience and seal the pact. You can return and make other pacts with the Witch Father, assuming he presents his other two faces to you.

Interesting enough in some of the older Witch lore around the Greek sabbatic gatherings of Witches, the God of the Witches is the invisible Hermes. Later myths make him the father of Pan, but in elder images, he had goat feet and the wings of his helmet could be envisioned as horns. A god of magick and trickery as well as the mysteries, he later was associated with the master Hermes Trismegistus, triple wise. Interesting that the sabbatic lord has three aspects to himself – primal amphibian/reptilian, clawed and horned/hoofed.

CONGRESS WITH SPIRITS

Tantra is a powerful form of magick for the magickal seeker. Tantra means a lot of different things to different practitioners. Basically a tantra is commonly a text, though the root of the word is related to a Sanskrit word meaning "to weave."[3] Tantra is typically equated with various forms of sex magick, and while sexual energy can certainly be a part of it, it really refers to the continuation of consciousness, and the practices to attain what we might think of as mastery and enlightenment through proper use of energy and consciousness. While sexual tantra can occur between flesh and blood partners, it can also occur on a psychic level between aspirant and spirit ally, often a deity. To a western magician, such tantra is akin to our modern meaning of theurgy, or god magick.

The Witch's sabbat gives us a markedly different image of tantra, in conflict with standard symbolism found in Eastern teachings of sacred sexuality and the western archetype of the Hiero Gamos (sacred marriage) and Wiccan Great Rite. Rather than focus upon the heterosexual couple as embodiment of the divine couple, be it Shiva and Shakti of India or the Lord and Lady of Wicca, the sabbat presents the image of group sex, of the orgy. While its original form might have been a shared space of couples as in Wicca today, as implied in the controversial *Aradia, or The Gospel of the Witches* by Charles Leland, sharing sources of what he believed to be genuine Italian Witch lore, there is a decidedly different aesthetic at work at the Witch's Sabbat.

> *In honour of thee I will hold this feast,*
> *Feast and drain the goblet deep,*
> *We will dance and wildly leap,*
> *And if thou grant'st the grace which I require,*
> *Then when the dance is wildest, all the lamps*
> *Shall be extinguished and we'll freely love!*

> *And thus shall it be done: all shall sit down to the supper all naked, men and women, and, the feast over, they shall dance, sing, make music, and then love in the darkness, with all the lights extinguished: for it is the Spirit of Diana who extinguishes them, and so they will dance and make music in her praise.*

— *Aradia, Gospel of the Witches* [4]

While one can automatically assume this is another corruption of the traditional teachings by Christian Witch hunters who would be both appalled and titillated at the idea of an orgy, could there be a deeper teaching here? When the diabolical element is removed, the imagery is more like one would image in the worship of Dionysus and Bacchus. While seemingly indiscriminate, is it not really an embrace of the all? Dionysian worship breaks down the barriers of separation, internally and externally, and allows spirit, energy and love to flow freely between all. The Maenads and Bacchante, while fiercely dangerous, are associated with the wilds of feast, drink, animals, people and spirit. Joining them were the man-animals of the satyrs, fauns and nymphs associated with Dionysus and Pan. One could see the orgy in the Witch's sabbat as apotheosis, deification, through group sex. Through the union with another, one communes with the spirit of divinity within the many, and therefore can see the spirit of divinity, or magick, in all.

Fig. 22: Maenads Worshipping Dionysus

Again, it is important to remember, to the best of our understanding, this orgy is happening in spirit vision, not necessarily in the flesh. In that context, this deeper truth in safety can be explored, while boundaries and concept of what is moral, just and good sexually challenged, particularly to the Medieval Christian mindset, but perhaps no less so for the mind of a modern Witch. Simple sexuality with an individual in a ritual context, and sexual connection with a spirit ally, without the images of group sex, can be challenging enough as we walk this path. And modern Stregas, Italian Witches, might cite that the Gospel of Aradia never specifically mentions group sex. "Freely love" and "then love in the darkness" can refer simply to couples.

Yet spirit congress has its place in many mystical traditions, and does in our own. Though most are not explicitly taught it, many Witches working with these themes have experiences of spirit sex. They experience sensual union with gods, angels and particularly faery allies, exchanging energy and creating bridges between the worlds. Such students will approach me as a teacher, fearing they have strayed into the realm of fantasy and offended the spirits with their fantasy, and are pleasantly surprised to hear that there is both context and history for the experience.

Ecstasy of spirit is described in terms of sexuality. One cannot read the writings of St. Theresa of Avila without seeing sexual connotations in her love for Christ and his love for her. We see it in Eastern tantra, where one either envisions their physical partner as a god, or that god form is invoked into the partner for worship through pleasure. The same can be found in the Wiccan Great Rite, when formed in flesh, not in token with the simple ritual of blade and cup. The High Priest invokes the Goddess into the High Priestess, who in turn invokes the God into him. Together, their god selves make love in the *hiero gamos*.

For strictly spirit vision traditions, we have the concept of the spirit spouse, wife or husband, of Siberian and other Asiatic shamanic traditions. The primary ally and teacher of the shaman becomes their spirit spouse. In Voodoun, Santeria and other African diasporic traditions, one can find practices of a mortal "marrying" a loa or orisha, solidifying a close relationship with ceremony. Likewise in the faery faith traditions, the concept of the Faery Lover or Faery Bride/ Husband is more openly talked about now, particularly through the work of author and teacher Orion Foxwood. Mythically the faery queen would take a mortal lover, as in the ballad of Tam Lin. One can't help but wonder if this is the root of mythologies that involve the gods loving mortals and giving birth to demigods, and the fallen angels, or "Sons of God," mating with the "Daughters of Men" in Biblical lore.

The sexual union can really be seen as also involving part of yourself, mirrored in these different spirit beings. The first and foremost inner world tantric experience can be with your own self. Modern Norse traditions relate an evolution in the relationship of the fetch, or fylgia, from an animal beast, helping us with the primal intuitive connection, and then evolving into a humanoid ally of the complementary sex. Some debate if this ally will match your sexual orientation, or be complementary gender regardless of your own sexual orientation and gender identity. Perhaps the fetch takes on the form of other spirits because this union with self is too much to accept for most, or other spirits step in at this stage to facilitate the process and build a bridge of energy with a potential new soul alteration. Through a lasting sexual union with the self, the third and seemingly final stage of the fetch, which in truth at this point might really be the Higher Soul, is an abstract symbolic or geometric form through which the mysteries are experienced.

A common theme in the European Witch sabbat imagery, and in British folklore, is the image of nine maidens. They are equated with the nine muses of Greek Mythology, those who inspired the artists and the evolution of our culture, but the British root most likely comes from the nine sisters of Avalon mentioned in the work of Geoffrey of Monmouth. While all nine are named, most famous of these is Morgan, who evolved in our image of Morgana Le Fey in the Arthurian romances. The sisters are described as priestesses and healers, shapeshifters and magicians, and she is chief among them. She gives Arthur Excalibur when his sword from the stone breaks. Later her role is expanded upon and divided amongst the characters of Viviane, Morgan and Nimue. The nine can be found again in a different form, in the Taliesin poem known as *The Spoils of Annwn,* as the nine maidens or nine Witches whose breath heats the cauldron of the underworld.

> *From the breath of nine maidens it was kindled. The cauldron of the chief of Annwfyn: what is its fashion?*

> — *The Spoils of Annwn* [5]

Lastly they are found in the grail romance poem anonymously written and known as *The Elucidation,* as the nine maidens who guard the nine wells. They offer their waters to travelers in need, but are raped by the knights of King Amangon. With this unholy action, the blessings of the nine, and through them the Goddess, are withdrawn from the world, and the land becomes the wasteland, physically and spiritually, prompting the knights of the round table to seek out the Holy Grail and restore right relationship with the land and Goddess.

The nine can be equated with faery women, as Morgan and her eight sisters were seen as faery ladies dwelling in the otherworld of Avalon, taking in those in need of healing or magick. When the Sabbat is not presided over by the horned god of Witches, it is the Queen of Witches who holds court. Images of Holda and Hecate, darker queens, are common, but the image of Diana as faery queen, and otherworldly ladies like her, are also present. While considered classically a Moon goddess and maiden, Diana in European lore is Witch queen, ruler over nature and the faery realm. Unlike today, the link between nature and the Moon, and faeries and the Moon, was more apparent. Old occult traditions would equate lunar and Venusian energies with the realm of Faery. The Mountain of Venus was akin to the World Tree and within it both the realm of the faery queen and the Wild Hunt could be found.

While less frenzied than the Maenads, the ladies of Diana's otherworldly courts can also approach the initiate and confer the experience of spirit congress. Sexual union with spiritual entities can transmit energies of healing, blessing, power and knowledge. Shapeshifting, from animal form, to your lover's form, or in and out of a multitude of forms is not uncommon for those working with sabbatic images. Shapeshifting gives us the blessing of identifying beyond our own present limited physical form, and into the multitude of creation. When you become something, you understand it better. The indiscriminate orgy imagery gives way to the process of everything becoming everything else, akin to the Celtic concept of *tuirgen* and the Buddhist (not Hindu or Neo-Pagan or New Age) concept of reincarnation. Throughout time, everything has been a part of and connected to, everything else. Many of these lessons and blessings come with the experience of spirit congress, attuned automatically without a lot of prior planning or thought. They arise naturally. One simply needs to be open to them. By being open to them, you relate deeply to the god within you, for you are relating to the divine god within the entire sabbatic orgy.

Exercise: Seeking Union

Perform the start of the Dance with the Hidden Company, as it should be a core practice before attempting this rite. Focus upon the four foundations: Prepared your self and space, assume a comfortable body position to facilitate trance, perform the Three Soul Alignment, remember your Dedication Vow. Use this evocation to enter into the grove:

By All Acts of Pleasure
That are our worship and way
By the weavings of spirit
And the Flesh of Day
All lamps are extinguished
All candles are snuffed
With the dark call for union
And the blessings of lust
Lust for the mystery
Lust for the divine
Lust for the flow
Lust for the secrets to separate and to combine
Perfection in self
Perfection in the other
All is one
And All is the Lover
So mote it be.

What do you see when you enter the grove temple? Either the Temple will be empty or full, depending on your own tantric path. The dancing masses might not make themselves known to you, and your lover awaits you in the light of the central fountain of fire. You must find your lover in the eternal light.

Or, the Temple is filled with the sabbatic orgy. It is the Bacchanalia of the frenzied ones. All figures finding union with each other, and when you look closely, merging into each other, over and over again. The figures shape shift from human to animal to non-human, and the ecstasy is in everything that is pleasuring, and then becoming, everything else. The boundaries of separation dissolve, and there is a union of fluid energy.

If with the single lover, you might find your perfect opposite, your match, your fetch transformed to husband or bride. You will find a matching that is amazingly powerful, completing you in ways that are unlike traditional romantic encounters, unless one is practicing a tantric craft, projecting the ideal divine form upon a lover for union.

If with the sabbatic orgy, you will find your perspective shift from one to many, and your definition of self challenged in the pleasures and sometimes pains, of the gathering.

Either with a single lover or with the group, you will find a new measure of union, and in the mystery of the union, grow wise. It can start with an energetic union, a mingling of chakra energy points and develop from there. Go forth and experience the sacred union of the sabbat.

When you feel your experience has reached its peak, and then returned to equilibrium, you can retain both the sense of union and the separate identity. Say goodbye to your lovers. Keep this mystery in your heart, mind, body and souls. Return to flesh and blood, breath and bone. Ground as necessary. Record the details and insights of the experience.

THE SACRAMENTAL FEAST

While it is hard to separate the sabbat feast from both the initiatory rituals and the sex, particularly as the sabbat dreamtime is non-linear, and in experience, can be hard to decipher which experience came first, in embodied rituals, the feast usually is a culmination of other work. The sacrament is the main body of the ritual. One need only look at the Catholic mass to see its central importance, and Witches were said to practice a form of inverted, or "Black Mass" by the Christians. Entheogenic sacraments most certainly played a strong role in the rituals of the Mystery Schools of Greece, Rome, or even Egypt. Even the Wiccan Cakes and Wine/Ale are done near the end of the ceremony, as both sacramental identification with the body and blood of the gods themselves.

At its first and most innocuous level, the Sabbat Feast was an enjoyment of all the things denied in daily life. Dance and sex, certainly, but with the difficulties of fine food, and the appearance that lowly peasants, those most likely with stronger Pagan leanings, would be eating less well than the nobles high upon the hill while the peasants were both taxed and expected to contribute to their Church, created a certain level of resentment. The Sabbat was an opportunity, even if only in vision, to experience these fine foods. Regardless of how the nobility lived, the Church was most certainly against even a perception of gluttony, telling people such enjoyment of food could lead to damnation in hell. While there is a certain spiritual wisdom to moderation and not being too attached to any one circumstance or condition, because the nature of the world is change, the Pagan ethos is one of enjoyment. The world is sacred, and all in it is meant to be enjoyed. If good food is available, then good food should be eaten and enjoyed. While we are a middle path, we are a crooked path, winding between extremes. Everything in moderation, including moderation.

In some descriptions, the only things that could not or would not be served in the feast was bread, oil and salt. While I find such a strict prohibition unlikely overall in terms of the spiritual sabbat experience, the reasons behind this included that they were too holy, too good and pure to be part of this "demonic" gathering. They are used in the Christian sacraments. Bread for the communion feast (yet wine, which was also used, is okay at the sabbat), oil in the anointing of the ill and dying, and salt mixed in the holy water. For more metaphysical reasons, salt might be avoided before doing spirit work as some say it's an anathema to the spirits of the dead. It is too protective and can bar spirits that you do want to summon. Modern sabbatic practitioners use bread and wine, though the bread is often dark, while the bread of communion wafers is white. In other traditions looking at the mystery of bread, the components of the bread were symbolic of the three selves. The salt is the terrestrial body, as it is in alchemy. The oil is the connecting medium, like the Lower Self or spirit. Its alchemical cognate is mercury. The honey, distilled in the hexagon containers of heavenly bees, is the soul, or Higher Self, aligned with sulfur. Flour is of the Higher Self, the part that reaches towards the light and grows gold. It transforms with the making of the bread.

The wine of the sabbat, or *vinum sabbati*, should be given special attention. Modern practitioners mix it in the cauldron, as they imagine our ancestors doing. Apple slices, food of the dead as they are white and red, are added to it today, particularly around Samhain. Most likely it was made or flavored with specific herbs, to act as a sacrament of plant powers, or even chemical entheogen. Drinking vessels dating all the way back to the use and building of Stonehenge by prehistoric people, have traces of henbane and belladonna in them. It is assumed these aided the trance work at rituals in the stone circle. Some versions of the myth of Sekhmet have her red beer spiked with mandrake, to create her true peaceful stupor, preventing her from killing all of mankind. Wine is equated with blood in many traditions, and power, for the grape is a powerful solar herb, considered premiere in the Western traditions. Associated with Dionysus, it makes a perfect sacrament for the sabbat celebration. In terms of energetic symbolism, if the salt, oil, flour and honey all constitute the three souls, the wine is the prana, the mana, the life force, that connects them all. It is solar energy turned dark red and purple, turned inward towards the mysteries. It is the connecting thread between the "beads" of the three souls.

Vinum Sabbati Infused Wine

Bottle of Red Wine

1 teaspoon of Mugwort

1 teaspoon of Wormwood

1 teaspoon of Dandelion Root

1 teaspoon of Poppy Seeds

1 Tablespoon of Honey

Bring the wine to a low simmer and add the consecrated herbs and honey, one by one, to the wine. Some potentially foolish practitioners might add small amounts of belladonna berries, henbane or true European mandrake root, but it is not recommended. Cover and let simmer for thirteen minutes. Then cool, strain and use in ritual. You can bottle it again and refrigerate to keep for a short time.

Soul Cakes

2 ½ Cups of Flour

½ Teaspoon of Baking Soda

2 ½ Teaspoons Baking Powder

1 Cup of Honey

½ Cup of Vegetable oil

4 Eggs, beaten

3 Tablespoons of Pomegranate Juice

½ Teaspoon of Poppy Seeds
1 drop of Lavender Essential Oil

Mix the flour, baking powder, baking soda, oil and eggs together. Slowly add the honey to the mix, along with the juice, seeds, and essential oil. Preheat your oven to three hundred fifty degrees Fahrenheit. Grease a 9x13-inch baking pan and pour the mixture into the pan. Bake for about thirty to forty minutes. Let it cool, then cut and serve.

Beyond the decadent food of the sabbat normally unavailable to the Witch, and its mystical associations, the most horrid accusation is that the Witches ate human flesh, particularly the flesh of babies, and/or made the sabbatic unguents of entheogenic herbs with the fat of unbaptized babies. When looking at the breadth of history, from at least Greco-Roman times, those who were outcast and ostracized faced the same heinous charges – cannibalism, infanticide and desecration of graves. The destruction of the last generation and the destruction of the next generation are considered the worst crimes imaginable to western man. Add animalistic traits, such as having horns, cloven feet or forked tongues, and whatever that society would consider diabolism, and you have the most popular accusations thrown against all outcast people by the dominant society.

The Jews were accused of all these things at one time. Sometimes they still are. This dehumanization empowers anti-Semitic thoughts and actions. The early Christians were accused of these things by Roman Pagans. Much was written on the barbarism of the Christians, claiming to eat human flesh and drink human blood, of their savior no less, in their communion sacrament. The Pagan religions knew it was a symbolic ritual. They were not killing people in their rituals, creating the first great misunderstanding between Pagans and Christians. Then later with the dominance of Christianity, those who perhaps held to older Pagan faiths were accused of the same things as Witches. The earliest forms of persecution against those we consider "Witches" were from the late Greeks and into the Roman Empire. Everyone in power feared those with knowledge of poisons. The Roman persecution of Witches intensified to horrific proportions with the dominance of the Holy Roman Empire and continued into Protestant forms of Christianity. The main difference between the Jews, Christians and Witches were that modern history considers two of the three groups real and historic, and one, Witches, because there is no evidence of these crimes, and a lack of a cohesive written testament and lore, fictional. Only relatively recently have educated scholars come to openly discuss the possibility of a shamanic origin to the sabbatic lore.

So as a modern Witch looking to the wisdom of my ancestors, I see no evidence that any Witches really practiced cannibalism or infanticide. If not, then do these images have any meaning for us today? While we don't desecrate graves, we do visit graveyard today, gather dirt and make offerings. We do gather at crossroads and in the woods when possible. So if stereotypes can contain a grain of spiritual truth, what do these things mean?

When asking my own guides within the Hidden Company about it, I got several interesting answers. One is to look at the traditions of Sin Eating as the allegory for cannibalism and the traditions of Psychic Vampirism for the myths of blood drinking. Both are expressions of very similar themes, the assimilation of life force energy by another. Both are sacramental consumptions when performed with the highest standards and integrity. Both have potential for going terribly wrong or being misunderstood by outsiders. And both have naturally inclined practitioners in the Witchcraft communities. The otherness of the Witch is often the otherness of the Vampire, crossing over. Many modern day Psychic Vampires identify in some way as Neo-Pagan.

The infanticide had a more complex meaning. As a religion of life, the death, and/or consumption of a child is particularly heinous. Many Witches identify strongly with the Great Mother archetype, and even without such identification, the idea is revolting and horrific. Yet the Great Mother is both dark and light, and myths have her, and other elder gods, such as Cronos/ Saturn, devouring his children. Life and death are sides of the same coin and such devouring means something different on the level of gods than it does on the level of humans. The God is seen in Witchcraft as child – Sun King, Child of Promise, Babe of Light. We too, ritually consume the light through bread/cakes and wine/ale. The devouring of the child is not literal, even in spirit vision, but it is the consumption of the divine child, and you become whatever you identify with magickally. To consume the child is to become your child self, an integral and necessary part of the evolutionary process as a magician. One of my favorite passed Witchcraft elders, whom I know only through story, but whom I'd like to think is among the Mighty Dead based upon the stories, is the American Witch Lady Circe, who advised:

"If you would walk the Witch's way, observe with care a child at play."

Through that observation, like a sacramental sun child cake, we become like the child. We become free and imaginative, and believe anything is possible. And when we do, it is.

On its most mystical level, the sacramental feast is the marriage feast, celebrating after a period of tantric union with your spirit ally or especially fetch partner, a more permanent union.

It is the wedding feast, as all in the Sabbat are in a perpetual state of celebration in the union of the Witches with everything else in nature. But it is also the funeral feast, a perpetual celebration of the life lived and the need to move from the realm of flesh to the realm of spirit. In that sense of paradox, between life and death, joy and mourning, we find the mystery of the feast.

Exercise: Sacrament Vision

Have the sabbat wine and sabbat cakes prepared for you for after the ritual, to reinforce in the flesh what occurs in the spirit. Also have a smaller offering plate and cup for making an offering to the spirits of the Mighty Dead.

Perform the beginning of the vision for the Dance with the Hidden Company. Focus upon the four foundations: Prepare your space and yourself, assume a comfortable position, align the Three Souls, and remember your Dedication Vow. Use an evocation to enter into the grove:

> *By oil, salt and honey*
> *By grape and by grain*
> *We seek to visit at the eternal feast*
> *Held by the Lord and Lady beyond all name.*
> *By that which has died,*
> *Burned in the ovens*
> *And drowned in the tombs*
> *Resurrected like the Sun*
> *Renewed as the rose that blooms*
> *We seek to partake in the feast*
> *We seek to be like the eternal star*
> *We seek to be born again and never again*
> *To walk with the wyrd and the bizarre.*
> *Where all is one and one is all*
> *And all is naught*
> *Naught but the stars*
> *So mote it be.*

When you enter the sacred grove of the Hidden Company, you find the feast table laid before you. It is the sacrament of the grand sabbat. All manner of food and drink is before you. The

Lady and Lord of the Sabbat invite you to join in at the table. It is up to you if you decide to join with them. If this feast is a manifestation of the Faery court, folklore tells us not to eat, or we'll be trapped in the realm of Faery forever. Others feel this was a worldly ruse of the Church, and to eat of the faery food is to be empowered by them. Opinions vary. But if it is a true manifestation lead by the Mighty Dead, this is a sacramental act helping you attune to the cycles and alignments beyond life and death, an initiatory experience. It can be a seal to the previous work in the dance, the pact and the union. The initiatory work is celebrated at this vision working and anchored within you.

Experience the sabbat feast. Make your own decisions. Commune with the participants gathered, as well as the Lord and Lady of the Sabbat. If you choose to eat, you might feel shifts within your energy bodies, corresponding to the alignments you are taking within you by the food and drink. Along with the food, there could be additional dancing and all forms of otherworldly entertainment. Each will be not only good cheer, but a deeper lesson in the symbols, movements and images. Take care to observe, remember and understand. Like the Grail Knight, do not make the error of not asking questions. Ask!

When you feel the feast has concluded, or at least your time has concluded as the feast is never ending and eternal, say farewell and politely excuse yourself. Return from the grove through the ancient hall to your perception of flesh and blood, breath and bone. Ground yourself. If you chose to eat, now make a sacrament of the cakes and wine. Leave a portion on a separate plate and glass for the spirits and place it upon your altar, and eat and drink your own portion. You can dispose of the offering in nature, at a sacred tree where you leave offerings, or upon the land of the garden, forest or field.

THE GOOD BATTLE AND THE WILD HUNT

Though somewhat different phenomena, the concept of the sacred battle and the procession of the Wild Hunt in its many forms, are connected in theme. Both involve a form of moving sabbat, a ghostly procession of deities, dead, faeries and spirits, through the land, just above it, or through the sky. The Wild Hunt is seen by others, and usually is an omen of death for the one who sees it, or an omen of ill fortune for the land. The sacred night battle, of those like the Benandanti, are usually only "seen" by those who participate in it, but their success or failure is felt by the entire community.

In the Wild Hunt, a range of entities with the tools and weapons of a hunter, are led through the land, seemingly hunting someone or something. They are joined with horses, wolves, dogs, birds and all manner of creatures depending on the version of the myth. They can be led by a figure, male or female, an intermediary or psychopomp god, such as Wotan, Gwyn Ap Nudd, Holda or Herodias, though some historical figures play a role in the lore as leader. It is found in central, northern and western European myth.

The hunt occurs on the darker half of the year, from fall equinox to spring equinox. Christian interpretation of the hunt is a parade from Hell, either lost souls escaping, or hunting the ones who have escaped from Hell. A Neo-Pagan interpretation of the Hunt is the rise of the dark god's power in the waning half of the year, protecting and guarding us during the this time, as the light of the Sun god once did in the waxing half of the year. The huntsman tracks down those forces and spirits that would harm, those malignant forces and lost souls from the year, and gathers them up. Modern crafters, for Samhain celebration, might join the Wild Hunt astrally, helping protect and guide the lost souls back to the otherworld. In the version known as Odin's Hunt, those who mocked it would be punished and mysteriously disappear, but those who joined the hunt would be rewarded with gold. The hunt is said to follow the tracks associated today with geomantic forces, but previously known as faery roads or ghost tracts, the same lines associated with the Witch's flight and the gatherings of the Sabbat. By the dawn, or the crow of the cock, they would retreat into the spirit world. Some say that three cocks will crow, one of red, white and black, before their enchantment withdraws.

The Benandanti on the other hand, were not a group of hunters, but spirit warriors, and only those identified as Benandanti can join in their battles. Traditional shamanic practitioners in tribal societies are described as spiritual warriors, "healing" by fighting the spirits of illness, as well as spirits of misfortune, bane and hungry ghosts. The Benandanti possibly appear to be a remnant, and further development of those traditions from a European perspective, surviving through Christian times until believed to be a form of diabolism from the Catholic Church. There is evidence their own people saw them as "good witches" protecting them, akin to the modern interpretation of the Witch by Neo-Pagans. A wide variety of cultural comparisons have been made to other traditions fulfilling similar functions, along with imagery not just of Witches, but also werewolves, vampires and faeries, including the Livonian werewolf traditions, Dalmatian kresniki, Serbian zduhaćs, Hungarian táltos, Romanian călușari and Ossetian burkudzauta and African Kelengu.

Fig. 23: "Wodan's Wild Hunt" (1882) by Friedrich Wilhelm Heine

Exercise: *The Night Battle*

This working is best done on the Ember Days, just before the solar holidays. Technically the Ember Days are the Wednesday, Friday and Saturday after specific holy days in the Roman Catholic calendar. Usually they fall in the first week of March, the second week of June, the third week of September and the week before Christmas Eve. Many believe they are more likely based on the times before the Pagan solar holidays of the equinoxes and solstices, and modern Pagans who look to these days as special usually hold to the Wheel of the Year associations. In Catholicism, a partial fast was held, one full meal and two meatless smaller meals. Fasting could be the process that helped facilitate the trance for the Good Walkers of Italy.

This work is not for everyone to do. Only certain Witches are called to the Night Battles. Others might find the experience of the Wild Hunt, the nocturnal sky or forest ride of the Wild Hunt, rather than the Battle itself. If so, go with the Wild Hunt ride experience. It will involve gathering up lost souls of the dead, offering blessings upon the land and those who hold well with the land and spirits, or a communion with either faeries or angelic beings.

Those who experience the battle enter into something very real and potentially dangerous. I only write about it as I've known people who experienced it, and much of the modern literature has nothing to offer in terms of practical advice. In fact much of this vision working is based on the testimonies and advice of fellow practitioners who have had this experience far more viscerally than I, but I felt it was an important experience to write directly about, rather than simply quote *The Night Battles* text as an anthropological survey of Italy. Those who enter the battle can be injured by the spirit beings, the Malandanti or Bad Walkers, who invite plague and pestilence. One I know experienced injury as illness, like a poison was running through her. Her mentor guided her through a process of seeking out aid from an elder being that was able to demand the remedy formula for the poison from the offending parties. The potion had to be made and soon resulted in a full healing with a long recovery.

Begin with the Dance of the Hidden Company vision, to meet in the nexus of the Mighty Dead, though when we start with our evocation, we might find ourselves gathered in the Valley of Josaphat, the forest, crossroads or even the graveyard of a church before ever getting to the grove temple. Begin as always with the four foundations: Prepared space. Comfortable position. Soul Alignment. Dedication Vow.

By the Ember Day
Between the Light and the Dark
By the Call of the Horn
And the drum's holy marks
Armies of Heaven
Armies of Hel
Armies of Spirits
By those who survive
And those who have fell
By the call of the Master
By the call of the Huntsman Wild
To defend the tribe of art
To return the light of the child
Green Spirits, Red Spirits
Black Spirits, White
in the Night Battles
Where we all fight
Victory is mine
Success in the War
The Magick of the True
The Magick of the Warrior
The Magick in the Core.
This circle I draw
The boundary is cast
By the Will of the Good Walkers
This Boundary will last.
May blessings be upon us
Blessings upon us all
May all thrive and heal
Before we wither and fall.
By the Ember days
Between the Light and the Dark
When the Battle of the Night
Leaves its holy mark.

You might start with hearing a horn, drum or other music as a call to arms. Your totemic animal ally might join you as steed, or you could find yourself transformed, shape shifted, into your own central animal spirit. Participants are armed not with steel, spirit or otherwise, but with plant spirit weapons, particularly stalked herbs. They shall be your allies.

Once gathered with your compatriots, you will find yourself in a hunt, chase or battle against those forces that seek to cause harm, illness, terror and misfortune. Your work to counteract these forces will lead directly to changes in your own community and the world. Follow your higher guidance and your ally's direction. Do as you must. Like the practitioners of old, defend your village.

When the battle is complete, usually with the images of dawn or the cock crowing three times, follow your path back home to flesh and blood, breath and bone. Say your farewells to those who you fought with and fought for. Tend to your own wounds and those wounded and then return. Know if you were successful, the land will prosper and the people will be healthy. Ground yourself. Take note of your experience in your journal.

Some might see this vision working and the paradigm it's based upon continuing in the mentality of duality conflict, us versus them, and reminiscent of the paradigms both in fundamental Christianity and many New Age traditions of the light versus the dark in a winner-take-all contest for the souls of the Earth. Today we must be looking for "win-win" solutions and "us" mentality. I agree wholeheartedly, but there are many who experience this phenomenon as a Witch, lightworker or spiritual warrior. It's a classic theme in shamanic traditions and predates our oldest mythologies of the European Night Battles, but if there wasn't truth to it, it would not have survived for so long. For some it is a necessary stage to be engaged in the conflict in a certain way, until a new way is understood and implemented. Perhaps this conflict is one stage to experience in a greater process.

For those familiar with the personal Inner Temple or Soul Shrine, you might find that the Grove of the Hidden Company becomes a home base, or "launching pad" of sorts for you to gather. It brings us many allies and teachers who desire to help, but requests must be made. These allies will not simply interfere even though they wish you well, akin to the bodhisattva of the east. It is akin to the Inner Temple of a collective group consciousness, rather than the personal psychic space of an individual. The grove is a nexus of many different realms and opens the way to deeper journeys.

1 Holman, John. *The Return of the Perennial Philosophy: The Supreme Vision of Western Esotericism.* Watkins Publishing, London, UK: 2008. P 32.

2 Martin, Lois. *A Brief History of Witchcraft: Demons, Folklore, and Superstition.* Running Press, Philadelphia, PA: 2010. p. 29.

3 Webster, Sam. *Tantric Thelema.* Concrescent Press. Richmond, CA: 2010. P 3.

4 Leland, Charles G. *Aradia, Gospel of the Witches.* "The Sabbat: Treguenda or Witch-Meeting – How to Consecrate the Supper – The Conjuration of Diana." *http://www.sacred-texts.com/pag/aradia/ara04.htm:* January 19, 2012.

5 Higley, Sarah. *Preiddeu Annwn:* "The Spoils of Annwn" *http://www.lib.rochester.edu/camelot/annwn.htm:* January 19, 2012.

CHAPTER TEN
THE MIGHTY DEAD OF HISTORY

While the occult traditions are rich with various masters and entities, not all of them have an association with Witchcraft or magick. While I believe the masters are truly beyond religion, even though they may have a particular mission, it can be helpful to seek out our own traditional ancestors, and look at them in the context of past occult and religious masters.

Occult tradition divides mastery into three levels: Masters of Masters, Greater Masters and Lesser Masters. The Masters of Masters are considered to be the greatest, teachers to those who already have a great level of attainment and responsible for shifting major events in the evolution of the Earth. They are considered "redeemers" by some, who rule their ray in the Theosophical definition of the term. While this would appear to include the three major masters of Manu, Planetary Teacher and Mahacohen, as well as the seven individual cohens, or masters of the Seven Rays, it is also said the Masters of Masters have to go beyond the terrestrial expression of their ray, of their mission, and become the "Star Logos" of their Ray. The Seven Rays are said to emanate to us through the seven major stars of the Pleiades and the seven stars of Arcturus. Listed among these redeemers are usually the masters of Osiris, seen as not a god but an enlightened man, Krishna, likewise not seen as a true avatar but another ascended immortal and Jesus Christ. In earlier Theosophical tradition, Christ was not seen as full master, as much of his virtues were attributed to another master overshadowing him while on Earth.

According to this tradition, the Greater Masters are seen as the law givers. They regenerate traditions, but do not redeem whole civilizations. The great prophets are considered to be the Greater Masters, though they usually have little to do with the overall Theosophical systems, except at times as past life incarnations of masters from other cultures. They are the giver of the "Law" or what one could see as the dharma, of their time and nation. Moses is the giver of the Law to Israel in the form of the Ten Commandments and the covenant with the Jewish people. Gautama, the Buddha, is the giver of the Law to Asia, in the form of Buddhism. Mohamed is the giver of the Law to Africa, and much of the Middle East, in the form of Islam. And strangely St. Paul is considered one of the Greater Masters, as the giver of Law unto Europe in the form of Christianity. Others connected to Hinduism, Taoism, shamanism, alchemy, and Paganism are not listed, nor are more "modern" religions such as Sikhism or Bahai. It's unclear where, if anywhere, the eight Taoist immortals fit.

If, as a Witch, this seems like less than helpful information, let me remind you that by these definitions, Aleister Crowley would be considered a Greater Master, the giver of the Law (Love is the Law. Love under Will) to the new aeon in the form of Thelema. I'm sure he would consider himself as a Master of Masters, achieving the rank of Ipsissimus, but I'm not sure I'm ready to view his mastery on the level of Osiris or Krishna.

Lastly, the Lesser Masters are the saints, the body of Just Men Made Perfect. Here we find more relatable teachers, and those perhaps most common to our vision of the Mighty Dead. As a Witch, I do like to see both Osiris and Crowley as a part of my spiritual heritage, but I feel most of the entities I deal with at this time are in the overall body of masters.

One could look at this division, upon the Tree of Life and Qabalistic and Thelemic teachings, as the top three ranks of Magister Templi, or Master of the Temple for Binah, where the 8th rank is equal to the third sphere of Binah, the Magus, of the 9th rank and second sphere of Chokmah and the Ipsissimus, or 10th rank of the first sphere Kether. The Just Men are those who have crossed the Abyss and made their way to the City of Pyramids in Binah. The Greater Masters are known to have given the Law to their people. What is the Law, but the Word of the Magus, uttered to change the aeon? They each started new movements, though I would wonder if we could really put St. Paul in the category with the others. And lastly the cosmic masters would be at the height of the tree, the Ipsissimus.

The following is an interesting list of historic and folkloric characters that could be considered among the Mighty Dead. I make no verifiable statement to their level of enlightenment or mastery, if any. If we believe that the Mighty Dead are outside the bounds of space and time, all, including ourselves, could be considered among their number on some level. There are figures that could be most helpful or healing for those of us on the path of the Witch. While the New Age lore has a wide range of masters articulated, it can be helpful to have a name or image of those with whom we feel a spiritual kinship and alignment, and use that lore to further our own evolution. Did any of these figures consider themselves a "master?" Who knows? Did they have that frame of reference? Most likely not for the vast majority. But do they have access to wisdom and the possibility of sharing it with us? Thus far, the answer in my practice has been yes.

While far more can be added to this list, including those with an even more spectacular and mythic history, such as King Arthur and Merlin, this gives us a wonderful starting place for some active, yet less well-known figures relating to magick and Witchcraft, and can widen our practice from the more standard mythic figures found in popular teachings.

Aconia Fabia Paulina

A Roman high priestess and initiate of the ancient mystery cults of Eleusinian Mysteries and Lernian Mysteries, as well as devoted to Hecate, Ceres, Magna Mater and Isis. She was a proponent of the ancient Roman religions and tried to save their practices from decline in the Common Era. She was married to Vettius Agorius Praetextatus, a leader in the Roman Senate. Call upon Paulina for her knowledge of the mysteries and her passion to preserve them.

Alice Kyteler

One of the earliest and more prominent European Witchcraft trials was for Alice Kyteler in Kilkenny, Ireland. Dame Alice was born in 1280, an Irish noblewoman who was married four times. When her fourth husband, Sir John LePoers was ill, he suspected poison and Alice's step-children accused Alice of poison and Witchcraft. Alice, along with ten of her servants as well as her first born son, William Outlawe Jr., were accused of practicing Witchcraft with her, including animal sacrifice, demon worship and blasphemy. A variety of magickal charms and powders were found in her home. In her trial, we have allegations of intercourse with a demonic figure named Robin, Son of Art, or Robin Artison. Many consider him her incubus, familiar, or perhaps a guise of the Devil. Her powerful and influential friends protected her for a time, even having the Bishop of Ossory, who was presiding over the case, arrested. She was convicted in 1325; the night before she was to be burned alive at the stake, she escaped to England and vanished into history. The Bishop persecuted her "followers." William was convicted, but like his mother, escaped death after recanting his heresy and magick. One, Petronella de Meath, was tortured and burned at the stake in 1324, as the first person in Ireland to be executed by burning. Alice is an excellent ally in learning when to retreat from a difficult situation.

Agnes Waterhouse

Agnes Waterhouse was most likely the first person put to death for Witchcraft in England. Along with Elizabeth Frances and Agnes' daughter Joan, they were accused of Witchcraft. Agnes confessed to having a shapeshifting familiar named Satan, appearing as a cat, toad, or dog, and it supposedly terrorized her twelve year old neighbor, Agnes Brown. Agnes would feed it her own blood, or the blood of a chicken. Elizabeth was hung for another charge twelve years later, though cleared of the original charge, and Joan was found free of all charges.

Aglaonike

An ancient Thessalian Witch of 200 BC with knowledge of the Moon and lunar eclipses. She is credited with the ability to pull the Moon from the sky, but this most likely refers to her knowledge of lunar eclipses and the nineteen year Meton cycle. She is credited as the first female astronomer of Ancient Greece and is mentioned in the writings of Plutarch. She can be called upon for aid in astrological studies, lunar magick and ancient Witchcraft.

Ambrose Bantam

Also known as Bantam the Sorcerer or the Grey Wizard, Ambrose was a Quaker and cunning man who lived in Somersworth, New Hampshire, found in the 1790 census. A reference to him is found in John Greenleaf Whittier's 1865 poem "Snowbound," referencing his "conjuring book" which is believed to be an English edition of Agrippa's *Three Books of Occult Philosophy*. Whittier wrote about him again in *Supernaturalism of New England,* as a "conjurer and skillful adept in the art of magic." While we tend to think of only Europe as a home for the cunning craft, with nothing but Witch trial hysteria in New England, here we have another view that might show the concepts of magick were ingrained and brought to the New World. Perhaps such people in rural New England were not rare oddities, but more common than we think. Call upon him for healing, divination, occult lore, and aid in grounding European traditions in the United States. For the modern Witch, this is traced in the book, *The Rede of the Wiccae* by Robert Mathiesen and Theitic.

For those of us in America, it can be helpful to have a connection to the cunning craft right in our own country.

Amergin

The name Amergin can refer to two semi-mythic Irish poets. The most popular is the author of the *Song of Amergin*, a shapeshifting poem declared as his people, the Milesians, landed upon Ireland. His words parted the storm allowing them to safely land upon the shores. As the Milesians are the last of the races to reach Ireland, becoming the modern day Irish, they faced the ruling gods, the Tuatha Dé Dannan. Amergin made a pact with the goddess of Ireland, Eiru, who then invited them upon her land. Amergin is considered a bard, poet, and Druid, and holds the mysteries of his people. Amergin is compared to figures such as Taliesin and Merlin, being a more Irish equivalent.

Apollonius of Tyana

Considered to be a contemporary of Jesus Christ, and compared to him in a less than flattering light, Apollonius was a wandering teacher and philosopher who has had many miracles and unusual circumstances attributed to him. It can be hard, like many ancient magickal figures, to determine what is fact and what is myth. It appears he traveled widely, from Asia Minor and Syria to Rome and possibly into India. Tradition tells us he established a school based upon his teachings, and Alexander of Abonoteichus was a descendent of his philosophical teachings. His magick and miracles were considered analogous to Christ, and evidence that a non-Christian could perform such feats. Some tried to make him a hero of anti-Christian sentiment. This lead to accusations that he was a demonic sorcerer from Christian authorities. Theosophists often consider him a reincarnation of Master Jesus, right after the crucifixion, continuing his work. He was considered a Hermetic philosopher possibly of the Neo-Pythagorean style, an alchemist, seer and a maker of talismans for healing and protection. He was said to be able to raise the dead and maintain his youth and vigor with the use of magickal rings and a strict meditation practice. Due to the name associated with Apollo, he was later associated with Sun worship, though myth tells us he was the son of the sea god Proteus, not a solar figure.

In the Theosophical movements, Apollonius is considered to be an ascended master, a teacher of the deepest philosophies and mysteries.

Aristoclea

A priestess at the Temple of Delphi she was considered to be a well-educated, wise scholar who tutored Pythagoras. She greatly influenced his own theories and understanding of the divine, focusing on divinity as light and truth.

Biddy Early

Biddy Early was a nineteenth century Irish folk healer and Witch. Born in 1798 as Bridget Ellen Connors, she was always known by her mother's last name, Early, even though she had four marriages, as her magickal gifts were said to be passed down each generation from mother to daughter. Her mother passed on the family secrets, the lore of herbal healing. Both her parents were dead by the time she was sixteen. She had to leave her home and wandered the roads, working where she could and starting her healing practice. The home she shared with her third husband, Tom Flanner, a cottage on Dromore Hill in Kilbarron overlooking a lake later known as Biddy Early's Lake, was strongly associated with her in the role as healer or wise woman.

There she saw many people who came seeking advice and healing. Her fame grew due to her success rate in healing people, both herbally and through her insight and what we would consider to be psychic ability. She was a creative problem solver as well as a talented herbalist. She did have an intuitive knack to know if someone saw a doctor or priest for help before her and, if they did, she would often refuse to work with them, feeling it showed a lack of faith and respect in her abilities, though if she was in a good mood, she would disregard that particular "rule." Farmers would seek aid for themselves, their animals, and the farm itself, including issues with the well or butter production. Most famous was her magick blue-green bottle, kept in a red shawl. According to legend, her son Paddy won it playing a game of Hurley for a team of strangers who disappeared. Biddy would look into the bottle as a scrying device, to see images of the past and future and get advice. She stated that she spent time among the Sidhe, the Irish faeries, visiting their land. She learned their language, and they instructed her in magick. She gave herbal remedies and potions, insisting her clients not drop the bottle on the way home, or they would lose the magick of the cure.

In 1865 she was charged with Witchcraft and heavily opposed by the local clergy, but the case was dismissed as no one would testify against her. Many stated she did nothing but good works. Biddy was an independent woman and refused to kowtow to the authority of the village as expressed by clergy and landlords, though she did befriend some priests and encouraged people to listen to what the priests had to say. She supplied her household with everything needed through her healing work. Her husbands did not need to work, and it is believed they all died from alcoholism, as many gave her gifts of strong liquors as payment. She didn't charge, but allowed her clients to decide how much to compensate her. Alcohol was a popular method of payment.

One tale says her fourth husband, Thomas Meaney, was a patient who agreed to marry her if she cured him, though he died two years after they were wed. She died in 1874 soon after Thomas' death, and asked a local priest she made friends with to prevent the magick bottle from falling into the "wrong" hands. He threw it in Kilbarron Lake, and while many have attempted to find it, none have. She was buried in Feakle Graveyard in County Clare, though her grave is unmarked. In retrospect, many now consider her a healer and holy woman, even though she was considered evil by the clergy of her time. Her cottage has been restored and become a tourist attraction. Call upon her for advice and healing, particularly if you seek to open your own cunning craft practice ministering to people.

Black Eagle

A Native American shaman/sorcerer spirit guide who aided Austin Osman Spare in his magickal work. Black Eagle became the focus of many of his magickal drawings and much speculation surrounds the nature of the spirit. Theories range that he is actually a South American sorcerer of an Aztec, Mayan or Toltec variety, to a facade for sinister extraterrestrial intelligences. Others see him potentially as a manifestation of the horned god, Devil or Baphomet, or even the animus/alter ego in spirit of Spare's teacher Mrs. Paterson. In any case, he proved to be very educational and inspirational to Spare, and appears to continue to influence those involved in Sabbatic Craft and Typhonian O.T.O. practices.

Cassandra

A mythic Greek figure, Cassandra was beloved by Apollo and given the gift of prophecy by him. In some versions of the story, she sleeps in the Temple of Apollo, and the python licks her ears clean to hear the future. Sadly Cassandra did not love Apollo back, and he cursed her so none would believe her predictions. She was the daughter of King Priam and Queen Hecuba, and sister of Helenu and Hector. As a prophetess, she foresaw the end of Troy, the death of Agamemnon and her own death, but could do nothing about it. Though not a Witch, some see her as a Priestess of Apollo. Her aid can be frustrating and tragic, as some believe anything she can help you foresee will not be believed by others, just as in her own life.

Cathbad

An Irish Druid serving at Emain Macha in Northern Ireland. He fathered a son who would be King Conchobar Mac Nessa and a daughter, Findchoem, who would marry Amergin. He was both a Druid and a warrior, teaching the ways of the Druids to many pupils and declaring the divinely blessed days for warriors to face battle. He is best known for declaring a day that if a warrior took up arms on that day, he would be famous forever, but live a short life. On that day, Cuchulainn decided to take up arms. Cathbad was a skilled prophet, with the gift of foresight.

Cathbad can be called upon for aid in divination, and all the Celtic mysteries of the Druids.

Cornelius Agrippa

While Cornelius Agrippa did not self identify as a Witch or even Cunning Man, but an occultist, magician, and alchemist, he advocated the defense of Witches and was accused of Witchcraft himself, causing him to lose several positions. Though a theologian, he was excommunicated from the Church for his studies. He studied under several renowned occultists of his time, such as Johannes Trithemius and Ramon Llull, and taught at university. Agrippa, as a public defense lawyer, successfully defended a woman in Germany accused of Witchcraft, and he gained a reputation as a supporter of Witches. He eventually moved with his family to Switzerland. He used his medical knowledge to help treat victims of the plague when in Holland. He is best known today for his *De Occulta Philosophia,* or the *Three Books of Occult Philosophy*. They are still in print today, and considered classics to the modern occultist. He was persecuted by the Spanish Inquisition, forcing him to move extensively to avoid their influence, until he died in 1535 in France.

Cornelius is an excellent ally when you feel persecuted for your beliefs and need support. As a scholar of ceremonial magick, he is an excellent ally to help the aspiring Witch learn High Magick.

Eliphas Levi

Eliphas Levi was an occultist and necromancer, famous for the publications of *Dogma and Ritual of High Magic* and *The History of Magic*, as well as a ritual in London where he summoned the spirit of the master Apollonius of Tyana. He is also well known for his depiction of Baphomet as the hermaphroditic goat headed figure, the sabbatic goat. He fused Baphomet imagery with alchemical and Qabalistic lore.

Born Alphonse-Louis Constant in Paris in 1810, he later adopted the name Eliphas Levi and had a very short career in the Catholic priesthood. He was a socialist and wrote a small work known as *The Bible of Liberty*, for which he was imprisoned for eight months. Eliphas was a proponent of the philosophy of the eternal secret doctrine, an underlying wisdom mystery found all over the world, guarded and guided by secret adepts. He was the first to correspond the Major Arcana to the letters of the Hebrew alphabet, though his correspondences are different than the popular ones of today. His ideas about Tarot and Qabalah inspired later magicians in the Golden Dawn and their own system. While late in life he made peace with the Catholic Church and warned against the practices of magic, his work lived on. He died the day Aleister Crowley was born, leading Crowley to believe he was the reincarnation of Levi. The adepts of the Golden Dawn brought Levi's work back into popular occult circles, and A. E. Waite translated his texts into English.

As Eliphas Levi summoned Apollonius, we too, can call for aid from Eliphas. Call upon him for understanding correspondences and Qabalistic studies, as well as the mysteries of Tarot and the sabbatic goat.

Erichtho

Another Thessalian Witch with the ability to speak to spirits who reveal the future. Considered the Crone of Thessaly, she was consulted by the Roman Sextus, son of Pompey, to know his future. She was also a skilled herbalist as well as a necromancer. Her historic reference appears in the work of the poet Lucan, in Pharsalia, and she appears as a character in both *The Divine Comedy* of Dante and Goethe's *Faust*. Erichtho is an ally in the ways of the Thessalian Witches, and in particular, necromancy, divination, and herbcraft.

Erma Hardinge Britten

An English born spiritualist and medium who operated primarily in New York City and Boston, Massachusetts. Born in 1823, by age thirteen in England she worked as a psychic or seer, using crystal scrying and astral travel for an occult group. She most likely received the name Hardinge from this group, and had some eye opening experiences on sexism and economics while in this group's employ. In adulthood she developed into a Spiritualist medium, teacher and eventual historian. She is credited with defining the seven principles of Spiritualism. She used her spiritualism platform to encourage the re-election of Abraham Lincoln. In 1870, she married spiritualist William Britten, but kept her Hardinge surname.

While most spiritualists identify as Christian, in numerous articles, Britten emphasized she was not. She would also refer to herself as a Witch and had the belief that all occultists speaking with the deceased, be they spiritualists, magicians, witches, prophets or mediums, are using the same skills and principles. She wrote two books she credited to a European occultist who had been a member of the group she acted as the child seer for, Chevalier Louise de B. One, *Ghost Land*, was more autobiographical of Chevalier. The other, *Art Magick: or, Mundane, Sub-mundane and Super-Mundane Spiritists: A Treatise…. Descriptive of art magick, spiritism, the Different orders of Spirits in the Universe Known to Be Related to, or in Communion with Man,* was published in 1876 and synthesized witchcraft, ceremonial magick, mesmerism and spiritualism. Some believe she simply edited the books, rather than received them spiritually. Under her own name, she wrote *Modern American Spiritualism*, released in 1870, and Nineteenth Century Miracles, released in 1884, documenting the modern spiritualist movement in America. In 1872 she started a magazine in Boston known as *The Western Star,* but discontinued it after six issues. After the Boston fires, her readers could no longer afford it. She then went to New York again and co-founded the Theosophical Society, being one of the six founding members with H.P. Blavatsky until a personal disagreement ended their relationship and Erma left the organization. She is an unknown and unsung Witch in the modern occultist movement.

Felicity Bumgardner

Felicity Baumgardner or perhaps Bumgardner is the name of the Witchcraft teacher of Laurie Cabot. Claiming knowledge and initiation from the Witches of Kent in England, she immigrated to the United States when she married an American and worked in the Boston Public Library, where she met Cabot as a teen and subsequently taught her to control her psychic abilities and initiated her as a Witch. Very little evidence can be found to verify her existence, though she continues to be a spiritual ally and ancestor to the Witches of the Cabot-Kent Hermetic Temple.

George Pickingill

If Gerald Gardner is considered the father of the modern Witchcraft movement, then perhaps occultist see George Pickingill as the grandfather or great grandfather of our Craft. Born in 1816, he was an English cunning man who worked in the village of Canewdon in Essex. He saw clients for curing illnesses and finding lost or stolen property. He was known to curse and use other harmful magicks, setting him in a different light than most "white Witches" of his time. Author Bill Liddel, in *The Pickingill Papers,* claims an illustrious occult tradition to George. Beyond his simple cunning folk work in healing and his work as a farm laborer, he was the founder of nine covens across England, one of which became the descendants of the New Forest coven of Gerald Gardner. Rumor stated he could control horses and other animals, and had a gaggle of imps at his disposal to do manual labor. Rumor also considered him a "Witch master" with nine other malevolent witches owing allegiance to him. This might be the source of the "nine covens" material to be publicized later. Reportedly members of the London occult scene also came to visit him and a controversial claim by Liddell states that Aleister Crowley was briefly a member of one of the nine covens and it influenced his later work, particularly aspects of Thelema. It also provided a further link between Crowley and Gardner, and that Crowley did not necessarily write the Gardnerian Book of Shadows, but Gardner sought him out to supplement material with his memories as a Pickingill initiate, and similarly flavored material made their way into Thelemic liturgy. Pickingill was adapting his own "traditional craft" to prepare it for the modern world through his nine covens, including the introduction of female leadership, as many souls from ancient Greece would soon be incarnating in England, and drawn to Witchcraft. This would prepare the way for them. This occult view of Pickingill is not accepted by conventional historians as fact. To many, he is like the patron saint of the Traditional Craft movement, with members from many different traditions seeing him as a spiritual ancestor.

Giordano Bruno

A heretical Italian Dominican friar, Giordano Bruno was born in 1548 and grew to be a philosopher, mathematician, philosopher, astronomer and scientist. Unlike Catholic friars of the time, Bruno was considered a pantheist, believing God and nature to be one. Such belief was considered heretical. His exploration of forbidden books and free thinking caused problems with the Church, leading him to flee the influence of the Church, though eventually he was caught and burned at the stake. He was most likely influenced by Neo-Platonism, Hermeticism, and Middle Eastern mysticism, and theorized even beyond Copernicus; he correctly believed that our Sun was a star. He created a cosmology vastly divergent from his peers. More controversially he believed that around the many stars were many more inhabited worlds, and multitudes of the "Garden of Eden" both on Earth and on other worlds. He also believed that Jesus was not God, but a skilled magician, that the Devil will be "saved" or "redeemed" and that the Holy Ghost is the Soul of the World. Among his many charges were also divination and magick. He wrote a large body of work on a wide variety of topics, radically different for his time period. Modern Strega (Italian Witch), teacher and minister Lori Bruno claims Giordano Bruno as a direct ancestor and sees her own magick as a descendant of his.

Grattidia (Canidia)

Grattidia is the actual real Roman Witch, pharmacist and perfumer upon whom the figure of Canidia in the work of Horace was most likely based. As the hag Canidia, she has two fellow Witches, Sagana and Veia, which have a match with the archetypes of the Fates and the Norns and in combination might have inspired Macbeth's three Wyrd Sisters. This image of the Witch as the repulsive hag versus the seductive enchantress appears to find popularity with the Roman writers, which then influenced the Christian perception of Witches. It was a deliberate move to discredit a belief in Witchcraft. She is associated in these poems with cypress, fig, owls and toads for her magick. As Grattidia, her knowledge would be as a Venefica, an herbalist and herbal magician and maker of medicine.

Hildegard of Bingen

A Christian mystic and visionary, Hildegard was a German nun who was also a healer, composer, poet, linguist, and philosopher. Born early in the eleventh century, she was cloistered at a young age, due to her visions. In the care of the Church, she developed her gifts, eventually becoming the magistrate of her community of nuns. She sought more independence and battled officials in the Catholic Church until she got it and continued her work in earnest. Today she is a point of study both in feminism and metaphysics, as she is considered a pioneer in holistic health, herbal medicine and gem healing. She particularly favored the golden topaz, emerald and amethyst. Her holistic system of visions, medicine and spiritual understanding represents a powerful system of health and what some would consider "magick." She can be called upon to gain new techniques and insight to illness, and the use of herbs, oils and crystals to gain a cure.

Honorius

One might wonder why a modern Witch would consider Pope Honorius among the Mighty Dead. He was the Pope of the Church of Rome from 625 to 638. During his reign, he was part of the controversial monothelitism, a philosophy that believed while Christ had a human and divine nature, he had only one will, a divine will. It was in contrast to those of the dyothelitism, or the mainstream Church, who believed Christ had two natures and two wills, human and divine. Honorius wanted to reconcile the monothelites with the greater body of the Church. After his death, Honorius and his fellow monothelites were considered an anathema and heretical to the Catholic Church. His name has been used to call into question the infallibility of the Pope. This alone gives him a warm spot in my own heart. But the figure of Pope Honorius is then connected with Honorius of Thebes, a potentially mythical character of the Middle Ages, who wrote *The*

Sworn Book of Honorius and created the Witch's Alphabet, or Theban Script, as presented by Cornelius Agrippa. The first version of *The Sworn Book* appeared public in 1629 and covers the typical grimoire traditions of demon summoning and finding lost objects. A later manuscript, *The Grimoire of Pope Honorius,* is possibly from the 18th century, and is a book of magick to be used specifically by a priest. Neither is a book of Witchcraft, but have gone on, like many grimoires, to influence the occult and Witchcraft traditions. The Theban script became the first code of Gardnerian Wicca, used by Gardner on initiation bracelets.

Hypatia

An ancient Greek philosopher from the Alexandria library. Hypatia was a Neoplatonist, mathematician, philosopher, astronomer and teacher. She was the last librarian of the Library of Alexandria. She taught a wide range of students, from Pagans to Christians and a wide range of foreigners beyond the borders of Egypt and the Roman Empire. She was both an editor of classical works and an author herself, and contributed to astronomy and science. She was considered an enemy of the Alexandrian Christians and a point of political jealousy between factions in the city. In 415 AD, during Lent, the Christians came in a mob to attack her. Led by a man known as Peter the Reader, they stopped her chariot, pulled her from it, stripped her naked and dragged her through the streets to the Christian Church, where they flayed her skin off her body, tore her to pieces and burned her. The Christians supposedly believed this "Pagan woman" enchanted others, though by all evidence she was a philosopher and scientist, not particularly a ritualist. Her death by the hands of a Christian mob was one of the signals of the end of the Classical period of antiquity when Hellenistic philosophy declined.

Hypatia is the patron saint of scholars, and particularly many of our ideas of equal rights and feminism. She embodied the powerful, liberated and educated Pagan woman of the ancient world. She is also a symbol of tolerance, being a victim of intolerance and cruelty herself. Some see her, including Christians, as a symbol of purity, as many accounts give her virginal status, though others say she was married.

Imhotep

Both an ancient high priest to the Sun god Ra and the chancellor to Pharaoh Djoser. Imhotep's name means "He who comes in peace." He is considered by many the first architect and doctor in ancient history, as well as a poet, philosopher, magician and artist. To many, he is a founder of what is now known as ancient Egyptian culture. Many myths gave him divine parentage, including Ptah, Sekhmet, Nuit, Hathor and Ma'at. He was equated with Asclepius by the Greeks. After his death he was deified, an unusual accomplishment for someone who is not a pharaoh and he became a guiding spirit to later scribes, priests and doctors.

In the modern Craft, despite popular movies painting him as villain, many experience contact with Imhotep, particularly those involved in medicine and engineering, or simply the ancient Egyptian mysteries. One of my students involved in the medical technology industry made spontaneous contact with Imhotep, who then became his master-teacher and ally in his magick and his medical career.

Fig. 24: Imhotep Statue

Isobel Gowdie

This Witch is sometimes titled the Queen of the Scottish Witches under her Witch name Janet. She is famous for her spontaneous confession to Witchcraft, with details that have become classic images of the Witch and adopted into many traditions that have no direct ties to Gowdie, or even Scotland. She describes practices and traditions, while mixed with the Christian Devil that seem to be a genuine folkloric magickal tradition. She was the first to proclaim that a coven is made up of thirteen witches, and gave accounts of meeting the Devil, being initiated and marked, flights, communion with the Faery Queen and King in the land of elves, and shapeshifting into a hare. The faeries taught her to fly, and she appeared to be able to eat the faeries' food but come and go from their land as she pleased. Most who consume faery food are trapped in Elphame. Many believed she gave her confession because she was mentally ill, while others think she was hoping for a lenient punishment, rather than being discovered by others. No record of her death exists, though stories say she was both hung and burned. Her confessions preserved an unusual amount of poetic lore about the supposed practices of the time that have gone on to inspire many Witches today. The Confessions of Isobel Gowdie is a symphony by composer James MacMillan, created as a modern day requiem to her.

Jacques de Molay

The controversial and last Grand Master of the Knights Templar. Becoming the 23rd Grand Master in 1292, he led the Order until its dissolution and his death by the orders of Pope Clement V and the machinations of King Philip IV of France, burned at the stake, in 1307. The Order amassed a great amount of wealth and power in Europe, and those in debt to the Order, such as Philip, sought to disband and discredit the order. Under torture, de Molay and other French Templars confessed to Witchcraft, heresy, idolatry and homosexuality. These confessions were used to disband the order and its power base, absorb its wealth and put many of the knights to death. Though he recanted afterwards, Jacques de Molay was still put to death. Legend says, perhaps incorrectly, that he cursed both the Pope and the King while dying, and both did die within a year of his death. He was said to die with composure even when burning, and many considered him a martyr spiritually greater than the King and Pope.

Many occultists believe the Templars were an occult organization drawing upon Middle Eastern secrets from the Temple of Solomon and Sufi mystical practices. Some believe they were heretics, while others believe their own worldview was thoroughly Christian. One confession under torture was the worship of a bearded idol head, considered to be Baphomet. While the same name as the sabbatic goat image of Eliphas Levi, it was not the same description. Many think it is simply a misspelling of Mohamed, and the Templars were practicing some form of Islamic mysticism. The Templars were associated with a wide range of magickal relics, from the Shroud of Turin and the Ark of the Covenant to even the Holy Grail. Others look to his curse as evidence of his magickal prowess and knowledge. Modern expressions of Freemasonry have adopted Templar images and lore into their teachings, which have gone on to influence modern occultism, ceremonial magick and Wicca so, in many ways, Jacques de Molay has contributed to our modern understanding of the Craft.

Joan of Arc

Joan of Arc is an unusual historic character for both Witches and Christians. Born in 1412, she was raised as, and self-identified as Catholic as would be typical for France at the time. Joan felt she had a mandate from God to remove the English invaders from France in the Hundred Years war. She was told this by "voices" she heard, claiming to be various saints, such as Saints Michael, Catherine, and Margaret, and she believed they were sent by God to instruct her. They instructed her to dress as a man, cut her hair and take up arms. She convinced enough people of her mission, including a theological board, and assumed command of a group of troops, becoming a captain. She led a victory in the Battle of Orleans, and she was later called the Maid of Orleans. Her faith and the faith she could instill in her troops inspired a formidable battle force, creating fear among their enemies. She helped France achieve victory and was given recognition at the coronation of Charles VII of France in 1429. She was later captured by the Burgundians, turned over to the English and then a pro-English court of the Church, which tried her for Witchcraft and heresy, and particularly focused upon her cross dressing. She was convicted and burned at the stake at age nineteen in 1431 and sadly King Charles VII never attempted to aid her. In a posthumous retrial, she was proclaimed innocent and then canonized in 1920 as a Catholic saint. While not a traditional Witch or cunning woman, she is honored because she died under the charge of Witchcraft, had obvious psychic powers (often perceived as mental illness), was a powerful warrior and perhaps unconsciously was a champion of transgender rights.

John Dee

While not a Witch, or even a Pagan, the Elizabethan magician John Dee is considered the continuation of the image of Merlin, the magician of Britain, and has a place in the Witch's heart. While ostensibly operating in a Christian magickal framework, he was an occultist, alchemist, astrologer and Hermeticist, with a wide education in "Pagan" arts and sciences. He was also a mathematician, astronomer and general scientist, who did not see a division of the magickal and scientific, but extensions of the same study. He is best known for his work with Edward Kelley, communing with angels and creating the Enochian system of angelic magick, which he never truly used. Shakespeare's character Prospero, from *The Tempest*, is most likely modeled after him. As such, he is an excellent patron of angelic magick, Hermetic teachings, and understanding the science behind the occult.

John "Jack" Brakespeare

Doreen Valiente's spirit contact who taught her about more forms of Traditional Witchcraft and the concept of Witchdom. Through psychic contact, though undocumented in any known historical text, he said he lived in the early 19th Century and led a coven in Surrey England. He shared basic philosophy and technique of his craft. Doreen, as an avid reader and researcher, disagreed with his stance on books. She made contact with him only between 1964 to 1966, usually at his urging, and incorporated some of his messages into her own practice. As far as I know, no other modern Witches claim communion with him.

John Cunningham (Doctor Fian)

John Cunningham, also known as Doctor John Fian, one of the North Berwick Witches of Scotland, along with seventy others, including Agnes Sampson, Agnes Tompson, Barbara Napier and Effie MacCalyan. A schoolmaster from Saltpans by day, he was considered a sorcerer and diabolical Witch, accused of trying to kill King James VI of Scotland by crashing his ship. He endured tortures of having his head bound with rope and jerked around, his feet crushed and his tongue pricked with pins until he confessed. He was forced to confess to a variety of charges, mixing diabolism with what might appear to be more genuine Witchcraft, including spirit flight, "ecstasies and trances," raising storms and casting horoscopes. One of the most interesting "crimes" was a love spell he supposedly cast upon a local girl. The spell required three pubic hairs, and he bribed her brother to obtain them while she slept. The brother was unsuccessful and ended up waking her, and the young lady complained to their mother, who gave him three hairs from a cow's udder for Doctor Fian. Fian cast the spell, and soon had a love sick cow following him everywhere, including church. People then began to suspect Witchcraft. While he recanted his confessions each time, no one cared, and eventually he was strangled at the stake and then burned for good measure at Castle Hill in Edinburgh in 1591. While a spiritual ancestor to us as he died in the name of Witchcraft, whether he was one or not, I wouldn't call upon him for success in love spells.

Fig. 25: Doctor Fian from "Newes from Scotland"

John Winthrop, Jr.

John Winthrop the Younger is a fascinating figure in New England history. Born in 1606, son of John Winthrop the founding governor of Massachusetts Bay Colony, John Winthrop the Younger came to Massachusetts with his father and went on to become the governor of the Connecticut Colony. When he returned to England for a time, he was elected as a Fellow to the new Royal Society and he wrote two papers for the society's Philosophical Transactions. He was part of a European network of natural philosophers specifically involved in alchemy. While Christian in orientation, Winthrop shaped the development of New England's settlement, culture, and medicine. He supported religious tolerance and advocated for the Pequot Indians. He acted as an authority in New England Witchcraft cases, putting an end to Connecticut Witchcraft executions. He died in Boston in 1676.

John Wrightson, The Wise Man of Stokesley

A famous cunning man who used a method of fasting to receive knowledge. While the seventh son of a seventh daughter, he claimed no special wisdom and power, just the ability to gain knowledge through fasting, including methods to cure people and animals, remove bewitchment, find lost and stolen objects and know what is occurring at a distance. He advertised his business, specializing in animal healing, and believed he could diagnose and cure bewitchment if someone "sent their water" or urine, a common practice among horary astrologers. While considered "wise" there was some disrepute to his character, and he favored violent counter-spells against those who bewitched others, with pins and fire. When working to find a lost object, Wrightson is an excellent ally.

King Edward III

King Edward III was the founder of the Most Noble Order of the Garter sometime in the 1340's, the oldest chivalrous order in the United Kingdom. In modern Wiccan mythos, generally not accepted by mainstream historians as having any truth to it, but providing some powerful resonance for Witches, King Edward founded the order as a secret nod to the Witches of England. This idea was generally popular among the Witches of Gerald Gardner and Doreen Valiente's era, and has lost popularity in the modern Neo-Pagan movement.

While at one of the King's court balls, the Countess of Salisbury (possibly either Joan of Kent or more likely Catherine Montacute) lost her garter while dancing. While history sees the reaction as ridicule and laughter, Witches believe the garter to be a sign of the Witch Cult, and the loss of a garter at this event as a revelation and scandal of the Countess' status as a Witch Queen of the Old Religion. The King picked it up with the words "Shamed be the person who thinks evil of it" and put it on. It was his unsaid approval of her status as a Witch and a statement that none would persecute her. It was his recognition that her Craft, despite popular opinion on sorcery, was not evil, but an aid to the monarchy.

Many see it as an understanding of the linked power between the Witch Cult and the Sacred King mysteries. The garter plays a powerful role in the mystic poem Sir Gawain and the Green Knight, so many see connections between the coded lore in Sir Gawain with events of King Edward's life. He was compared to King Arthur and was very popular in his own life, and only received any great criticism much later on. Crowned at age fourteen, he made England into a military power. He ruled until his death at age sixty-four in 1377.

La Voisin

Catherine La Voisin was a very controversial French Witch during the reign of Louis XIV. While she was a practitioner of divination, medicine and midwifery, it appears she was also involved in the celebration of the Black Mass and poison for personal gain. Based upon the reports, it is hard to depict her as the innocently persecuted cunning woman, as her work seems a mix of helping and harming. She gained enormous wealth catering to the upper class of Paris until she was caught in what would be known as the Poison Affair, an investigation of aristocratic murder by poison and Witchcraft. She was burned at the stake in Paris in 1680.

La Voisin has become a popular figure in media and art, but as a spiritual guide, she can probably best help us not only with her knowledge, but learning not to make similar mistakes of power without love and wisdom.

Lee R. Gandee

A modern cunning man in South Carolina going by the title of Hexenmeister or Hex Master in the Pennsylvania Dutch Pow Wow Tradition. Born in 1917 and passing in 1998, his life was filled with unusual encounters with magick as both a child and adult, including astral projections, hauntings, and the effects of hexes upon himself and others. He learned the craft of Pow Wow, aiding others as his own life became more bizarre with strong past life experiences and unclear sexuality and gender identity. He wrote the book *Strange Experience, The Autobiography of a Hexenmeister*, published in 1971 that included many Pow Wow secrets. While he took on many students and mentored other practitioners, his book was a legacy of his craft. He is also featured in the book *American Shamans*, written by his student, Jack Montgomery.

Leonora "White Crow" Piper

Though not self-identified as a Witch, Leonora Piper was a trance medium and spiritualist born in New Hampshire in 1857 and operating in her Boston area home. Her abilities and reputation attracted a wide variety of researchers, with some believing she was truly genuine and others insisting she was a fraud. She was tested to a great extent by researchers of her time. Spiritualist churches and temples across the United States hold her in the highest regard. She began at age eight with a sharp blow to the right ear, followed by an extended sound of the letter "S". Then she soon "heard" that her Aunt Sara was not dead but with her still. Her mother made note of the day and time, and later found out that Aunt Sara died that very moment. Interestingly it is possible that her intermediary spirit guides, her "controls" may not have been deceased historic humans as claimed, but perhaps symbols and aspects of her own self, but the spirits they connected her with for others were genuine. One of her guides, Phinuit, supposedly a French doctor, did not appear to know anything about medicine or the French language. But her messages through Phinuit appeared to have merit to those receiving them. Phinuit seemed to be "inherited" from her own flesh and blood teacher, Dr. J.R. Cocke. While Phinuit seemed to be her primary control for the mediumship early on, later in her career the allies and entities changed. A researcher for the American Society for Psychical Research (SPR), William James, was so impressed he nicknamed her White Crow with the statement, "If you wish to upset the law that all crows are black, it is enough if you prove that one crow is white. My white crow is Mrs. Piper."[1] Later James seemed to withdraw his support when her messages were claimed to come from a psychic researcher who had worked on the Piper case for the SPR and later died of a heart attack. Despite the controversy, Leonora was one of the most prominent and respected trance mediums of her time, passing in 1950, and provided the role of the Witch as communicator with the dead for her people and community, even if she never called herself a Witch.

Maatkare Mutemhat

In ancient Egypt, during the 21st Dynasty, Maatkare was high priestess and considered a "wife" of Amun. She is depicted as the high priestess in the Temple of Khonsu in Karnak, the Temple to the god of the Moon. To work with the Egyptian lunar mysteries, seek the aid of Maatkare.

Marie Laveau

While not a practitioner of European Craft, but of New Orleans Voodoo, Marie Laveau is a Witch by vocation and calling. The Voodoo traditions in many ways have a much better understanding of the Mighty Dead and ancestors, and see a fluid line where veneration can elevate the spirit of someone to become one of the powers, or lwa, of the tradition. Marie Laveau is considered a lwa by many practitioners, the guiding spirit and matron of New Orleans magick. Born a free person of color on September 10, 1801 in New Orleans, she made her home in the French Quarter. After the apparent death of her first husband she became a hairdresser who serviced wealthy families. She took Christophe Glapion as her lover and common-law husband until his death in 1835 and had many children, including a daughter also named Marie Laveau, in 1827. She and her mother were often confused for each other, and played into the mythology that the elder Marie could magickally regenerate and become young once again. Marie senior became a Voodoo Queen, running rituals and preparing charms, all while maintaining her Roman Catholic religion, and mixing it with African religious concepts as is traditional in both

New Orleans and Haitian Voodoo. She ministered to the sick, poor and those in prisons while also making a living with her magick and her hairdressing. Many believe her magick was really from gossip gained from her profession as a hairdresser and trafficking with prostitutes and servants, who would provide sensitive information on Marie's wealthy clients, making her psychic abilities all the more impressive with minute details, but she is also credited with doing great healing work, and effective magick for successful court cases. Marie died on either June 15 or 16, 1881, reportedly at age 98 and is buried in Saint Louis Cemetery No. 1 in the French Quarter, where she continues to be venerated, though there is some dispute as to which grave is actually hers. Offerings are made and many wishes granted are attributed to her power.

Mother Shipton

One of the most colorful "Witches" of folk history is Mother Shipton. While a very real person, many of the details of her mythos were admittedly fabricated by the editor of her posthumous book, Richard Head, including her birth in the Knaresborough Cave and her monstrously deformed appearance, referred to her as being "Hag Faced" even as an infant. We can assume she had a fairly normal birth for the time, 1488, and a fairly normal appearance. Her birth name was Ursula Southeil, born to a sixteen year old Witch named Agatha Southeil. As the mythos grew, some suspected the Devil was her father. Strange happenings seemed to follow Ursula, including poltergeist-like phenomenon and mysterious goblins harassing her enemies. Her reputation as a Witch grew, and she married Toby Shipton, a carpenter from York in 1512. Part of the mythos said she used a love spell upon the poor man, but by all other accounts their marriage was normal. She soon became known as Mother Shipton and her predictions and psychic abilities became better known. She started with local predictions and readings, and like any village wise woman, helped settle disputes, return stolen goods and right other wrongs, though healing did not seem to be one of her talents. Later her predictions turned to a more national or global stage and she was held in the same high regard as Nostradamus. Some believe her somewhat vague prophecies predicted modern boats, cars, submarines, planes and the internet. Some forgeries were added to Mother Shipton's prophecies when her book was reprinted. Regardless of the forgeries and embellishments, in her own time she was a well-known Witch, so there must be some kernel of truth to her talents. She died in 1561, buried not in a Church yard, but on the outskirts of York.

The spirit of Mother Shipton can be called upon in any prophetic work. Due to her mythos, if not her facts, she is also helpful for those seeking to accept themselves and their appearance, and find love and marriage, even if one is unpopular or feared.

Fig. 26: Mother Shipton

Mrs. Paterson

Austin Osman Spare's teacher and magickal "mother." She was supposedly a descendent of the Salem Witches of Massachusetts which Cotton Mather failed to kill and her descendants returned to Britain at some point, with knowledge of American Indian sorcery. Perhaps she was the contact of Black Eagle, whom she passed at her death to Spare. Paterson befriended Spare and initiated him into her brand of the Craft, teaching him for eight years, including the mysteries of the Witch's Sabbat, and encouraged him to use his art in magick. According to Spare, she had the ability to transform herself into a beautiful younger woman, although being chronologically very old, proving to him her claim of genuine magickal powers. Like many other initiators, there is little physical evidence to back up the story of Mrs. Paterson, other than story and hearsay. Some critics believe the emphasis of Mrs. Paterson and Black Eagle upon Spare's work is fabricated by author Kenneth Grant, though they continue to be magickally potent ideas for those working on the inner planes, and some in the current of Spare perceive contact and connection with them.

Paolo Gaspurotto

One of the male Benandanti who lived in the village of Iassico. Paolo was known to give healing charms for those who had become ill, and did so for the son of a miller in Brazzano named Pietro Rotaro, who let the information come to the attention of the local priest in 1575.

Gaspurotto was brought before the inquisitors and testified, as he believed the Benandanti were fighting the Witches. When brought up again for investigation five years later, he denied being a Benandanti or having anything to do with them. He was imprisoned for a time and his testimony was warped to fit that of the traditional Witch Sabbat imagery of the Catholic Church. It's possible by the end he began to doubt his own beliefs and experiences.

Paracelsus

Paracelsus, or Auroleus Phillipus Theostratus Bombastus von Hohenheim, was a pioneering healer and alchemist who has influenced modern occultism and holistic health. His name is said to mean "equal to or greater than Celsus" meaning he was greater than the Roman Aulus Cornelius Celsus, an encyclopedist and writer on medicine. He studied a wide variety of healing arts, including alchemy, surgery and general medicine at the University of Pasle. He began a quest for true cures to disease, going deeper into his exploration of alchemy as medicine and an understanding of the underlying life force. Abbot Trithermius, teacher of Henry Cornelius Agrippa, initiated Paracelsus into the mysteries of alchemy. He continued to travel and study all subjects, occult or not, that would aid his work, including the practice of astrology and necromancy, moving all over Europe and possibly the Middle East. He studied not only with scholars, but with Witches, sorcerers, gypsies, necromancers, astrologers and cunning women. He returned to Europe and eventually taught at his alma mater in Germany with a tremendous zeal. He was a vocal critic of the work of Galen and his ideas. His behavior and successful healing work made quite a few enemies. Many suggest that the word "bombastic" got its meaning from his characteristic behavior, though most etymologists would disagree. Eventually he was forced to leave and began to wander again in his work and education. Throughout his life, Paracelsus was a prolific writer though much of his work was published posthumously. Among his important writings are *Nine Books of Archidoxus (Neun Bücher Archidoxus), The Great Surgery Book, Philosophia Sagax, Astronomia Magna, Seven Defensiones, Wundt und Leibartznei, Philosophia Magna, Tractus Aliquot, Von den Krankheiten so die Vernunfft Berauben, Kleine Wundartzney, Opus Chirurgicum, Bodenstein,* and *Liber de Nymphis, Sylphis, Pygmaeis et Salamandris et de Caeteris Spiritibus.* Though he didn't believe in the magickal superstitions of his time, he believed in the principles of alchemy, correspondence, astrology and the virtue of nature in healing. He pioneered alchemical medicines in the art of spagyric tinctures and ens tinctures, the alchemical trinity of sulfur, mercury, and salt, as well as the theories around the four elemental entities familiar to us today as sylphs, salamanders, undines, and gnomes. Paracelsus is also said to be the first to identify zinc and to use both mercury and opium in medicine in the west, as well as being the first modern systematic botanist. His view on alchemy can be summed up as: "Many have said of Alchemy, that it is for the making of gold and silver. For me such is not the aim, but to consider only what virtue and power may lie in medicines." Paracelsus was eventually invited to live in Salzburg, where he soon died at age forty-eight. The cause of his death is unknown and, while conspiracy theories abound, most believe that it was natural causes.

Considered a wizard by some, Paracelsus can be called upon for aid in the art of alchemy, medicine and healing, as well as speaking up and speaking your mind.

Fig. 27: Paracelsus

Shamhat

Shamhat is a priestess of Inanna in the story of the Sumerian king Gilgamesh. Shamhat uses her talents in the arts of love and sensuality to tame the wild man Enkidu, who goes on to become the companion of Gilgamesh on his adventures. Sadly after she brings civilization to Enkidu his own animal companions then fear and recoil from him, as he is no longer one of them. She teaches him how not only to love a woman, but to eat and drink and dress in the Sumerian custom. Often called a temple prostitute in the tale of Gilgamesh, she is better understood in her role as sacred prostitute, a priestess of the goddess of love and war. Shamhat is a teacher of the mysteries of the cults of the Goddess in these Middle Eastern traditions.

Simon Magus

Usually seen as a Biblical figure, Simon Magus was actually a renowned Pagan magician competing with the Apostles after the death of Christ. He is considered the first Christian heretic. While a skilled magician, reportedly being able to fly, he got baptized as a Christian and offered payment to the apostles for initiation into the art of laying on of hands with the Holy Spirit. He was refused, and his "sin" for offering money in return for a position in the Church is known as simony, though many would believe despite their initial protest, the practice is alive and well in the Catholic Church. In one version of the tale, the apostle Peter prays to God to stop Simon's ability to fly while levitating high above, and he falls and breaks his leg and severely injures himself. The once benevolent crowd of followers turns on him with Peter's help and stones him to death. One could consider him the first magician-witch killed by the Christian Church. In the work of Lynn Picknett, *The Secret History of Lucifer*, she depicts Simon as a goddess reverent sex magician following the tradition of John the Baptist, and John as a rival, not precursor to Christ. His death was a method of annexing his followers to the new Christian Church.

St. Christopher

Another beloved folk saint is Saint Christopher. While Catholics can still venerate him, he is considered controversial. His official feast day in the Roman Church was removed, and due to an inability to verify him historically, many don't consider him a true saint, though he is beloved by folk magicians who use his charm as an amulet for protection when traveling. In his legend, Christopher was considered a giant from Canaan, who sought to serve the greatest king. He traveled far and wide, and found that one king, possibly a demon or monster, feared the sign of the cross, and the name of Christ, so he sought out Christ. He was instructed in Christianity and dedicated himself to service in Christ by bearing people safely across a river upon his shoulders, making him somewhat of a psychopomp figure. One day a small child seeks to cross and he carries the child, who grows heavier by each step. Christopher almost drowns and feels as if he has the weight of the entire world upon his shoulders, giving another nod to the archetype of Atlas. The child reveals he is the Christ, and Christopher's work is serving Christ. Christopher later goes to aid the martyrs of Lycia and faces temptation from the local king. He refuses and is decapitated, making him a martyr. Interestingly, many depictions of him in the Eastern Orthodox Church, most likely due to a mistranslation of his name, depict him with a dog's head. In one version of the legend, the Christ-child granted him a human head after successfully carrying him across the river. While having no direct connection to figures such as Anubis, many modern Pagans make such a link. Due to his giant proportion and his dog head, he is depicted as the patron saint of monsters in the Vertigo Comic *Midnight, Mass.* Today he is most called upon for protection during travel and from sudden death.

Fig. 28: St. Christopher (1423)

St. Cyprian

A favored patron in the Hoodoo and folk traditions, Cyprian, despite being a saint in the Catholic Church, is considered the patron saint of Witches, sorcerers, necromancers, root workers, occultists, and magicians. Before converting to Catholicism, he was from a wealthy and respected Pagan family. After his baptism he quickly became a deacon, an educator, and eventually a Bishop and martyr. He apparently turned from Paganism to Christianity due to the decline of Paganism in the late Roman era, seeking to escape its moral lapses and excess. His association with Witchcraft and magick most likely comes from a book associated with him. Along with his Christian writings and teachings, he is credited with authorship of *The Great Book of Saint Cyprian*, although most scholars do not believe Cyprian wrote it, just as they do not believe Old Testament King Solomon authored the various *Keys of Solomon*. In fact, the St. Cyprian of this grimoire refers not to Cyprian of Carthage, but to Cyprian the sorcerer of Antioch. Cyprian sought a sexual relationship with a Christian virgin named Justina, and used his magick to have devils pursue her. She banished them with the sign of the cross several times. In his frustration, he made the sign of the cross, and this freed him from the Devil's grip, and he went on to become a Christian, bishop, and then saint. Justina headed up a convent. But his book of spells, this *Great Book*, was not destroyed upon his conversion or death, and continues to guide those in his magickal tradition.

St. Germain

While the Catholics refer to the Bishop of Auxerre, a Pagan convert to Christianity, as St. Germain, in occult circles, St. Germain most often refers to the Count de Saint Germain, a European alchemist and magician with quite a controversial history. While cited in historical documents, none are sure if they all refer to the same man due to the span of time. He was said to travel the courts of Europe, remove flaws from gems, grow precious stones larger and turn lead into gold as needed. He was said to live an immortal existence upon the Earth in a body, due to his alchemical enlightenment, or, as some rumors have it, due to vampirism. He was associated with another ascended master figure, Prince Rakoczy, also known as Master R in Theosophical lore. Some say the two are the same figure, while others see Master R as Germain's own teacher. He is later associated in Theosophical lore as an ascended master, the cohen of the Seventh Ray of ceremonial order, and channeled the I AM Discourses through Godfrey Ray King. While European, he seems to have a special link with Mount Shasta, California. Past incarnations associated with him through New Age lore include Samuel the Prophet, Joseph of Nazareth,

Proclus the Philosopher, Christopher Columbus, Sir Francis Bacon and the Merlyn of King Arthur's Court. He was also considered a High Priest in ancient Atlantis and today is associated with the healing system that was first known as Shamballa Reiki. Called the Wonder Man of Europe, he's been equated with the Wandering Jew and some reports say he can fly. Today most consider him the patron saint of alchemists, magicians, Freemasons and occultists. As "master" of the New Age, he is also considered the patron of individualism and global consciousness. He is the "master" of the violet flame, invoked to bring transformation to any situation or illness. In the coming New Aeon, rumor has it he will ascend from being the master of the Seventh Ray, or Violet Ray, and become the Lord of Civilization, or Mahacohen of the Third Ray, guiding us in a new age.

Tamsin Blight

Cornish Witch Tamsin "Tammy" Blight was born in 1798 and known as the White Witch of Helston. She was married to a fellow cunning conjuror, James Thomas, but had her own practice prior to the marriage. They practiced together in the classic cunning folk tradition, seeing clients, both human and animal, for healing, divination, magickal charms, casting spells and communication with spirits. Born in Cornwall, England, during the closing years of the 18th Century, Thomasine Blight (as she was more properly known) achieved great success as a conjuror in West Cornwall, at first during her time at Redruth, and later after her removal to Helston. She was said to be able to remove a curse or spell that had been cast upon someone, as well as to put spells on those who displeased her. She also engaged in shamanic trances using hallucinogens to help predict the future and to communicate with spirits. She was particularly known for raising the spirits of the dead to answer questions, and possibly used plant substances and other shamanic techniques in her craft. She became separated from her husband after he was threatened with arrest for proposing to sleep with another gentleman who subsequently reported him to the authorities. Tamsin passed in 1856, celebrated as a popular and successful cunning woman.

Call upon Tamsin for aid in all forms of spiritualism and necromancy. As the classic "white Witch" archetype, she can help in many forms of magick, curing and charms.

Tituba

Potentially the only real "Witch" involved in the Salem Witchcraft Trials of the 17th Century. She was one of the first to be accused and to confess to Witchcraft in Salem Village. Many see her as the first victim, or the original cause of the hysteria. Tituba was a slave belonging to Samuel Parris. Tituba married another slave, named John, and had a daughter named Violet. Many believe she was a fortune teller, reading palms and tea leaves and would share her stories with Abigail Williams and Elizabeth "Betty" Parris, and then others. Those who heard Tituba's stories soon entered into fits, and described visions of Witches. Parris' daughter, Betty, suffered from these strange symptoms, which some now speculate was ergot poisoning. Parris found out, and the girl accused Tituba of hexing her or at the very least, relating stories of magick to them, and Parris beat Tituba until she confessed to her "crime" to avoid further pain. She claimed she loved Betty and never meant to hurt her, and went on to name Sarah Good and Sarah Osborne as Witches, painting an amazing picture of a Salem community of Witches. Tituba "admitted" to trafficking with the Devil, and signing his book in blood. She later recanted her confessions. Parris was enraged by her recant, and refused to pay to have her released from prison. Someone else paid for her, and most likely John, to leave prison and she began a new life with a new owner.

Tituba and the Children.

Fig. 29: Tituba and the Children by Alfred Fredericks (1878)

Tituba's race is in question. She could be of African, South American, or Arawak descent, as she was said to come from the Spanish West Indies. Documents from the time list her as "Indian" but modern speculation has that in doubt, and often suggests a mixed background. The magick that she did practice is speculated as a form of Voodoo from the Caribbean, though that does not mean she was necessarily African, and even the assumption of Voodoo is not found in any records from Tituba herself. The nature of her confessions seems much more in line with post Christian images of European Witchcraft. Is she a figure to vilify, for being the starting point of the Salem Witch trials, or a simple a folk practitioner and oppressed slave, doing what she felt she needed to do to survive? As one of the few early Witches accused who escaped with her life, was she any wiser than the rest? She was honored by Laurie Cabot when Cabot opened her Tituba's House of Voodoo as a secondary shop within her own Salem store.

Walpurga Hausmännin

An example of the village healer and midwife vilified can be found in the story of Walpurga Hausmännin. Walpurga was an old widow acting as a midwife in the city of Dillingen, in Bavaria. Along with accusations of Witchcraft, she was also accused of vampirism and child murder. Under tortured confession, she said that she was seduced by a demon named Federlin. Federlin brought her to the Devil to strike a contract that was bound by their sexual intercourse. Among her tortured confessions were stealing the host from the Church for the Devil's black masses, eating roasted babies, killing children and pretending they were stillborn and then drinking the murdered children's blood. Federlin gifted her with an ointment rather than bring her to the Sabbat so she could harm people, livestock and crops. Prior to these accusations she apparently had a successful midwifery practice. She was executed after torture and mutilation by burning at the stake in 1597.

The blessings of Walpurga are those ideally of child birth and midwifery, her love in life despite what happened to her.

The Witch of Endor

Never named, she appears in the book of Samuel I, Chapter 28 of The Bible. She is the woman who "hath familiar spirit" and is called upon by King Saul to conjure up the spirit of the prophet Samuel, who as the first king of Israel, is seeking advice on how to defeat the Philistines. Like many oracular readings, the king does not hear what he wants. Samuel prophesizes Saul's failure and defeat. While witchcraft and mediumship was outlawed in the land, this brave spirit worker remained and when called, used her craft. The fate of the Witch is not specifically revealed, but her home inspired the name Endora in the popular television show on Witchcraft, *Bewitched*.

Why would we seek to commune with these dead? First, they are a part of our magickal roots. But if they are not enlightened in life, how can they be a part of the Mighty Dead? Do we not seek out to work with, to remember and venerate those who are "higher" on the path than us, to help us across the veils and abyss to more refined levels of consciousness? Yes, we do. But in the Witch's world, we are not necessarily focused on the higher or lower, but in the cunning traditions, it is about helping people, including yourself. True, it would be hard to claim every historic cunning woman and man in folklore to be enlightened, but when setting beyond the bounds of space and time, how do we not know they weren't enlightened masters before incarnating, to fulfill a mission? How do we know that in subsequent incarnations, they did not reach the rank of great master? We don't. In the end we are all helping each other. Much like the tantric Buddhist ideal, we are all dedicating the work we are performing to the evolution of all, no matter where we might be currently in this incarnation.

Many are cunning folk who were "white witches" of a more Christian persuasion, who used their magick to reveal the "work" of the "evil" Pagan oriented Witches of the old religion, seen as Satanic. While we look to the wisdom of the cunning folk, critics would cite that modern Witches of a Pagan persuasion would have more in common with the stereotypical Satanic Witches than the Christian cunning folk, but the eclectic nature of the cunning folk, mixing herbalism, astrology, Christian prayer, faery faith and Hebrew magick is akin to the New Age eclectic. Those modern Pagan Witches who are Witches by vocation, helping people, see a kinship to the cunning folk, post or pre-Christian. White Witches of the Christian orientation were performing the vocation in their society, at a particular place and time, as we do, though we have more freedom now. Many of the occultists of Europe were born into a Christian framework, and were recognized as such, though their current associations and practices can be sympathetic to Witches today.

Many of those listed in this chapter are Witches accused of Devil worship. How is that helpful in our own quest for enlightenment? History tells us now, they were most likely not even Witches in a sense that we'd understand, but practitioners of folk healing, if at all, and victims of their communities' suspicion, greed and paranoia. Yet, they are all martyrs. Whether they believed in it or not, they died in the name of our religion. I suspect many had more to do with the Craft than most researchers would like to think, due to unusual folklore elements in their confessions, but regardless, they were innocents who we honor, and in that exchange of merit, they help us.

Figures, such as Mother Shipton, have had wildly exaggerated myths, which have been proven to be untrue. Yet, does the lack of physical truth prevent us from a spiritual truth? Many of the Eastern saints, such as the very popular Quan Yin, have verified histories much different than our current understanding or view of them. Evidence shows that the original image of Quan Yin was most likely male and was changed to a feminine figure for political reasons, to distinguish her from the male figure of Buddha. In the realm beyond, Those Who Promise change shape and form to best meet our needs and understandings. If not enlightened in life, we know them from our work with them that helps their evolution through time, and we commune with their already enlightened nature, successful in the quest beyond space and time.

Exercise: Communion with the Historic Dead

Prepare to commune with the Mighty Dead. Decide upon which figure from the historic dead of the grand order you wish to commune with and set an appropriate space for the being. You need not be restricted to the previous list, but can work with any spirit you feel appropriate for your path. If working with an ancient figure, symbols and tools that match the feel would be appropriate. For example Egyptian tools for Imhotep would be appropriate. Perhaps more medieval cunning craft images and tools for Isobel Gowdie or Tamsin Blight and even Christian symbols for any of the saints would be appropriate Even if you have few tools, make sure you have a central candle to be your spirit fire. I prefer a white candle, with the spirit candle glyph (following) carved upon it, and the following oil used to help commune:

Spirit Contact Oil

1 oz. Base Oil

5 drops of Mugwort Essential Oil

1 Tablespoon Mugwort

1 Tablespoon Wormwood

1 Tablespoon Bay Leaf

1 Tablespoon Tarragon

½ Tablespoon Parsley

¼ Tablespoon Poppy Seed

Put the dried herbs into a jar and add the base oil, such as grape seed oil, to the mixture. Either gently heat in a double boiler for thirty minutes on low heat, or let it sit in the sun for six weeks. Shake regularly. Ideally start it on the dark of the Moon. It will be done on a full Moon. Place it under the light of the Full Moon and add 10 drops of Vitamin E oil. If you have any Mugwort essential oil, add 5 drops. (Do not use Mugwort or Wormwood if pregnant.) Bottle it in a dark bottle without exposing it to sunlight again.

Fig. 30: Spirit Candle Glyph

Once the tools are prepared, prepare your ritual space and self for this spirit communication. If you are well served by spirit boards, pendulums and other oracular devices, by all means have them available to you. Get into a comfortable position for spirit contact. Perform your soul alignment of the three selves. Remember your Dedication Vow. Put these four foundation stones into place to go forward and enter into a meditative state. Light your central spirit candle. If you'd prefer to be in a traditional sacred space or circle, you can perform those rituals, and in the four directions, feel the four Orders of Masters attend your work, and the spirit flame in the center of the space. From that flame, call to the spirit with which you wish to commune. Make both a heartfelt evocation, and one that demonstrates knowledge and sympathy for their Earthly life, as it is through that particular incarnation they will manifest and aid you. By knowing something about them, you honor them and through that honor, they might speak to you. Unlike many traditions of necromancy, we are not summoning and forcing their participation, but willingly inviting them to attend. Sometimes the answer is no.

The presence of the master you've called will be indicated by some shift in the central candle. The light will flicker, or grow brighter. Begin to psychically commune with the master. You can use any technique that works for you: oracle devices, automatic writing, scrying, clairaudience or inner vision and journey techniques. Ask your questions of the master politely. Many have great success asking specific questions on magickal technique, formulas and healing methods.

Thank the spirit when done, and make it clear that while you are giving license to depart, you are simply opening the door and thanking the illustrious dead for their time. I usually end with the phrase "Stay if you will, go if you must. Hail and farewell." When done snuff the central candle and release your space. Return your awareness from any trance state and ground as needed. Bring your awareness to flesh and blood, breath and bone.

For those looking for help from more modern Witches and occultists who influence what we do today, including figures such as Aleister Crowley, Alex Sanders, Andrew Chumbley, Austin Spare, Dion Fortune, Doreen Valiente, Gerald Gardner, Kenneth Grant, Robert Cochrane, Scott Cunningham, Sybil Leek, and Victor and Cora Anderson, I suggest reading *Ancestors of the Craft*, a compilation of ancestral biographies I have edited. More detailed biographical information about each figure is listed, often by those who knew them personally, have a deep spiritual connection, or are in their initiatory traditions. I've found amazing help from modern Craft allies, and know many Witches who have had encounters in vision and ritual with figures such as Doreen, Alex, Sybil, and Victor. I have had many psychics describe a figure that would correspond with Scott Cunningham near me, and have felt his support in my work, as I've been blessed to know many of his friends as I walk this path. Sybil Leek called upon Aleister Crowley in ritual. Many call upon Alex Sanders. Reach out and make these connections to the recent dead as well as the ancient dead.

Mythic Dead

Some powerful figures, arguably more powerful to work with than those in the previous list, have less of a clear connection to a historic figure. They are the mythic dead who have made themselves known to our tradition. They are primordial, ancient dead, master sorcerers, whose line in some way we carry on. We cannot prove their lives, and perhaps they are no longer individual souls, but complex amalgams of entities. But they are strong-willed, filled with personality and willing to help those who ask with respect.

Aradia

Aradia is the daughter of the Witchcraft deities Diana and Lucifer as depicted in *Aradia, or The Gospel of the Witches* published by Charles Leland in 1899. The controversial book was based upon a document given to Leland by his Italian Witch informant Maddalena, outlining the beliefs of some Witches of Italy. While some consider Aradia as a goddess herself, or an avatar for the goddess Diana upon the Earth, in the myth, it is believed she walked the world as a mortal woman. Her birth was said to be in 1313, coinciding her adulthood with resurgence of Witchcraft in Italy. Her mother was the goddess of the Moon and queen of faeries and her father the Roman god of light, with the name many Christians equate with the Christian Devil. According to the fable, she came to the Earth to teach Witchcraft to the peasants of Italy so they could worship Diana and return to the old ways, throwing off their Christian oppressors.

Baba Yaga

Baba Yaga, or Grandmother, is an ancient Witch figure showing up in a wide range of Slavic and Eastern European folk tales. Usually depicted as the harmful Witch, she nevertheless often aids, sometimes unwillingly, the protagonists of the tale. Questing for the help of Baba Yaga is considered a dangerous task. She is the archetypal fearsome Witch of the forest sometimes equated with the Witch of Hansel and Gretel, living in the gingerbread house. She flies through the night in a large mortar, steering with a pestle, and sweeping away her tracks with a birch broom. She lives in a wooden hut standing upon giant chicken legs, letting it walk around, and her home is surrounded by a fence of human bones and skulls. She has invisible servants in her hut, and is sometimes depicted with three knight riders, possibly sons, in white, red and black. They stand for the day, the Sun and night. While never quite equated as a goddess, she is sometimes seen as a threshold figure guarding between the living and the dead. She is fierce and requires good manners to interact with her, though some tales depict her, or possibly a series of old wise women called *baba yaga*, or grandmothers, as entirely benevolent figures.

Fig. 31: Baba Yaga by Ivan Yakovlevich Bilibin

Cuchulain

Sétanta is the child who would become the man Cuchulain, or "Chulain's Hound" in Irish. Found under a variety of spellings, including Cú Chulainn, Cú Chulaind and Cúchulainn, he was the son of the Irish god Lugh and the mortal Deichtine, sister to the King of Ulster, Conchobar mac Nessa. While she was married to Sualtam, most assume Lugh of the Tuatha de Dannan was Sétanta's father. Sétanta gained his name after killing the dog of Chulain, and vowing to replace the dog until a new one could be raised and grown fully. The Druid Cathbad was the one to name him Cuchulain. He is also known as the Hound of Ulster because of this. As a demigod, Cuchulain's life was prophesized to be powerful and memorable, but short lived. Cuchulain had the ability to enter into a battle frenzy and wielded powerful magickal weapons and a chariot. Many classic scholars compare his story to that of Achilles. He had a fractious relationship with the goddess Morrighan, who acted as both tutor and nemesis at times. His life was filled with glorious battles and ultimately his death occurred when the geasa, or sacred prohibition, was broken. He was not to eat of his namesake, the dog, or refuse hospitality. When offered dog meat by an old woman, most likely the Morrighan, he was weakened and went to his death on the battlefield.

Cunning Woman

Cunning Woman has no historical context, but her spirit is akin to the Western Pagan image of the Medicine Buddha. She is the first healer, the first bone setter, the first herbalist and spirit caller. She is the spirit of the Stone Age shamaness, using all of these talents to heal. She is the originator of medicine and continues to guide, teach and heal with these skills. She appears to me as neither young nor old, neither heavy not thin, neither solid nor ethereal. She is between, and resides in a great garden with many trees and herbs and gems, each with a secret to share. She sees me at a table, sometimes wood and sometimes stone, and spends more time counseling to the issues beneath the illness than the illness itself. She is funny with a dry sense of humor, and while timeless in her wisdom, savvy about the modern world and her advice is applicable to us no matter our background or culture. She will give information to help cure, actions, and often spirit remedies consisting of the spirits of plants, minerals and even animals to "drink" while in vision. Keep note of any formulas she gives you to make and take, as she rarely gives them twice. If you don't heed her wisdom, she will shorten her time and attention with you.

Dame Abundia

The Lady of Abundance, also Dame Habonde, is the leader of the Wild Hunt or nightly visitation in European myth, leading the band of women, often in spirit, house to house where offerings are left for them and granting prosperity to those who do so in accord with the old ways. Most likely a mythic survival of the Roman goddess Abundantia, the goddess personifying good fortune and prosperity. Others interpret Abundia as a faery spirit. As she leads the procession of the spirits, equated with the dead, she could possibly be a spirit of the dead, for the ancestors can bring prosperity and blessing to the land of the living. Many theories see the old gods as some of our eldest ancestors, deified.

Gilgamesh

Gilgamesh is a Sumerian demigod and the fifth King of Uruk, where modern day Iraq is now. While a historic figure, his more mythic tales are found in The Epic of Gilgamesh, confusing his nature. Mostly likely his deification arose over time as his stories became more impressive, or he truly was a priest-king, operating in several worlds at once. He built (or had built) the walls of Uruk to protect his people from invaders. He had a tumultuous relationship with the goddess Inanna/Ishtar, similar to the role between Cuchulain and the Morrighan as both a tutor and sometime adversary. In the epic, his friend, the wild man Enkidu is killed by the gods as punishment, and Gilgamesh becomes obsessed with finding the secrets to immortality. His quest brings him to the sage who survived the Great Flood, Utnapishtim. Utnapishtim instructs him on a miraculous anti-aging herb at the bottom of a lake. Gilgamesh gets it, but it is then stolen by a serpent when he bathes. The tale of Gilgamesh is similar to the search of other heroes' quest, and some are guided by the spirit of Gilgamesh as an ancient priest-king, becoming an ancient sage to us much like Utnapishtim was to him.

Hercules

Hercules (Heracles to the Greeks) is a demigod, the son of Zeus and Alcmene. Being both human and divine, his story is looked upon as the quest for immortality through heroic acts. Hera/Juno resents this demigod son as a sign of her husband's infidelity. Further, Zeus has Hercules suckle on Hera's breast while she sleeps, to increase his power and divinity. She causes all manner of problems for Hercules as revenge.

To atone for his past, killing his family in a wild rage (some say caused by Hera/Juno) he consulted with the oracle of Delphi on how to atone. He was instructed to serve the king of Mycenae, Eurystheus. King Eurystheus sent him on twelve labors reminiscent of the twelve signs of the Zodiac and seen as a mythic pattern. Later through trickery, Hercules dons a poisoned robe which sets his skin on fire. He finishes the job by having a funeral pyre built and is consumed within it. His spirit rises up to Olympus and is made into a god by his father Zeus. Modern occultists see the story filled with symbolism of the process of initiation to join the ranks of the gods themselves.

Hermes Trismegistus

Is Hermes Trismegistus a god, several gods or a man? The answer might be yes to all of these. Usually he is considered to be an amalgam of the Greek Hermes with the Egyptian Thoth, or more properly, Tehuti. Both are considered magicians and psychopomps, though Hermes embodies more of the messenger archetype, and Thoth the scribe and elder. Hermes Trismegistus is said to be an elder scholar, embodying the best of both of these figures. The thrice great title has been theorized with many meanings, from the three parts of a true deep breath (clavicular, thoracic and abdominal) to the three worlds of the shaman (heaven, earth and underworld). The body of lore known as the *Corpus Hermeticum* is attributed to him, which was most likely written by the hands of several different individuals, all under his name. Many deified Egyptian scribes and scholars were later associated with Thoth, and it appears that the tradition continued, perhaps anonymously in the Greco-Egyptian period. He is associated with the legendary Emerald Tablet of the alchemists and a wide body of occult lore. Some consider him not one individual, but the incarnation of many individuals who bring magickal science and civilization to humanity. Among his incarnations are said to be Moses, Athothis, Imenhotep, Zoroaster, Idris, Enoch and Buddha. Like the Buddhist view of the various Dali Lamas as the incarnation of Avalokiteśvara, he can be an eternally incarnating spirit, bringing the mysteries of alchemy, of transformation and magick, to humanity in every era. As Hermes can be quite tricky, we simply don't have a protocol to recognize him in each life time, and I think that's the way he'd prefer it.

Fig. 32: Hermes Trismegistus

Herodias

In Medieval Witchcraft lore, Herodias is seen as the leader of the Witch cult and master of the night assembly and procession of Witches. Some believe this to be the Herodias of the New Testament. Others equate her with Lilith, Adam's first wife in the Old Testament, or Aradia of Italian Witchcraft. Historically Herodias is known as a Jewish Princess, wife of Herod Antipas and mother of Salome, who called for the beheading of John the Baptist. In the Ysengrimus, a twelfth century manuscript attributed to Nivardus, she is known as Pharaildis and equated with Salome, the daughter of Herod. She wanted to have sex with John the Baptist and, upon hearing this, Herod had him beheaded. She clutched the severed head mournfully and the head of the saint breathed fiercely upon her, blowing her through the roof with a whirlwind. She was cursed to fly through the sky by this whirlwind at night, dwell in oaks and hazels by day, and be accompanied by "one third of humanity" as an "afflicted sovereign." Similar legends are found in Spain.[2]

So on one hand we have a deity oriented interpretation of Herodias, and another a more mortal and historic figure. The idea of a woman who lives in oaks and hazels seems to point to a deeper folkloric wisdom to the image of Herodias, rather than simply being cursed. Call upon her to understand the mysteries of the Night Assemblies of the Witches.

King of Salem

While many in Salem, Massachusetts might vie for the crown as King or Queen of the popular tourist community based upon Witchcraft and the history of the Witch hunts, the King of Salem is none other than the master Melchizedek, found in ceremonial and Theosophical lore. Not an obvious choice as a Witch ancestor, and many would assume he is a Judeo-Christian ancestral contact, not Pagan. He is credited with initiating Abraham who went on to start the Jewish tradition. His priests are said to be a saintly order in which either Christ was a member, or a leader of the movement. Yet, he only claimed to be the King of Salem, where we get the name Jerusalem, or New Salem, from. He was the priest of the "god most high" a title, not a specific god, though this deity is most often equated with Yahweh/Jehovah. But Qabalistically minded Pagans realize there is a difference in the manifestation of the spoken name Yahweh and the unspoken name of the divine godhead marked by the four letters YHVH.

Melchizedek's name is said to be "my king is righteous." He simply taught Abraham the sacrament of bread and wine. One could argue it was quite a Pagan ritual, not necessarily the harbinger of Christ's sacrifice. In some lore, he is considered immortal, the man who lived the perfect life, and he is equated with the Shamballa/Agartha immortal World King. Dion Fortune considered him a Lord of Flame and Mind, and he became a guide to her in her own work.

In my own work, my communications with him, he appears as a "Witch King" for lack of a better term – sorcerer king, perhaps what the ancient Buddhist would call a Dharma King. I see him more akin to the three wise men at the nativity of Christ than a rabbi, a divine and royal astrologer, ruling in secret, keeping wisdom to his heart. Living so close to Salem, Massachusetts, and growing up in Salem, New Hampshire with its America's Stonehenge, and thinking about all the spirituality, prophecy and strife around Jerusalem, I think of all the magickal lore, real and perhaps undeserved, associated with this name. I think of him as the ruler of the archetypal perfected city, the New Jerusalem in the Western World written about by William Blake in his poem "And did those feet in ancient time". This New Jerusalem is associated with Glastonbury, sacred to Christians and Witches. If he was guiding Dion Fortune so strongly, he obviously had something to do with the Witchcraft revival, as she was the High Priestess ushering in the New Aeon.

Master of the Head

Master of the Head is another figure who is more of a mythic theme than an individual identity. He is the spirit of the severed head, found in many tales, from the Celtic tales of Bran who guards the eastern shore of England to the tales of John the Baptist, possibly worshipped by the Templars as Baphomet. The head is an oracle of wisdom, guidance, prophecy and protection.

Master of the Hunt

The Master of the Hunt is the leader of the Wild Hunt or Phantom processions of spirits in European folklore. While often it is a female figure, such as Diana, Holda or Abundia, it is just as often a male figure as well. Some are deities, others faeries, and still others human, such as King Arthur, making the lines and roles blurred. When working with the imagery of the Wild Hunt, I find the Master of the Hunt as the primal hunter figure stretching across time and space and manifesting in various forms and names locally. To me, he uses the name Huestia, reportedly a name for the Wild Hunt in Spain.

Merlin

While we consider the Merlin consciousness as a title, and an order of spiritual beings, it is hard not to list him as a composite figure among our mythic dead. Merlin manifests as a mighty magician and prophet, ranging from the wild man of the northern woods to the more commercial blue robe and pointed hat Merlin. Merlin is a consciousness of western Pagan magick, helping us get in harmony with the Earth and stars and discover our true destiny.

The Queen of Sheba

The Queen of Sheba is a semi-historical figure found in Jewish, Christian and Islamic lore. Usually unnamed, the Ethiopian accounts name her Makeda or Magda, meaning Great Queen, while her Arabian name is Balqis. Considered to be an African Queen, or possibly a ruler in Egypt or Arabia, some accounts list her as the Queen of Sabia in Yemen. The Queen of Sheba was intimately tied with King Solomon of the Old Testament. While standard Biblical accounts simply depicts the two as fellow rulers and she visits the Temple, esoteric tradition depicts her as a High Priestess of an ancient Pagan fertility cult, possibly Astarte, and King Solomon as her lover and later priest as they explored the mysteries of the hiero gamos, or sacred marriage. Possibly he was her student, or they traded magickal training, rituals and secrets. According to this line of belief, The Song of Songs is a magickal document of their work together.

Tubal Cain the Blacksmith

Tubal Cain is a Biblical character with strong associations with Witchcraft lore. He is the descendent of Cain, the child of Adam and Eve exiled to wander. He is the son of Zillah and Lamech, the brother of Naamah and an accomplished blacksmith. He is described as a craftsman, artificer, chemist and miner, and linked with forged gods such as Vulcan. The Clan of Tubal Cain looks to him as a Witch god figure.

Utnapishtim/Deucalion/Noah

The patriarch survivor of the Antediluvian, or pre-flood world. Utnapishtim is considered the survivor of the Great Flood in the Mesopotamian story of Gilgamesh. Deucalion is the Greek version, and Noah is the Hebrew survivor. There are other survivor myths who help regenerate the next world and people, but these three are the most well known in the Western Mystery Tradition. The survivor of the old world is charged in esoteric tradition to the keeper of hidden knowledge from the last age. Noah and Deucalion are both known as wine makers and wine drinkers, and wine plays a great role in the esoteric traditions. Noah was said to possess the mythic Book of Raziel the Angel to help him construct the ark, and the book later passed into the hands of King Solomon. These figures are survivors because they listened to divine wisdom and guidance and can teach us how to do the same, as well as pass on ancient knowledge to us.

The Wanderer

The Wanderer is the ancestor we have who has wandered the planet, carrying seeds, songs, tools and culture from place to place. Many have been possessed by the spirit of this ancient ancestor, inspired to travel and connect different places and people. The spirit of the Wanderer can be seen in an anonymous old English poem with a possible origin point in the time of the Anglo Saxons, found in the Exeter Book. Mythically, the two more common figures of the Wanderer are not particularly Pagan. Cain is seen as the exile from the Garden of Eden, forced to wander the Earth. Many in the Gnostic traditions of Witchcraft feel that he wandered and taught the lore of agriculture, herbcraft, smithing, and magick as he did. The other is the Wandering Jew. A strange piece of Christian folklore, the Wandering Jew is said to be either a tradesman or servant of Pontius Pilate, who taunted Christ upon the cross, and was then cursed with immortality and the need to wander, never settling down, continually walking the Earth until the Second Coming. At various times the Wandering Jew has been an urban myth believed as literal truth and a symbol of the Jewish diaspora. In Medieval European literature, the Wandering Jew is equated with the Eternal Hunter, and has associations with Wotan. Wotan or Odin is equated with the Wanderer, and various gods would disguise themselves as wandering beggars to test humanity. The spirit of the Wanderer can be called upon for connections between lands and people and the need to be upon the spiritual walkabout across strange lands.

> *Often the lone-dweller waits for favor,*
> *mercy of the Measurer, though he unhappy*
> *across the seaways long time must*
> *stir with his hands the rime-cold sea,*
> *tread exile-tracks. Fate is established!*

— First Stanza of *The Wanderer* (Translation by Jonathan A. Glenn, 1982.)

First Mother and Father

The modern Witchcraft traditions have no universal first divine human couple. Those working in Gnostic or Christian lore of course have Adam and Eve. Lilith could also be counted for those who include the more esoteric lore, though most Witches now see Lilith as a goddess. The more esoteric template for humanity in Judaism is the Adam Kadmon. The Hindu have Manu, the Eastern Adam, and the Theosophist saw the Manu in a similar light to the perfected Adam Kadmon. The Norse have Ask and Embla, the first man and woman made from Ash and Elm. To the Greeks the first modern human couple was Pyrrha and Deucalion, though the first woman, ages before in the earlier races was Pandora. Pandora shared with Eve the role of scapegoat for the ills of the world. Modern science traces us to one or many Mitochondrial Eves in the Out of Africa theory of human evolution. Yet there is no common mythology for Witches. Still, well after the parental figures of Goddess and God was a first human mother and father, coming to many simply as the First Mother and First Father. These ancient ancestors have much to show us about where we have been and where we might go if we follow their wisdom. They have seen all the human wars, famines and diseases and all our triumphs, arts and civilizations, including those we have forgotten. Call upon them for ancient knowledge and wisdom.

Dangers of the Saintly Dead

There is an interesting paradoxical phenomenon that occurs when working with the saints and masters, depending upon your tradition and view. Many consider the working of the saints as an exoteric, mainstream practice of religion, while working with the masters is a hidden, occult practice of the mysteries, even though they are essentially the same practice. In working with the saints, it is said their communion is primarily mystical and devotional. The saints are personal in their work. You forge a direct friendship with a particular individual entity who aids you personally. The masters, on the other hand, are an exploration of the unknown and unknowable, seeking answers to the questions that have no direct linear answer. They help less with daily life and seek no devotion. They are teachers, and are anonymous or hesitant to reveal human form and identities. Working with them does not require devotion, and in fact, devotion can inhibit their work with you.

There is an old saying that if you see Buddha on the road to enlightenment, kill him. This is not an uncharacteristic call to violence from Buddhism, a primarily peaceful tradition, but an illustration on how important it is not to get caught up in the cult of personality. It becomes very easy, if you meet Buddha, to want to stop where he is and commune with him, and even worship him. While devotional practices can be quite helpful to reach higher and deeper levels of consciousness, they become problematic when they become the goal themselves, rather than a tool to advance and evolve. By "killing the Buddha" or simply moving past him, you follow your own path, rather than get stuck to any one image or idea of the divine. The Buddha that is on the road still is not the ultimate Buddha. Just as the Chinese say the Tao, or Way, that can be described or written about is limited, and is not the true Tao. The mystery is found beyond and while you are in a body, you need to keep going.

I was hesitant to outline these potential allies for devotional and personal experience for this reason. Yet their revelation can deepen the culture, art and practice of modern Witchcraft as we so desperately need. Many adepts of Hinduism, Tantric Buddhism and various forms of shamanism use the same principles for advancement and evolution and do not get stuck, though getting stuck is a danger. Many in the Theosophical influenced traditions get stuck upon their favorite ascended master. This teaching of "Killing the Buddha" should be kept in mind, so you too do not get stuck focusing on Mother Shipton, Paracelsus, or Tituba. Work with the dead for mutual evolution, rather than get trapped in sole devotion.

---

1 William James on Psychical Research compiled and edited by Gardner Murphy, M.D. and Robert O. Ballou, Viking Press, 1960, p. 41

2 LeCouteux, Claude. *Phantom Armies of the Night: The Wild Hunt and the Ghostly Processions of the Undead.* Inner Traditions, Rochester, VT: 2011. p. 11-13

CHAPTER ELEVEN
SAMHAIN AND THE
WITCH MASTERS

While all eight of the sabbats hold a unique magick, modern Witches have a particular affinity for Samhain, the Feast of the Dead. For many of us, Samhain was the first sabbat we participated in, the gateway into exploring the mysteries of the Witch. I know my introduction to the Craft was a Samhain Ritual taking place on Gallows Hill in Salem, MA with Laurie Cabot, on the 300th Anniversary in 1992. We gathered where the "Witches" of Salem were supposedly hung and recited the names of those dead in a magick circle, and later celebrated with cakes and ale. While it was an amazing experience for me then, full with the fanfare of three hundred people and television crews, I found the later celebrations in more private circumstances more meaningful, using this celebration to commune with the dead through divination, scrying, mediumship and journey work.

Traditionally Samhain, pronounced "Sow-ween," is considered the third and last harvest, the meat harvest when the herds would be slaughtered and the meat either salted or smoked for the winter. Between that association, and the final withering of the green world, the time is associated with death, dying and the afterlife. As so much energy is going into the spirit world, the veil is said to be thin, and the ability to contact spirits increases. This has led to our Halloween celebrations of wearing costumes and masks. Originally it was to fool the spirits, ghosts and demons who rise from the depths into thinking you were either one of them, or more fierce and scare them into leaving you alone. Jack O' Lanterns, originally carved from turnips, not pumpkins, were wards to scare off the unwanted spirits.

Today, Witches celebrate the ancestors, and use this "thin time" to commune more deeply with the ancestors. Offerings of food and drink are made. Questions are asked. Time and space are less distinct, and therefore knowledge of the future from the spirit world is also said to be easier or more accurate. Many do yearly readings at this time, to take the ancestors guidance into the entire year.

My appreciation of Samhain has only deepened with the work of the Mighty Dead. While I still honor all my ancestors, not only on Samhain, but retain an ancestral altar all year round, things become particularly intense with the Hidden Company at this time of year. They seek my attention more clearly. Their messages ring true. My "assignments" for the year become clearer.

Samhain in the Libraries of the Phosphorous Grove

This simple ritual will help you work with the Mighty Dead, in the celebration of Samhain, or adapted to suit other needs. While the true Witch's Sabbat is beyond space and time, eternal, we find a particular resonance with it at Samhain, for both are between and beyond normal time and space.

Altar

Traditional Witch Altar – Pentacle/Peyton, Crystal/Stone, Chalice of Red Wine, Athame, Wand (Wooden), Cauldron, Incense Thurible/Cauldron, Charcoal, Salt Bowl, Water Bowl, Broom, Dark Bread, Offerings (Alcohol and Food), Black Candle and White Candle (On the left and right respectively), Central Fire (Small Cauldron filled with Epsom salt and high proof rubbing alcohol, or an orange candle). You can further decorate with any other items – fallen leaves, statues, acorns, gourds. If you can have something to represent bone – a real bone, an animal horn or even a carved crystal skull, all the better. Wear a simple key upon a cord or chain around your neck. The key will be necessary to unlock the way of wisdom and understanding.

Cleansing Self and Space

Throw an appropriate cleansing incense upon the burning charcoal, such as frankincense and myrrh. Go around the circle three times, ideally widdershins, to cleanse the space.

> *By these creatures of Fire and Air*
> *By the spirits of the Green*
> *I cleanse this space.*

Mix a little salt with the water. Draw a pentagram over the liquid to sanctify it. With your fingers or a small evergreen branch, asperge the liquid widdershins around the circle to cleanse the space.

> *By these creatures of Earth and Water*
> *By the spirits of the Minerals*
> *I purify this space.*

If you have a ritual broom, move three times widdershins around the circle, sweeping the space of unwanted forces, and out to the Northeast of the circle if possible.

Circle Casting

Take your wand and starting in the north, cast a circle thrice round in blue light with these or similar words:

> *I cast this circle to protect me from all harm on any level.*
> *I cast this circle to draw in the most perfect powers for my work with the Ancestors*
> *on this Samhain night.*
> *I create a space beyond space and a time beyond time,*
> *Where the highest Will, Love and Wisdom reigns supreme.*
> *So mote it be.*

Feel the circle become a sphere of blue light.

Call the Directions

Face the north and say:

By Earth and Oak and Onyx Stone
I call to the foundations of our home
By timeless temples beyond the age
Come forth to this circle stage.
Hail and welcome.

Face the east and say:

By Fire and Holly and Ruby Red
I call to the hearth flame of our dead
By willful wisdom beyond the hedge
Come forth to this circle edge.
Hail and welcome.

Face the south and say:

By Air and Hazel and Agate Line
I call to the sounds of whispering signs
By the needed knowledge beyond all place
Come forth to this circle space.
Hail and welcome.

Face the west and say:

By Water and Willow and Moonstone Jewel
I call to the waters of the western pools
By mournful memories beyond the gate
Come forth to our maze of fate.
Hail and welcome.

Look above and say:

By the Stars and Sun and Moon's Pale Light
I call to the Powers at their height
By the Vault of Heaven beyond the nail
Where the barge of souls sets its sails.
Hail and welcome.

Look below and say:

By the roots and stones and heart of the Earth
I call to the Powers of Life, Death and Rebirth
By the Gate of Bone that holds the seal
To the fleshless lands beyond those that feel.
Hail and welcome.

Look at the altar/center and say:

By the Flesh and Blood and Bones of the Living and the Dead
To the Wisdom Powers of Cunning and Dread
By the Timeless Ancestors of all our lines
From the first note of creation to the end of time.
Hail and welcome.

Invocation of the Three Rays

By the Straight Line
By the Red Ray
By the First Ray of Power
I invoke the Divine Will
All Is Possible.

By the Bent Line
By the Blue Ray
By the Second Ray of Love

I invoke the Divine Heart
All Is one.

By the Crooked Line
By the Yellow Ray
By the Third Ray of Wisdom
I invoke the Divine Mind.
All Is Known.

Evocation of Goddess and God

By the light of the black candle
Of the night
Of the Moon
Of Severity
I call upon the Witch Mother
She who Weaves the Web from the Light of the Stars,
From the Light of the Moon
From the Deep Earthlight that dwells in the depths.
She whose voice is within the light and lightning
Hail and Welcome

By the light of the white candle
Of the day
Of the Sun
Of Mercy
I call upon the Witch Father
He who Sings the Song from the Music of the Spheres
The Seven Wanderers
The Seven Mighty Ones
The Seven Guardians of the Gate
He who is the Three Faced Master of the Sabbat.
Hail and Welcome

The Gate Between is open in balance.

Naming the Work

I seek the celebration of Samhain at the eternal sabbat. I seek communion with the Mighty Dead and their wisdom held in their arcane libraries.

Incense & Anointing

Use your appropriate incense, oils or potions upon your brow, back of the neck, wrists, throat and heart.

The Working: The Libraries of Stone, Wood, Blood and Bone

Put before you upon the altar, or the ground if sitting before the altar, within easy reach, the stone/crystal, the wooden wand, the cup of red wine and, if you have it, the representative of bone. Four can be before you in a line, or one in each of the cardinal directions around you.

We seek the libraries of the first ones, the first knowledge and how it grows. The most ancient teachers of humanity are the very stones of the Earth. They were the first masters. They in turn, were ground down to provide the rich soil that allowed the plant spirits and eventually the tree teacher to rise. They became the High Priestesses and Priests of the green realm. They in turn gave rise to support the creatures of flesh and blood, leading to the feathered, finned, fanged and furred masters of nature. The animal lords and ladies gave support to the maturing animal of humanity, allowing our first masters to rise and take sanctuary in the Phosphorous Grove, where everything glows with brilliant light. The four tools are aligned with these four risings. Stone to the Stone People, the Masters of Lapis. Wood for the Masters of Flora. Blood red wine for the Masters of Fauna and Bone for the Masters of Humanity.

Gaze into your central fire and imagine the fire that is at the center of the Sabbat. Conjure the images of the eternal dance around the Sabbat fire, your sisters and brothers in the Craft. Make your way to the center of the Sacred, Secret Fire in the center of all things. When ready, enter it, preparing to know the wisdom of the source.

Inside the Perfect Peace Profound of the white fire you have the four tools before you. You might experience a sense of bilocation in this vision, being perfectly aware of your body and the four tools, even possibly with your eyes one-tenth open still, and still fully immersed in the peace of the white light.

Touch the key around your neck, and hold the intention of unlocking the Library of Stone. In vision and physically, hold the stone/crystal. Open the gates to the Library of Stone. Project your consciousness into this stone, which is part of every other stone upon the Earth. Feel yourself attune to their crystalline structure. Ask for the wisdom of the stones. You might find yourself in a beautiful library of gems, stones and crystals, or perhaps ancient standing stones riddled with quartz deposits. Each one holds the records you seek, like a vast cosmic library of rock. What do they have to show and teach you, for they are your oldest ancestors, your eldest teacher? Ask questions. Wait. Listen. Feel. Envision. Learn.

When you feel your experience with the stone is complete, move on, thanking the Stone Masters and the Keepers of the Stone Library, and put down the stone. Touch the key again. Think of closing the doors to the Library of Stone, and then focus upon Opening the Library of Wood with the key.

In vision, and physically, hold the wooden wand. Open the gates to the Library of Wood. Project your consciousness into the wooden branch, which is a part of every other branch, every other tree that ever has been, is or will be upon the Earth. Feel yourself attune to the sap. Ask for the wisdom of the trees. You might find yourself in a vast forest of many different trees. Wisdom flows like sap. Wisdom can be licked off the leaves like dew. Wisdom is in the berries, nuts and fruits. Wisdom is written in the grain patterns of the wood. What do they have to show and teach you, for they are your elder teachers and role models? Ask questions. Wait. Listen. Feel. Envision. Learn.

When you feel your experience with the wood is complete, move on, thanking the Tree Teachers and the Keepers of the Wood Library, and put down the wand. Touch the key again. Think of closing the doors to the Library of Wood, and then focus upon opening the Library of Blood with the key.

In vision, and physically, hold the chalice of wine. Think of the blood of the Earth, all the creatures evolving from a few tiny cells, branching off to form all the animals upon the planet, all connected by the same blood. Open the gates to the Library of Blood. Drink a sip of wine to attune your consciousness to the blood of all creatures. Ask for the wisdom of the creatures of flesh and blood. You might find yourself in the flow of DNA, where your answers are written out in the entwining serpents of the double helix, or in a multitude of blood vials, cups and cauldrons in some liquid alchemical library. What do they have to show and teach you, for they are your healers and guides? Ask questions. Wait. Listen. Feel. Envision. Learn.

When you feel your experience with the blood is complete, move on, thanking the Creatures of Flesh and Blood and the Keepers of the Blood Records, and put down the chalice. Touch the key again. Think of closing the doors to the Library of Blood, and then focus upon opening the Library of Bone with the key.

In vision, and physically, hold the representative of bone. Think of your own bones, and the very knowledge of the ancestors that remains with them. When we die, our bones are the last thing to leave the world, our last link. Bones retain our power and wisdom. Saturn rules the bones, ruling both the Earth and the Air signs of Capricorn and Aquarius, where knowledge meets the world and can become wisdom. Attune to the structure of the bones, which is like the crystalline structure of the stones. Open the gates to the Library of Bone. Feel yourself knocking on, tapping or rattling your own bones, and thereby knocking on the bones of not only your direct ancestors, but all of human consciousness. Ask for the wisdom of the Mighty Dead. What do they have to show and teach you, for they are you reborn! You might find yourself in a vast necropolis, catacombs, burial mound or crematorium. The skulls, bones and fragments of the dead encode a special wisdom. Ask questions. Wait. Listen. Feel. Envision. Learn.

When you feel your experience with the bones is complete, move on, thanking the Mighty Dead who specifically keep the Bone Library, and put down the altar tool. Touch the key again. Think of closing the doors to the Library of Bone. Be at one with the Most Profound and Perfect Peace and when ready, return from the central fire into the dance of the Sabbat!

Sacramental Rite

Make an offering to the Mighty Dead. Pour out a bit of the remaining red wine onto the dark bread. Take a small bite for yourself and share the rest with the spirits. Other alcoholic spirits are appropriate offerings to the Mighty Dead. Vodka is considered the liquor of Saturn. Absinthe would also be an appropriate offering. I also favor the use of elderflower liquor known as St. Germain or the Italian liquor Strega. Apples or black beans are also appropriate food offerings.

> *To the Mighty Dead,*
> *The Hidden Company of our Timeless Tradition*
> *I offer this to you.*
> *May there always be peace between us.*

Final Blessing

Perform a circle of healing and blessing if you desire.

Devocation

> *By the Light of Severity*
> *I thank and release the Witch Mother, the Goddess*

The Weaver, the Web, the Voice of Lightning
Hail and farewell.

By the Light of Mercy
I thank and release the Witch Father, the God
The Singer, the Song and the master of the Sabbat
Hail and farewell.

The Gate between is closed in balance.

Release the Directions

Look above and say:

By the Stars and Sun and Moon's Pale Light
We thank and release you from our sight.
Hail and farewell.

Look below and say:

By the roots and stones and heart of the Earth
We thank and release you with joy and mirth.
Hail and farewell.

Look at the altar/center and say:

By Flesh and Blood and Bones of the Living and Dead
We thank and release you from our stead.
Hail and farewell.

Face the north and say:

By Earth and Oak and Onyx Stone
We thank and release you from our home.

Hail and farewell.

Face the west and say:

By Water and Willow and Moonstone Jewel
We thank and release you from this rule
Hail and farewell.

Face the south and say:

By Air and Hazel and Agate Line
We thank and release you from this time.
Hail and farewell.

Face the east and say:

By Fire and Holly and Ruby Red
We thank and release you from our stead.
Hail and farewell.

Release the Circle

I cast out the circle as a sign of our work.
May the circle be undone, but never broken.
So mote it be.
Merry meet, merry part and merry meet again.

Envision the circle expanding out infinitely as you trace its outline counterclockwise once, like a stone dropped into a still pool, with ever expanding ripples of light, reaching across the cosmos.

Chapter Twelve
Crossing the Veil

A key component to the work of the Witch is not only communicating with those who have crossed the veil, but helping those in transition to cross the veil and arrive safely in the shadowlands of the ancestors. In the mold of the Cunning Ones, we are considered the midwives to both the living, being born into the world, and the dying, those being born back to the world of spirit. We are the priestesses and priests of both life and death, and the funerary rite is as much our province as the healer's hut, for healing comes in many forms, and sometimes the most healing thing we can do is let someone go and help them make the journey to the next mystery.

Preparation For Crossing

Preparation comes in many forms, and the Witch as Cunning Healer will have to deal with both the dying and the family of the dying. Sometimes we are a welcome sight by the family, as death is a scary thing, so someone who appears comfortable with it can provide a tremendous release to the heart. Other times we are quite unwelcome, particularly by those who have not yet given up on the hope for life and recovery. Our presence as midwife to the dying process is a sign of no hope, and we can become the target of anger and fear. The very nature of our tradition, Witchcraft, is enough to give most pause and conjure fear, so we must do our best to alleviate those fears whenever possible. Yet, our first duty is to the dying who has called for our presence and aid.

In ministering to both the dying and the family, there is a great paradox. The family and friends are really seeking connection. They seek to maintain presence of their loved one, even beyond the veil. While that is possible for those with such perceptions, even for an adept, it is best to flow with the time of separation and readjustment to the new reality of life and the physical, if not spiritual, loss. On the opposite end of the desire spectrum, the dying one is simply seeking release, not connection, for it is connection that can hinder the release. A great step in preparation is that both the dying one has given their own souls permission to leave, and that the loved one has also given blessing and permission to leave. Even with such permission, body and soul can be stubborn and cling onto life, even in the midst of great pain.

Ideally preparation should start before the deathbed. There are two approaches we have as facilitators. When working with another Witch, or another magickal practitioner, the preparation can be much easier if they are truly initiates of the mysteries. Such a worldview can be summed up viscerally in the work of Carlos Castaneda. Many who do not follow his Toltec ways, or even know of his teachings have followed this principle, even if they do not personalize "Death."

"Death is the only wise advisor that we have. Whenever you feel, as you always do, that everything is going wrong and you're about to be annihilated, turn to your death and ask if that is so. Your death will tell you that you're wrong; that nothing really matters outside its touch. Your death will tell you, 'I haven't touched you yet.'"

— Journey to Ixtlan

To the Witch, our allies are the Goddesses and Gods of Death, for magick is change, and they rule over the greatest change of all. Hecate, Persephone, Pluto, Morrighan, Hela, Osiris, Cernunnos and Ereshkigal are all found in our practices and devotional traditions. By framing our life by death, we seek to live life to the fullest. By experiencing true initiation, we experience a kind of death that can prepare us for the next journey.

Magickal preparation work for a practitioner can include:

- **Letting Go Meditation:** Reflection upon letting go of all earthly concerns and all treasures you hold dear. Train yourself to let go of any things to which you have attachment. This can include possessions, but also people, your identity and your body.
- **Passing the Power:** It is said that a Witch must pass her power at least once before death, or the power will anchor her here to the world in pain and sufferings. Letting go of your Earthly power can pass your virtue and blessings onto a worthy successor, through formal initiation, or simply laying on of hands. Some say the virtue and power passed also carries some of the karma of the Witch, to be worked out and healed by their spiritual descendent.
- **Communing with the Dead:** Communication with the ancestors, and asking them for help and guidance when the time is right is an excellent form of preparation. Asking questions of your passed loves ones, guides and teachers can be helpful, even if the answers are not always clear or what you wish to hear.
- **Unraveling the Knots:** Some traditions look at the energy system as a knotted cord. Each point, such as a chakra, is a knot within the cord. In death, we untie the knots. Our triple souls disengage from the body matrix and pass from this world. Many advocate the dying practice gently releasing more and more, and practice projection through the crown, the highest chakra, for the clearest and most conscious journey to the next world.
- **Books of the Dead:** Reading and meditating upon death bardo texts, the transition texts guiding the dying to the next life can be quite helpful. They are preparation for later rituals of the death journey. Most famous are *The Tibetan Book of the Dead* and *The Egyptian Book of the Dead.*
- **Preparation to be with the Mighty Dead:** Practitioners should focus on this time of keeping the Three Soul complex together as one if they seek to be with the Mighty Dead. Three soul alignment should be practiced and maintained for clear and conscious transition.

Those who are not initiates of the Mysteries or practitioners of a deep spiritual discipline can be aided in other ways, and in fact these other aids can also be used by initiates, for initiation helps us go beyond our human self, but does not negate it, and these works aid in the preparation of the human self for death.

- **List Unresolved Issues:** Make a list of unresolved issues, unfinished business that could prevent the consciousness from freely transitioning. Unresolved conflicts, regrets, fears, guilts, judgments and angers should be made conscious. Some will involve others. Some will involve larger situations, institutions or simply the self.

- **Real World Resolutions:** Whenever it is possible to reach a resolution with someone in the flesh, do so. Speak your peace. Ask for forgiveness. Whatever is necessary to bring resolution.
- **Ritual Solutions:** For situations where personal real world resolution is not possible or appropriate, construct rituals that will aid this resolution. Such rituals can include letter writing and then burning the letter, visualizations and cleansing rites.
- **Explore:** If the dying has no strong faith or metaphysical philosophy, explore various philosophies regarding death and dying. Point out the similarities between many cultures as a marker of truth in consciousness behind the grave. Speak of your own mystery traditions to alleviate fear of death.
- **Flowers of Death:** One of the most appropriate healing aids to make peace with this transition is to use flower essences of particular plants that aid us in the process of accepting death and transitioning peacefully. These flowers include Datura, Belladonna, Aconite, Hemlock, Hellebore, Nettle, Carnation, Rose and Lily. Flower essences are non-toxic preparations of these plants.

Preparing the Body

Preparation for death includes preparation of the physical body. The use of anointing oils, both in last rites rituals to help the consciousness release from the body, and in funerary rites to prepare the body after death, are quite traditional and date back to ancient Pagan practices. Many of the favored gods of the ancient Pagan world are involved in the art and science of embalming, and many of our traditional spell ingredients, such as salt and myrrh, are also a part of funerary processes.

When performing a last rites blessing upon one preparing to cross over soon, anoint the power points of the body, from the bottom up, to help release the consciousness through the crown chakra, granting the greatest clarity upon passing. Those who attain a cohesive consciousness to be at one with the Mighty Dead usually perceive the experience through the crown chakra, though we could perhaps see it as stepping aside through all the chakras equally and simultaneously through unity of consciousness.

While we might perceive a normal death as the breakdown of the three soul matrix, with the lower soul naturally descending and the upper soul rising, the final moments of the matrix soul in the body appear to exit through a chakra power point. The qualities of the chakra, and their personal relationship with that energy center in life, will influence the quality of their passing. Particularly those who pass through the lower three chakras, when unclear, can experience a crossing of fear and pain. Those who pass through the heart can have a very emotional crossing, joy or sorrow. Those through the throat or brow might be more detached and abstract in their death process, while the crown grants greatest illumination.

The ritual is also said to help "bar the door" in situations where there is absolutely no chance of recovery, preventing the consciousness from trying to come back into the body once it leaves. At times the three souls can disengage prior to death, with the Lower Soul powering the body, lingering, while the Middle Soul and Higher Soul have left, but hover until the final passing.

Here is a simple Last Rites ceremony to perform to bring comfort and aid in the transition. Use the oil formula below or one that you feel is appropriate.

Last Rites Oil

$1/8$ oz. Base Oil

4 drops of Myrrh Essential Oil

2 drops of Rosemary Essential Oil

2 drops of Carnation Essential Oil

1 drop of Mint Essential Oil

1 drop of Lemon Essential Oil

Pinch of Salt

Anoint the soles of the feet.
Blessed be thy feet that have walked thee on the path. Now walk with those in spirit.

Anoint the root/perineum point.
Blessed be thy root that has kept you in this body. Now release and root in the world of spirit.

Anoint the belly area.
Blessed be thy belly that has held the gifts of trust. Now trust in the world beyond the veil.

Anoint the solar plexus.
Blessed be thy fire that has held the gifts of fire. Now see your light beyond the veil.

Anoint the sternum.

Blessed be thy heart that has held the gifts of love. Now love is found everywhere.

Anoint both palms.

Blessed be thy hands that have crafted your life. Your work in this world is now done.

Anoint the throat.

Blessed be thy throat that has held the gifts of voice. You shall be able to speak to your loved ones everywhere.

Anoint the Atlas bone/Well of Dreams.

Blessed be the well that has held the gifts of dreams. You shall dream among the ancestors now.

Anoint the brow.

Blessed be thy brow that has helped the gifts of vision. You shall see your loved ones everywhere.

Anoint the crown.

Blessed be thy crown that has held the gifts of heaven. You shall enter the starry realm from which we all return.

With these twelve points of blessing, you are free to go with the ancestors of blood and spirit on your next journey. You are loved and blessed.

Most ministers in the Craft do not have the opportunity to prepare the body for funeral due to social customs, local laws and lack of experience with the practice. Some may be given the opportunity to spiritually prepare the body before it is prepared physically for wake, funeral or cremation. If you have the opportunity to prepare the body for funeral on some level, the following customs might be helpful.

Place on either side of the body a bowl of salt and bowl of soil. The salt helps clear and cleanse the energies of the body and the mourners at the deathbed. It helps absorb any karma or wyrd of an individual, lessening its impact in the crossing. Salt also demonstrates the crystalline nature of consciousness, corresponding with the Middle Soul. The soil embodies the process of decay, as the body will return to the soil, and eventually become one with the soil. Having them present helps mitigate the heavy energies upon the Priestess/Priest doing this work as well as helps the deceased.

Wash the body with waters mixed with floral essence. It can be as simple as white carnations soaked in the water, as many customs see carnations as flowers of the dead, or a mixture of petals. Even oils or hydrosols can be used, such as rose or lavender. Other funerary herbs (in the following section) can also be used in the washing water.

To anoint the body when washed, take the oil, and mark a straight line down from the crown to the root vertically Then mark a horizontal line across either the shoulders-throat or sternum. Draw a circle around the crossed point, blessing the body, but also sealing it from return by the consciousness. Some traditions insist that two pennies be included in the body's preparation, as payment for the ferryman of the River of the Dead to take them into the afterlife.

The Witchcraft traditions, borrowing from a wide variety of cultures, have no universal custom to burial, but work within the framework of traditional society and its present options. In ages past, a Witch was always buried in unconsecrated (not owned by a church) ground, often at a crossroads, in a field, or upon the family's land. Today burial and cremation are the most likely options. Less commonly accepted is mummification, excarnation or burial by sea, despite their history.

Vigils are often kept with the body, between death and the funeral rite. Some customs believe that either the soul(s) remain near the body confused about their death and need the reassurance of loved one, or that possibly they, or the body, are spiritually vulnerable at this time and must be guarded. Most likely it comes from a time when wild animals could desecrate the body prior to the funeral if not guarded. The custom eventually developed in the practice of holding a "wake" or "visitation." Crying and wailing was said to not only express grief, but also to keep away evil spirits so the deceased could transition. The party atmosphere of telling stories, playing music, and prayer also did the same.

Magickally it can also be acceptable to meet with the body three times a day prior to the funeral to offer prayers of blessing and protection. Offerings traditional to the ancestral altar can also be made, particularly offerings of flowers and candle light, to help energize the consciousness for true release and transition.

Some magickal traditions believe the magickal tools of the Witch, at least the primary tools, should be buried either with the body or in a special place where they could potentially be retrieved by the new incarnation of the Witch. I feel that the wishes of the practitioners in regard to the tools should be respected beyond any custom or tradition. Tools are a way of passing the power and knowledge onto the next generation and beloved friends through inheritance and gifting.

THE WAY OF THE PSYCHOPOMP

The psychopomp is the guide of souls, both into the world of the living and, more often, out to the realm of the dead. It is the province of the gods of the crossroads, of gateways and travel. They open and guide the way. Most popular in the Witchcraft traditions are Hermes and Hecate, yet you see the function fulfilled by the attendants of Ra, as his barge descends into the Underworld, and in particular Anubis, who prepared bodies for death. Likewise with a boat motif, you find the Greek Charon guiding souls on the rivers of the dead, and in Celtic myth with the seafaring god Manannan Mac Lir. You find it in the Norse Valkyries guiding warriors to the halls of feasting with Odin or Freya.

The lore of the psychopomps was eventually transformed into the classic books of the dead. Just as the chariot, or *merkava*, mystics provided maps to the Jewish mystics, paving the way of the Qabalistic maps of reality, the early psychopomps, invoked with the power of these gods in some manner, mapped out the territories of consciousness after death and from them came elaborate funeral and burial rites. They depict the transition experience, or *bardo* in the Tibetan tradition, of life to death. *The Tibetan Book of the Dead* is very popular today, though in its current form is a relatively recent addition to the Tibetan literature. Many feel it was a terma, or mystical treasure, returned by magickal means when people were ready for it. Due to its popularity in both the east and west, I'd say people were ready for it. It is traditionally read to those on their deathbed, even if unconscious, as spiritual instructions preparing them for what to expect and how to navigate it.

Clearer documents are the pyramid and funeral texts found in the Egyptian tombs, carved upon the walls of pharaonic graves and eventually culminating in *The Egyptian Book of the Dead*, also known as *The Book of Coming Forth by Day*. It is full of techniques to navigate the underworld to attain immortality in the other side using spells, charms, and words of power to pass through trials. While we're not sure if the instructions were read to the dying pharaoh, or available to the general public, they were written on the walls of the tomb to help the dead king safely navigate the underworld realm as the soul descended through to duat and faced many trials and judgments.

One could argue the impressionable consciousness is imprinted with a map. If that is what they expect, then the energy beyond that is beyond shape and form, takes the shape and form conforming to the deceased's beliefs and expectations. While you could argue it is therefore "not real" it demonstrates a remarkable ritual technology, for using belief to navigate what would otherwise be dominated by a wide variety of mismatched images and themes, like a random dream. The unseen forces take on some form for us to perceive, and will use the symbols in the memories and consciousness to manifest. It is far better to choose the setting and protocols based on a spiritual pattern, than to try to find that pattern in the potential random chaos of our death throes.

Today the same concept can be used by spiritual practitioners, not simply reading the instructions, but guiding meditations, both prior to death, to establish a clear path, and near the transition, to help one along. Today's Witches can be psychopomps, guiding the dead to the next realm with ease and grace. The belief in many traditions is that the more conscious one is about the passing, the more clear, both the more pleasant the experience is, and the more conscious choice one has as to what comes next. You can respond rather than react. For those not present, the journey can be done seemingly in "token" without conscious involvement of the dying, but in reality, the journey will still guide their consciousness, even after some time from their death.

In our three-soul model, it can be difficult to determine which of the souls we are guiding. For some, the three do not divide fully until after crossing. We perceive ourselves as ourselves, with all three aspects. Others believe the divide comes immediately upon death, with no body to link the upper and lower souls. For this method, it only matters to initiates of three soul teachings. For all practical purposes, the consciousness after death can be perceived as one unit, to experience its separation in its own time and way. In reality the psychopomp might be dealing exclusively with the higher soul, or more likely the lower soul, as most psychopomp imagery is for the underworld, and involves a lot more personal feelings and release than what would be expected from the very impersonal and detached higher soul which simply returns to the heavens. The imagery in the suggested psychopomp work of this chapter does often favor one aspect of the soul complex, and that will be noted below. For those practitioners of the three soul model, the Three Soul Prayer and alignment should be practiced regularly, in an effort to attain union with the Mighty Dead upon death, or at least be one step closer to it. You can do several different journeys to help each aspect of the soul release over time, or one longer journey combining imagery if that feels more helpful to you.

The process should be started by making contact with your own spirit allies, including your own contact among your ancestors and Mighty Dead. For some, the initial connection won't be the ancestors, but with other allies, such as animal spirits or angelic contacts. Calling upon specific psychopomp figures is an excellent idea, so that you act primarily as their intermediary and assistant, but they are doing the actual guiding once you usher the newly dead to the gates beyond.

Traditional imagery usually follows the four elements. They can be adapted to suit your own intuition, and what appears in your own inner vision as the type of aid each of us needs to cross is fairly unique, even if it follows some classic patterns.

- **Water:** The crossing of water, or the travel upon water, is the most common image of crossing. Literally one is crossing over to the other side beyond the watery divide. The image of water tends to emphasize the lower soul, or Shaper, as its nature is to flow back to the underworld ancestral pools of wisdom.

- **Air:** The consciousness of the deceased ascends to the heavenly realms, free from the weight of mortal life, it is naturally buoyant and capable of flight. One might fly or climb to the upper branches of the World Tree, or to the top of a mountain peak, or even a world above the threshold of the clouds, closer to the stars. The air imagery emphasizes the Higher Self, or Watcher, often described as a soul bird residing in the branches of the great tree after death, awaiting a new incarnation cycle.

- **Fire:** Consciousness moves towards a light, be it above, below or on a horizontal axis. The imagery of a funeral pyre is helpful for some, as the fire releases the accumulated energies and consciousness moves towards a light of higher awareness. While this can be used for any of the soul selves, it often favors the Namer, or Middle Self, as it is the lynchpin connecting the three selves, and cremation helps separate the connection and release the soul complex if a strong vessel of consciousness to join the Hidden Company has not been created.

- **Earth:** Earth imagery included the sacred tomb, the grave, decomposition into the land and most importantly a tunnel within the Earth that the consciousness moves through to its next destination. Earth images tends to also favor the Namer, for when the body returns to the Earth, the wisdom of the personal Middle Self rejoins the Earth as well.

- **Spirit:** Light can simply be envisioned and the consciousness absorbed into the light itself, or through a tunnel of light. This technique is good for all three souls.

When performing a psychopomp working, with the person physically present, or in spirit form, encourage them in your heart and mind to release their connection if the time is right and give them permission to journey onward when they are ready.

Invite all of the beloved ancestors of the one passing to join you. Allow the ancestors appropriate to each aspect of the soul to welcome them. The ancestors of blood will welcome the Shaper. The ancestors of bone and breath welcome the Namer. The ancestors of spirit will welcome the Watcher. Or the Mighty Dead will welcome them all. Often in the following vision, a full triune entity will go on the journey, gently shedding each part as needed when the appropriate element manifests. Follow the ancestors' guidance and lead in the psychopomp work.

Call upon any psychopomp divinities you feel comfortable working with. Ask them to aid and attend in this work and follow their guidance.

It is said that the soul, the Watcher self, visits four places upon death, and walking with the Higher Soul on this revisitation can be a helpful preparation for the passing consciousness, as well as giving you insight and information on their passing. The revisitation is not just going to the place as it is, but as it was, making a visit back in time. The four places to visit are:

- **Place of Death (Water):** Where the deceased actually died and the physical body stopped. This is the place to accept that death has occurred and is a reality.

- **Place of Burial (Earth):** Where the presumed resting spot will be. This is where one lets go of the world and the hope to still be in it.

- **Place of Birth (Air):** Where this consciousness came into the physical world. This is where the individual reviews life, moving from the end, burial, to the beginning, birth, and thinking of all the things to occur in between.

- **Place of Initiation (Fire):** Where the individual awakened to the spirit life. For Christians this is the place of Christening or Confirmation. For Witches, it is the place of initiation. For those who have not undergone formal initiation, it is the place of awakening to the reality of magick. This is the place one reflects on the reality of spirit. If one is to step out of the soul of incarnation as the Mighty Dead, it will be at the place of revitalization of initiation.

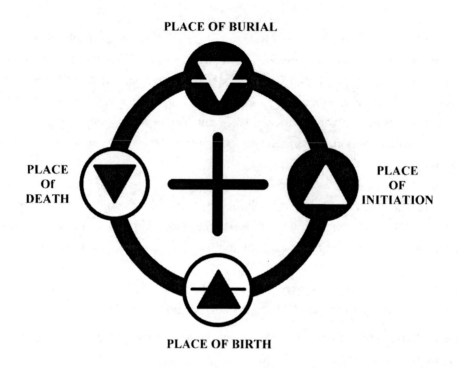

PLACE OF BURIAL

PLACE Of DEATH

PLACE OF INITIATION

PLACE OF BIRTH

Fig. 33: Visitations Upon the Circle

These four revisitations can prepare the individual for the true crossing experience. We can look at it like four points of a compass, the unwinding of the circle of their life. The order of these place visits can be different in each journey. The order, and corresponding elements, might prove an interesting meditation on the nature of their crossing. Once the visitations are complete, either under the guidance of the ancestors or psychopomp divinity, you might find yourself aiding the crossing by cutting any energetic cords that bind them to the world, so they can move freely on their journey.

While the Higher Soul of the Watcher seeks to return to the heavens, it often has to travel through the underworld to get back up. Witches say the darkness of the underworld is the same darkness that is in the starry heavens. The light of the heavens can also be found in the stars of the Earth. The Higher and Lower Souls accompany the Namer back into the Earth and elements as they progress into the depths of the underworld. The two remaining reach the rivers of the underworld. They cross the River of Memory/Forgetfulness, reviewing the many images of life. The wounds and hurts can be washed away by the river. At this point the human psychopomp must leave them at or on the river and return once they have reached the first land of the ancestors. The underworld realm is envisioned as seven leveled, each with a gate. An initiate, one who has experienced the passage in life, can help them go through these gates. Various descent mythologies can be read as a "map" to this experience. At the heart of the underworld, in the realm of the Lady and Lord of the Dead, they will be challenged, blessed or healed, and released to their next journey on the Mysteries. Usually the lower soul remains with the pools of ancestral wisdom to add to it and return again through the blood lines, while the Higher Soul ascends the world tree to await a new cycle of incarnation. If all three aspects together in union make it to the heart of the underworld, they could possibly join the Mighty Dead in union and harmony.

Initiation of the Psychopomps

One who seeks to do this work regularly should seek out initiation by the psychopomps and guardians of the threshold. Some who are called to do the work are initiated by these powers spontaneously. The initiation can come in the form of their own N.D.E., or Near Death Experience, or through a visionary journey, where they are taken beyond where most humans go on the path guiding the departed.

One could argue that anyone who has undergone true initiation has the spiritual access to do psychopomp work, for they have died and been reborn already, but receiving the blessing of the psychopomp gods is beneficial for all involved.

If you seek the initiation or blessing of these entities to continue your own spiritual work, make a talisman of the traditional payments for access to the realm of the dead. In the ancient Greek traditions, the dead entered with two copper coins, today two pennies, typically placed upon the eyes or in the mouth. For the living, however, the payment was the golden bough, a plant said to have golden leaves.

Vast debates have been created on the identity and origin of the seemingly mythical plant. It is the key that allows the hero Aeneas to pass into the underworld, as recorded by the poet Virgil in the epic *The Aeneid*. It is equated with the Sacred Tree of the cults of Diana. Occult tradition says that the Golden Bough is either oak or the plant that was prized by the Celtic Druids when it grew upon oak, mistletoe.

In the northern traditions of Paganism, those in the Celtic lands gain access to the otherworld through the Silver Branch, equated with the apple, having either silver or gold fruits that ring like bells, opening the gates to the spirit realm. Apples have a rich history with the otherworld, being red and white, the colors of the dead, and associated with the magical realm of immortality and faery women, Avalon. Make a charm of apple, oak and mistletoe, and even copper, to aid you in your psychopomp work to come and go freely. Key imagery, both for protection and for opening and closing the gates, would be appropriate for this charm. A small bag filled with the herbs, with a brass skeleton key tied outside it, worn as a necklace could work well.

Fig. 34: Skeleton Key

Create your sacred space. Light any appropriate incense and candles. Wear any appropriate oil, including oil used to consecrate the dead. Wear your charm of apple, oak and mistletoe.

Contemplate the four stops you make as cardinal points of your space: the place of death, burial, birth and initiation. Walk the path you will walk when you well and truly die, but do it this time to give yourself greater understanding and empathy for those who have departed and those whom you will be aiding.

In the sacred space of ritual, call to the gods of the ways and make your request with this invocation, or one of your own heart and hand.

By the Silver Branch,
By the Golden Bough,
By Apple, Oak and Mistletoe
I seek safe passage along the rivers of blood and forgetfulness
Beyond the rivers of the five senses
To the Rivers of Dread
Seeking the river of stars across the black sky
Where the secrets of immortality lie.
I seek the psychopomp in the wilderness of souls
To be initiate in the ways of the wanderer and guide
To cross freely from one realm and back to the other side

To aid those carrying coppers
While I bear silver and gold
To speak with them again,
Hearing secrets never told.
Hear me now, for I am called to guard and open the gate
Here me now Two Face God and Pale Lady of Fate.
Initiate me in the mysteries of the Wayfarer of Souls.
Grant me the torch to fulfill this role.
So mote it be!

Enter into vision and seek audience with the psychopomp through the gates of death. Ask to be initiated and blessed. Each experience will be unique to the gods appearing and your relationship with them, but usually involves receiving a spark, an ember or flame to guide you along the way, or a revealing of the light already within you.

When the experience is complete, touch your talisman and consecrate it in a manner you deem appropriate. Return your awareness and close your ritual space in the appropriate manner for the method by which you created it.

Funerary Rites

While many religions have standard funerary rites, most Witches believe a Witch's funeral should be as unique as their life, and in fact, the same can be said of all people. While there are some basic principles of remembrance and blessing, the rituals can be adapted to suit the individual and the mourners. The purpose of such rituals is two-fold. On one hand, it is a magickal act of support to the departed, to adjust to death, release ties and have the necessary energy to cross to the next mystery. On the other, these rites are just as much for the living to remember, grieve, make peace and let go, or at the very least, set the stage for this process to begin. Most importantly, I believe they are as much a celebration of life as they are a process of death and grief. In that celebration, both sides of the ritual can be honored.

If ministering to a non-Witch who is deceased, or in dealing with a family who is not Pagan, sensitivity should be given to both what the deceased would want for the service, as well as the needs of the family. When the lines of communication are open, a respectful balance and harmony can be created. Deeper rituals of magickal crossing can be performed in a more appropriate setting, and the larger public ritual can be created as a safe space for mourning and celebration of life.

The following can be used or adapted as needed for a funerary rite. If appropriate, the various herbs and stones can be used in funerary incense, candles, flower arrangements, or in any other way considered appropriate for the ritual.

Funeral Herbs

Basil	Marjoram	Poppy
Bay	Mint	Rosemary
Carnations	Myrrh	Sage
Ivy	Parsley	Willow
Lavender	Pennyroyal	Wormwood
Lily	Periwinkle	Yew
Marigold	Pomegranate	

Create Sacred Space

Create a sacred space for the ritual in a manner that is appropriate for the setting. This can be anything from a full magick circle, an opening prayer or simply an honoring of the directions.

Evoking the Gods

We call to the Goddess and God of the Underworld. We call to the Dark Lady and the Horned Lord. We honor you on this day, and ask that you open the gate to your realm so our brother/sister can gain entry to the Mystery of the Great Beyond in abode.

Light a black candle.

We call upon the Psychopomp, the guide of souls. Please guide our sister/brother through the labyrinth of worlds, truly leading her/him to the Great Beyond in the heart of Mother Earth and the Heart of the Stars.

Light a white candle.

We call upon the Divine Spirit, the Divine Mind, Divine Heart and Divine Will, from which all things come and to which all things return.

Lighting of the Candles & Bardic Sharing

We each light a candle of our choice, so the light and flame will feed the soul body of our sister/brother, to make the journey to the Great Beyond. We hold the candle with love, wisdom and power, and we bless those who have stepped across the veil. So mote it be.

Have all participants light a candle and say a few words as they do. It's a time to share short stories and memories with those gathered, as well as poems, songs or any other expression of love, memory and grief.

Anointing of the Oil

We bless this mixture of Myrrh, Frankincense and Cinnamon as the oils of the dead. Preserving the body, healing the spirit and guiding the soul. We anoint ourselves with this sacred oil as we know we too, live between worlds, both living and dead, touched by the gods. We anoint our sister/brother, so they might find the connection between worlds, take up their work beyond the veil. Blessed be.

Anoint body, casket or urn, depending on what is appropriate at this time.

Readings

Any appropriate reading can be used here, including any version of the Descent of the Goddess. Favorite poems or passages of the deceased can be read.

Cutting of the Cord

By the cutting of this cord, we release the earthly bonds so that their soul(s) may fly free to the next realm and seek peace, wisdom and rebirth.

A ritual cord, if not the cingulum of the practitioner, or the measure if a part of the British Traditional Wicca movement, is cut with a consecrated blade, to loose the bonds between the soul to this world, allowing free travel to the next great mystery.

Working

The group gathered does this joint guided vision together in an effort aid the crossing of the deceased to the next world. If the gathering comprises more experienced Witches, the more complex Journey for Crossing can be used.

All around us is the veil, and we part the veil that separates the world of spirit to the world of flesh. We seek the realm of the Otherworld. Imagine parting a curtain and before you is a great tree, the largest tree you have seen, with its branches reaching up to heaven and its roots digging deep into the underworld. Cross through the veil to this threshold place between. Call to our dearly departed sister/brother. Ask them to come to this place between. Touch the tree and open the roots. A cavern opens in the roots and through it we call to the Psychopomps, the guiding spirits. Who comes forward to help? Ask the psychopomp to help lead the soul of our departed to the next realm that is appropriate. Ask the ancestors who have crossed to help. Feel the between place at the tree fill with light, life, love, law and liberty. Feel it fill with these holy powers. Ask for help from the Goddess and God and wish the loved one well, knowing they are never truly far from us. Blessed be. Return through the veil and close it or leave it open as your intuition guides you, for perhaps the deceased is not yet ready to close it.

Devocation of the Gods

We thank and release the Goddess and God of the Underworld. We thank and release the psychopomp. We thank the Divine Mind, Heart and Will of the Great Spirit. Stay if you will, go if you must. Hail and farewell. Blessed be.

Release of Sacred Space

Release the sacred space in the method appropriate to how you created it.

Interment

If interring the body into the ground, many believe offering should also be made to the spirit of the land and Mother Earth herself, for taking the deceased into her body. Offerings of wine, bread, oil, incense resin, and many traditions use fava beans as an offering in any funeral or ancestor rite. The casket can be censed with incense prior to interment, and flowers can be placed upon the grave by participants.

Post Funerary Rites

Witches involved in the funerary rituals should "check in" with the deceased both after death and after the funeral rite, to see if any further aid in crossing is required, and if so, make appropriate contact with spirit allies to aid in that transition. Upon the initial crossing, the Witch looking in upon the dead can experience the different aspects of the soul—Namer, Shaper and Watcher—on different journeys. Depending on their relationship with the deceased, one may take dominance in their ancestral relationship.

Upon death, an individual ancestral shrine should be created as a temporary focus for "feeding" the deceased the appropriate energy. In particular, a white stone is representative of the dead. It is also amazingly helpful in the acceptance and grief process for those who do it. Offerings, particularly of favorite food and drink are left out. Along with the daily offerings, for a three to nine day period, one can converse with the deceased, saying anything left unsaid before death, offering love, expressing grief or anything else that the mourner feels called to do. Usually during this period the funeral rite takes place. Upon the end of the shrine period, the items of the individual shrine, including the stone, can be incorporated into a larger ancestral altar. The name of the departed is added to the book of the dead or list of the dead upon the altar.

Offerings to the whole can be made regularly, often weekly, and specific offerings to the newly deceased can be done on birthdays, anniversaries and other important life days. Such rituals of blessing and healing are important particularly to those who die violently, accidentally or unexpectedly, where little conscious preparation can be done for both the deceased and the loved ones. These offerings become an act of healing for the deceased and the loved ones who remain. A full memorial service upon the birthday or day of death could be appropriate. A "dumb supper," where the picture is left out and food offerings are made at the gathering, either traditionally silent, or in a normal spoken gathering, works quite well. When focusing work upon a specific ancestor, their picture and/or stone will be brought out. Offerings can be poured upon the stone as well, particularly oil and drinks and then later reincorporated back into the main altar.

In places where the dead are remembered in nature, be it a true graveyard, or, as many choose the option of cremation, a cairn can be erected. A cairn is simply a pile or stone built with intention. While they are found all around the world with various speculated purposes, they are also clearly used to house the remains of the dead. The pile can be quite small and nondescript, or larger. A cairn can be made in the forest or garden for the dead, particularly if you scatter someone's ashes. They are akin to grave markers in the ancient world.

Chapter Thirteen
The Mystery of
the Mighty Dead

I fervently believe that the Mighty Dead continue to guide our tradition in secret and unknown ways. Ministers to the gods and goddesses of Witchcraft, as we aid them in the world of flesh and blood, they implement the True Will of the Mother and Father of Witches upon the Earth through us.

In *An ABC of Witchcraft*, Doreen Valiente mentions the Mighty Ones in reference to Gerald Gardner, and his controversial approach to spreading the Craft in his time.

"However, some would argue that the method he used was unwise. It would have been better and more fitting, they say, to have proceeded by purely occult methods; because the Craft has its own guardians, the Mighty Ones who have been great witches in the past and who now dwell on the Inner Planes. They would not have let it die. It cannot be denied, however, that the world is changing and evolving, and the Craft cannot be static. It, too, must evolve, if it wishes to remain a living thing." [1]

Though I love the wisdom of Doreen, I must wholeheartedly disagree with most of her sentiment. Though I do agree that we have our own guardians and that the Craft must evolve to survive, I don't think Gardner should have proceeded with only occult methods. While the Mighty Ones would not let the Craft die, I don't believe they have the preternatural powers ascribed to the Secret Chiefs by Crowley and Mathers, and I think the ceremonialist's and Theosophist's view still dominated the era of Gardner and Valiente. They are simply spirits, powerful spirits, but in relationship with the living they effect change. I think the Mighty Ones method of keeping the Craft alive was through using Gardner, his blessings and faults alike, to ensure the continuation of the Craft into a time that will guarantee it will never be lost as it once was. Doreen seems to understand it in the last lines, but her general traditionalist sensibilities would still have preferred to keep the Craft more secret originally. But if she had her way, we would probably not have her body of writings, nor the entire global movement through which many of the readers of this book came to the Craft.

Many of the "changes" Gardner made that anger the traditional Witch helped ensure its fame would spread. Ritual nudity, scourging and the sacred fivefold kiss titillated the imagination, yet one of his self-proclaimed missions was to dispel the idea that Witches were "perverts." While they are seen by many as shocking for the sake of being shocking, he did put esoteric principles behind them, to give them reason, even if we don't all agree on the importance of the reasons.

Through Gerald they put "training wheels" on for those newcomers who would not have the benefit of deep lore and training in the initial forays of their magick. The Wiccan Rede and Law of Three, seen as alien to British Traditional Cunning Craft, helps those who are powerless and attracted to Wicca garner power with a development of ethics. These guides have helped instill a dynamic of power over self rather than the focus of power of others. Perhaps there is more truth to the lore of the cursing Witch than most of us would like to admit, and the Inquisitions were a horrible mechanism of balance for us to understand. Through Gardner, the Mighty Dead planted the seeds to grow a Wicca for the New Aeon that will take its place at the table of world religions, adding its wisdom without losing its mystery.

As we explore the great mystery of our Mighty Dead, a new truth becomes evident, often alarmingly so for the hard polytheist with no underpinning in Hermetics or Theosophy. As they stand outside the bounds of space and time, in a collective consciousness beyond our kin, we stand with them. In the third dimension it appears to be a silver or golden chain of initiates, from the first sorcerer to the last future Witch. We are all links of the chain. We are all beads upon a cord of Witchcraft. Yet when you step out of the linear, the links become a mass. The beads are all found randomly in a bowl, touching each other with no order or pattern. The first Witch is also the last Witch, and every Witch in between.

The Celtic concept of tuirgin says consecutive incarnations cross all boundaries as everything is continually in a process of becoming everything else. *Cormac's Glossary* for this transmigration of the soul is "a birth that passes from every nature into another... a transitory birth which has traversed all nature from Adam and goes through every wonderful time down to the world's doom." [2]

If everything is always becoming everything else, and we aspire to be one with the Mighty Dead, then beyond time, we have already done so, are doing so and will do so, all at the same time. Beyond time, all time is one time. Consecutive practitioners make this discovery viscerally, and no amount of discussion or text can bring the reality home until you do discover it for yourself. We already stand among the Mighty Dead. I've known ceremonial magicians, particularly Thelemites and Ma'at Magicians, realize this through their work, as they seek to mutate in the next evolution. New Age practices help you invoke your future ascended master self through sacred decree and visualization. And the Witches who helped me awaken to my own experience with the Hidden Company saw their own faces staring back from the Company one evening in shock.

Just because we have succeeded on one level does not mean we stop aspiring to become one with the Mighty Dead currently. It's our work now that will guarantee that result. Just like the client with the tarot reader who is warned that whatever is now shown is most likely, but just because you are working towards something and the reader predicts success you cannot stop working for it. Your work is the fuel for that success. Change your action and change your fate.

If the Witches of the Hidden Company, in fact, the ascended masters of all traditions, are in a collective consciousness, then the seeming three dimensional view of their separateness, of our separateness is an illusion. We are all one. This idea is sometimes embodied in the concept of the First and Last Sorcerer or First and last Witch. This is one continual ocean of spiritual ancestral memory, and we are all in it, all the time.

In Catholicism, this concept is somewhat expressed in the "Communion of Saints" who make up collectively a single church "mystical body" headed by Christ. This body includes not only the individuals that make the collective, but every holy thing they share – their faith, beliefs, and rituals. They are all a part of the mystical body of communion. It is a sacred bond linking the living and the dead. Those who are not *yet* "saints," still take part in this communion body.

The Buddhists have a story about the Bodhisattva Avalokiteshvara, who is equated with the Tibetan Dali Lama as a manifestation of Avalokiteshvara. Depicted as an androgynous, bisexual being, just as Avalokiteshvara was on the verge of Nirvana, he heard the cries of the birds, trees and all sentient beings. He decided rather than have all suffer, it was far better to have just one suffer, so in his vow he renounced Nirvana until all sentients reached it by taking on their karma and incarnations. All are manifestations of Avalokiteshvara, and all who existed before this vow have already gone "home" to nirvana. Our perceptions are just that. All are Avalokiteshvara wandering the cycles of karma until the end of time is done.

While the First and Last Witch, the One Witch is not doing so for the alleviation of suffering, S/he is like a multi-armed centipede stretched not through space, but through time, starting with the first cave drawings, drumming and spirits visions and ending in a place we can scarcely imagine beyond our wildest dreams. We are all one point, one segment in the chain that is not a chain. But through using the chain imagery, we can merge our identity with those before and behind us in the ancestral line to establish our magickal lineage, increase power, knowledge, connection and ultimately, realization of the One Witch who is all Witches. The Mighty Dead reach back through several identities through time and space backward and forwards.

The Mayan sorcerers and wisdom keepers have a greeting, *Lak'ech Ala K'In* or simply *Lak'ech,* meaning, "I am you and you are me" or in the modern interpretation, "you are another me." Essentially we are the same being looking through different places and time, through different eyes, but ultimately animated by and reporting to the same collective source. In this perception, we just learn to treat everyone and everything like us, and ultimately, like Spirit in the greatest sense, for within the concept of tuirgen, all is of the One Witch, which is us. We must question our assumptions of who is or isn't of "us" as Diana's Darling Crew, the Company of Witches, for those who are not of us in this life may be in the past or in the future. Time is not linear. Our vow, no matter what the tradition, is to serve in some capacity—serve the Mighty Dead, serve the Gods or serve each other matters not, for all are from the same source.

This is the true secret of the Witch Blood, the true secret of the Holy Grail conspiracies. The magick blood of the gods, fallen angels, faeries or messianic kings has mixed and mingled with all the races in all places, and we are all family here and beyond the veil. We simply need to look within to know it.

Exercise: Union with the One Witch

This ritualized vision working's purpose is to merge the personal identity, hopefully aligned with the three souls and purified through deeper rites of healing and empowerment, with the lineage of sorcerers before you in the future, behind you in the past and in all points in between. All past, future and distance is resolved, for all is within you and a part of you. From this point one can truly turn the Wheels of Fate, Justice and Judgment in the vast loom of the Goddess.

While it can be done as a simple but intense vision working, the more ritualized you can be, the greater impact the rite can have, as it emphasizes its importance on the path and the simple culmination of our work in this text. You can punctuate it with any of the crafted tools here, such as burning the Mighty Dead incense, preparing the spirit candle with glyph and the skull or other relic. In fact, if you can safely burn the candle upon the relic, all the better. Prepare a sacrament, such as the Dreaming of the Dead tea, or an alcoholic sacrament with appropriate magickal connotations. My preferred offering for the Mighty Dead is either St. Germain liqueur or Strega liqueur. So using it as a sacramental drink in this rite would be appropriate. Anoint yourself with sacred oil as well, upon the wrists, brow, back of the head and chakra points. While Spirit Contact oil would be appropriate, the Funerary Oil, as this can be quite initiatory, is also appropriate.

Create a sacred space, perhaps through a ritual circle or other method appropriate for your own traditions. Light any incense and candles and let them safely burn while performing the ritual. Lay your four foundation stones for spirit contact with the Mighty Dead: Prepare the space, appropriate body position, soul alignment, remembering your Dedication Vow. Take any prepared sacrament. Face magnetic north the place of true knowing and the Mighty Dead. While many think that knowledge comes from the sky and the voices of the wind, and it does, true knowing comes from the bones of the Earth and the whispers of the underworld. Here at magnetic north the masters are most easily found.

By the north star door,
And the three world spines,
By the True Knowing of the mountain bones,
And the ghost roads and dragon lines,
I seek the First Witch, the Last Witch

The One Witch of All Time.
The currents of wisdom
From before and behind
Hidden Ones come out
Make your way through my bones
Mark the way
To the Stars
Stars within stones.
First Witch, Last Witch,
One Witch of All Ages
In the wisdom books of flesh
Our lives are the pages.
Be one. Be many. Be none. Be all.
Be one with me.
Answer my call.

Imagine yourself in the very center of your space. Feel the northern gate open to you. Feel the light and life, love and law of the Hidden Ones pour through the gate like a river, or more appropriately, like a tidal wave of light. Feel it flow not only down upon you, but in you and through you. Feel quite literally the current of the Mighty Dead through your entire body – every cell, every fiber of your being, every layer of your consciousness. Their wisdom, their knowledge, and most importantly their pattern, flows into you and you for a time know it all. Feel the masters pass through you from North to South, everyone from the most ancient past to the farthest future.

Feel as if the entire light of the Phosphorous Grove is pouring through your flesh and blood right now. Feel your blood reach out to their spirit blood, and the blood remembers. Feel your bones tapped and resonate with their bones left within the earth. Feel your breath and know it is the same breath they drew in life, past and future. Feel your flesh moved by their current of wisdom.

A multitude of beings pass through you, though at the same time, it is only one. In some strange way, it is like a massive centipede, an insect consciousness of many legs and arms. Each individual is one segment, one unit, just as every incarnation of your life is one segment, and in fact, every moment of your current life is one segment, infinite links within a chain, and infinite chains running parallel, and opposite and diagonal to each other.

Feel the presence of the Four Orders from the Four Directions attending you. Soon you are in a sea of perfected souls. Rather than links within a chain, you are fibers within an ever widening tapestry of creation, being spun out and woven upon the loom of the Lady. And yet there you are with the Lady, feeding the threads in, weaving the fates with her.

Let all seeming paradox be resolved within this experience of the fibers of fate.

Reach out with your being, all the way back to the First Witch, the first one of us beyond time who had awoken to this magick in the Zep Tepi, the time before time.

Reach out and across with all of your being, all the way forward to the Last Witch, at the end of time, who helps close the door to this creation and return to source.

Feel yourself become the One Witch, who is both and all in between.

You have been burned by the fires of awakening and rekindled the initiation blaze.

Dissolve your identity in the flow, the stream of the Masters.

Find yourself again within the stream, your link as you feel it here and now.

Conjoin this awareness of self with the vastness of the One Witch.

You are alive.

You are dead.

You are unborn.

You are being born.

You are living.

You are dying.

You are all things.

You are nothing.

You are no-thing.

You have been made.

You have been unmade.

And you have been made again and again and again.

Becoming. Being. Becoming.

Xeph. Xepher. Xepheru. (Kep. Keper. Keperu.)

When you feel the process is complete and you are returning to a single identity yet retain this awareness of consciousness, ground yourself. In the grounding, expand your energy into the Earth, not just below yourself, but the entire Earth. You are blessing the Earth for all the Mighty Dead, come and gone.

Release your space and return from any trance state. Return to flesh and blood, breath, and bone, and do any additional grounding that is necessary. Take some time to journal, to relax and perhaps to eat and drink, to feast both in celebration of the experience, but also to return to some normalcy with day-to-day living human actions.

One might ask, if we are truly guided by the Mighty Dead, then why isn't the world of Witches, Wiccans, and Pagans—or the entire world, if they truly go beyond religions—in better shape? Why is there so much conflict and fractiousness in our communities and worlds?

Well, who is really listening to the Mighty Dead? Not as many as I would hope, but my fervent dream is this book can change that, at least in the Witchcraft communities. But the general world can barely follow the basic tenets of its various religions people claim to cherish, let alone heed advice from more mystical sources. And to the Mighty Dead, harmony does not equate with "good" and conflict with "bad" as long as we are evolving. Look at the process of alchemy. One must break down things, purify and recombine. Dissolve et coagula! The initiatory model to allow us to even have communion with the Mighty Dead is one of hardship. At a signing for her book, *Fire Child*, Witch elder Maxine Sanders summed it up best. When asked by an audience member the same essential question, why there was so much tension and why couldn't Witches get along as his idealized vision in the 1960s Summer of Love utopia, Maxine responded, "If you can't stand tension, never enter one of my circles! A good magician knows how to use tension to create change." [3] I don't think anyone can say it better. Magick uses tension to create change. All the seeming disharmony of this age is the birth pain to new and different consciousness. From beyond the veil of time, all of this is seen as good, no matter the result. All will grow wise.

Based upon these experiences and teachings, I tend to equate the various embodiments of enlightened dead in a collective universal communion, a level of consciousness where religion and outer form no longer matter when compared to inner form. There are much more conservative teachers and interpretations that would say each of the various communal bodies are separate and distinct, working with different gods and forces. Not only are the Mighty Dead different from the Lords of Shamballa, but each tradition of Witchcraft has its own Mighty Dead. I disagree, but I guess we won't know truly until we consciously get there and experience it. Channeled information often fulfills your own current beliefs and biases or speaks to your fears.

Ours is the way of magick. As Dion Fortune tells us, dividing the path of the occultist and the mystic:

The operations of occultism are based upon the powers of the will and the imagination; both blind forces. Unless they are controlled and directed by a motive which has relation to the universe as a whole, no ultimate synthesis is possible. The personality must be universalized by the ideal at which it aims in order that it may function as an organized part of the cosmic whole. It is this urge towards universalization which is the ultimate hunger of the soul; the lesser self seeks to achieve it by drawing all things into itself in a rage of possession; the greater self seeks to achieve it by transcending the bounds of self and becoming one with the universe. There are two unions to be achieved: the self may become one with the universe by means of universal sympathy—this is the goal of the occultist; the self may also be made one with the Creator of the universe by means of absolute devotion— this is the goal of the mystic. But the occultist, having achieved his own goal, has not yet made the ultimate integration, he has not yet passed from the manifested phenomenal aspect into the cosmic; and the mystic, having achieved his transcendent union, cannot hold it, but must lapse back into the phenomenal universe. The ultimate integration can only be achieved by means of universal sympathy and absolute devotion united in one nature. Into such a one all things are gathered by means of sympathy, and he is in his turn gathered into the All by means of devotion.

This is the ultimate aim of evolution for the manifested universe as a whole; and he who goes by the Way of Initiation does but anticipate evolution. It is the function of the Mysteries to assist the initiate to tread that section of the Path which has already been explored, but beyond lies a section that is known to no consciousness that is in a physical form; this section a man must tread alone with his Master; and beyond lies a section where a man is alone with his God. [4]

While the simple occultist has the danger of embodying the lesser self by only focusing on spellcraft, the true occultist gains union with the universe. The Witch is a balance between the occultist and the mystic. We speak and we listen. We learn and we feel. We do ritual and we meditate.

When one truly achieves this level of consciousness, one becomes ensorcelled on all levels, in the sense that one is encircled by the holy circle of our art and science that is truly a sphere. You stand in the Temple of Self. You stand between the worlds. Everything becomes enchanted in our circle that surrounds and interpenetrates and reaches beyond. The sphere reflects all but you. You become one of the invisibles, like the masters themselves. You step outside and forever dwell in twilight. You stand between and beyond time and space. You know that the direct line of time is really a wheel which is really a spiral. Where the line, wheel and spiral intersect, where all time is one time, the true crossroads, you can change the past, create the future and turn the wheel of fate. As all circles are one circle and all spheres are one sphere, you join the ranks of the Hidden

Company. "Harm none" then does become the true teaching, for consciously harming another is consciously harming yourself, for all is one and one is none in this mystery. Compassion to all is compassion to the self and can be one of the gates to that mystery, our key of Perfect Love.

Ultimately an understanding of this process plays into my generally optimistic outlook on life. While talking with a friend who is possibly more intelligent and educated, devout spiritually, balanced personally, and accomplished in her career that focuses on public service, I realized why. She sadly has a pessimistic outlook on the future of our world and life itself even though she wants things to be well. But despite her accomplishment and community, she is still disconnected and solitary in her wandering. I know I'm part of an illustrious chain of Witches and magicians that is not a chain and that, if I do my part and everybody in the chain does their part, as I know we all do, then the world moves forward as it should—from the First Witch to the Last.

---

1 Valiente, Doreen. *An ABC of Witchcraft*. St. Martins, New York, NY: 1973. p. 187.

2 *Three Irish Glossaries: Cormac's Glossary, O'Davoren's Glossary and a Glossary to the Calendar of Oengus the Culdee.* Williams and Norgate, London: 1862

3 Private Book Signing at Nu Aeon, Salem, MA: May 4, 2009.

4 Fortune, Dion. *Esoteric Orders and their Work.* The Aquarian Publishing Company, London: 1928. Pp 5-6.

BIBLIOGRAPHY

Albertsson, Alaric. *Travels through Middle Earth*. Woodbridge, MN: Llewellyn Publications, 2009.

Bailey, Alice A. *The Rays and the Initiations*. New York, NY: Lucis Publishing Co., 1960.

Belanger, Michelle. *The Psychic Vampire Codex*. San Francisco, CA: Red Wheel/Weiser, 2004.

Bertiaux, Michael. *Cosmic Meditation*. London, UK: Fulgar Limited, 2007.

Bhairavan, Amarananda. *Kali's Odiyya: A Shaman's True Story of Initiation*. Nicolas Hayes, 2000.

Butler, W.E. *Lords of Light: The Path of Initiation in the Western Mysteries*. Rochester, VT: Inner Traditions, 1990.

Castaneda, Carlos. *The Wheel of Time*. New York, NY: Washington Square Press, 1998.

Chapman, John. "St. Cyprian of Carthage." *The Catholic Encyclopedia. Vol. 4*. New York, NY: Robert Appleton Company, 1908. 1 Mar. 2012 <*http://www.newadvent.org/cathen/04583b.htm*>.

Cox, Robert E. *Creating the Soul Body: The Sacred Science of Immortality*. Rochester, VT: Inner Traditions, 2008.

Crowley, Aleister. *Magick: Liber ABA (Book 4)*. York Beach, ME: Weiser Books, 1998.

Cummer, Veronica. *Sorgitzak: Old Forest Craft*. Pendraig Publishing, 2008.

De Biasi, Jean-Louis. *Secrets and Practices of the Freemasons: Sacred Mysteries, Rituals, and Symbols Revealed*. Woodbury, MN: Llewellyn Publications, 2010.

DiFiosa, Jimahl. *Talk to Me*. Flying Witch Productions, 2008.

DiFiosa, Jimahl. *A Voice in the Forest: Spirit Conversations with Alex Sanders*. Southborough, MA: Harvest Shadows Publications, 1999, 2004.

Fortune, Dion. *The Cosmic Doctrine*. London, UK: The Aquarian Publishing Company, 1949.

Foxwood, Orion. *The Faery Teachings*. R.J. Stewart Books, 2007.

Foxwood, Orion. *The Tree of Enchantment*. San Francisco, CA: Red Wheel/Weiser, 2008.

Fries, Jan. *Cauldron of the Gods.* London, UK: Mandrake Press, 2005.

Gardner, Gerald. *The Meaning of Witchcraft.* Boston, MA: Red Wheel/Weiser, 2004.

Gardner, Gerald. *Witchcraft Today.* Citadel Books, 2004.

Guiley, Rosemary. *The Encyclopedia of Witches, Witchcraft and Wicca.* Infobase Publishing, 2008.

Grant, Kenneth. *The Magical Revival.* York Beach, ME: Samuel Weiser, 1973.

Hall, Manly P. *The Blessed Angels.* Los Angeles, CA: The Philosophical Research Center, Inc., 1996.

Hall, Manly P. *Lectures of Ancient Philosophy.* New York, NY: Tarcher/Penguin, 1984.

Huson, Paul. *Mastering Witchcraft.* New York, NY: Perigee Trade, 1980.

Johns, June. *King of the Witches: The World of Alex Sanders.* New York, NY: Coward-McCann, Inc., 1969.

Jones, Evan John & Robert Cochrane, editor Mike Howard. *The Roebuck in the Thicket: An Anthology of the Robert Cochrane Witchcraft Tradition.* Somerset, England: Capall Bann Publishing, 2001.

Jones, Evan John & Shani Oates. *The Star Crossed Serpent.* Oxford, UK: Mandrake Press, 2012.

Knight, Gareth. *Magical Images and the Magical Imagination.* Sun Chalice Books, 1998.

Knight, Gareth. *The Secret Tradition in Arthurian Legend.* York Beach, ME: Weiser, 1996.

LeCouteux, Claude. *Phantom Armies of the Night: The Wild Hunt and the Ghostly Processions of the Undead.* Rochester, VT: Inner Traditions, 2011.

LePage, Victoria. *Shambhala: The Fascinating Truth Behind the Myth of Shangri-la.* Wheaton, IL: Quest Books, 1996.

MacErlean, Andrew. "St. Germain." *The Catholic Encyclopedia. Vol. 6.* New York: Robert Appleton Company, 1909. 1 Mar. 2012 <*http://www.newadvent.org/cathen/06472b.htm*>.

MacEowen, Frank. *The Mist Filled Path.* Novato, CA: New World Library, 2002.

Martin, Lois. *A Brief History of Witchcraft: Demons, Folklore, and Superstition.* Philadelphia, PA: Running Press, 2010.

Mathiesen, Robert and Theitic. *The Rede of the Wiccae: Adriana Porter, Gwen Thompson and the Birth of a Tradition of Witchcraft.* Providence RI: Olympian Press, 2005.

Meier, Gabriel. "Sts. Cyprian and Justina." *The Catholic Encyclopedia. Vol. 4.* New York: Robert Appleton Company, 1908. 1 Mar. 2012 *<http://www.newadvent.org/cathen/04583a.htm>.*

Mershman, Francis. "St. Christopher." *The Catholic Encyclopedia. Vol. 3.* New York: Robert Appleton Company, 1908. 1 Mar. 2012 *<http://www.newadvent.org/cathen/03728a.htm>.*

Moss, Robert. *Dreamer's Guide to the Dead.* Rochester, VT: Inner Traditions, 2005.

Paddon, Peter. *The Crooked Path: Selected Transcripts.* CA: Pendraig Publishing, 2009.

Lindsay, Phillip. *Masters of the Seven Rays. Their Past Lives and Reappearance.* Newport Beach, Australia: Apollo Publishing Pty Ltd., 2000.

Lindsay. Phillip. *The Shamballa Impacts.* Newport Beach, Australia: Apollo Publishing Pty Ltd., 2000.

Ramer, Andrew and Mark Thompson. *Two Flutes Playing.* San Francisco, CA:1 Alamo Square Dist Inc., 997.

Regardie, Israel. *The Golden Dawn: A Complete Course in Practical Ceremonial Magic.* St. Paul, MN: Llewellyn Worldwide, 1986.

Ruiz, Don Miguel. *The Four Agreements.* San Rafael, CA: Amber-Allen Publishing, 1997.

Scott, Ernest. *The People of the Secret.* London, UK: Octagon Press, 1985.

Shah, Idries. *Oriental Magic.* New York, NY: Penguin, 1993.

Slater, Herman. *A Book of Pagan Rituals.* York Beach, ME: Samuel Weiser, 1978.

Suckling, Nigel. *Witches. Facts, Figures and Fun.* London, UK: 2006.

Thorsson, Edred. *The Book of Ogham.* St. Paul, MN: Llewellyn Publications, 1994.

Thorsson, Edred. *The Nine Doors of Midgard.* St. Paul, MN: Llewellyn Publications, 1991.

Thorsson, Edred. *Northern Magic Mysteries of the Norse, Germans & English.* St. Paul, MN: Llewellyn Publications, 1992.

Valiente, Doreen. *The Rebirth of Witchcraft.* Custer, WA: Phoenix Publishing, 1989.

Villoldo, Albert with Erik Jendresen. *Island of the Sun: Mastering the Inca Medicine Wheel.* Rochester, VT: Destiny Books, 1994.

Webster, Sam. *Tantric Thelema.* Richmond, CA: Concrescent Press, 2010.

ONLINE RESOURCES

Jones, Mary. *http://www.maryjones.us/ctexts/bbc19.html* : January 5, 2012.

Stavish, Mark. *An Interview with Dolores Ashcroft-Nowicki, http://www.servantsofthelight.org/aboutSOL/interview-DAN.html* : Jan 5, 2012.

Yronwode, Catherine. *http://www.luckymojo.com/saintcyprian.html:* March 1, 2010.

http://en.wikipedia.org/wiki/Taoist_Immortals : November 10, 2011.

http://en.wikipedia.org/wiki/Perfect_Master_(Meher_Baba) : November 22, 2011.

http://en.wikipedia.org/wiki/Qutb : November 22, 2011.

http://en.wikipedia.org/wiki/Tagzig_Olmo_Lung_Ring : January 15, 2012.

http://www.munay-ki.org/index.php?page=nine_rites : Jan 5, 2012.

http://en.wikipedia.org/wiki/Sodality : January 20, 2012.

http://www.fulgur.co.uk/authors/aos/articles/grant/ : January 22, 2012.

http://www.witchcraftandwitches.com/witches_laveau.html : January 22, 2012.

http://www.witchcraftandwitches.com/witches_kyteler.html : January 22, 2012.

http://www.witchcraftandwitches.com/witches_gowdie.html : January 22, 2012.

http://www.witchcraftandwitches.com/witches.html : January 22, 2012.

http://en.wikipedia.org/wiki/Benandanti : January 21, 2012.

http://en.wikipedia.org/wiki/Wild_Hunt : January 21, 2012.

http://en.wikipedia.org/wiki/Tituba : January 22, 2012.

http://www.shee-eire.com/magic&mythology/fairylore/healers,wise-ones&charmers/biddy-early/page1.htm : January 23, 2012.

http://en.wikipedia.org/wiki/Biddy_Early : January 23, 2012.

http://en.wikipedia.org/wiki/George_Pickingill : January 23, 2012.

http://special.lib.gla.ac.uk/exhibns/month/aug2000.html : January 23, 2012.

http://www.witchcraftandwitches.com/witches_blight.html : January 26, 2012.

http://www.witchcraftandwitches.com/witches_shipton.html : January 26, 2012.

http://www.witchcraftandwitches.com/witches_hausmannin.html : January 26, 2012.

http://en.wikipedia.org/wiki/Imhotep : January 26, 2012.

http://www.witchcraftandwitches.com/witches_agrippa.html : January 26, 2012.

http://www.witchcraftandwitches.com/witches_voisin.html : January 26, 2012.

http://www.witchskel.com/2/post/2010/2/history-101-the-ancient-witches-of-thessay.html : January 26, 2012.

http://en.wikipedia.org/wiki/Hypatia : January 27, 2012.

http://www.shee-eire.com/Magic&Mythology/Warriors&Heroes/Druids/Cathbad/Page1.htm : January 27, 2012.

http://en.wikipedia.org/wiki/Apollonius_of_Tyana : January 27, 2012.

http://en.wikipedia.org/wiki/Aristoclea : January 27, 2012.

http://en.wikipedia.org/wiki/Maatkare_Mutemhat : January 27, 2012.

http://w3.coh.arizona.edu/classes/mskinner/clas362/paulina.htm : January 27, 2012.

http://en.wikipedia.org/wiki/Giordano_Bruno : January 29, 2012.

http://www.the-cauldron.org.uk/witchesofgreece.htm : January 29, 2012.

http://en.wikipedia.org/wiki/John_Winthrop_the_Younger : January 29, 2012.

http://www.alchemylab.com/paracelsus.htm : January 29, 2012.

http://www.egs.edu/library/paracelsus/biography/ : January 29, 2012.

http://en.wikipedia.org/wiki/Paracelsus : January 29, 2012.

http://en.wikipedia.org/wiki/Jacques_de_Molay : January 29, 2012.

http://en.wikipedia.org/wiki/Order_of_the_garter : January 29, 2012.

http://en.wikipedia.org/wiki/Relic : January 30, 2012.

http://en.wikipedia.org/wiki/Thelemic_mysticism : January 19, 2012.

http://en.wikipedia.org/wiki/Afterlife : Feb 5, 2012.

http://en.wikipedia.org/wiki/The_Sworn_Book_of_Honorius : March 1, 2012.

http://en.wikipedia.org/wiki/Hermes_Trismegistus : March 1, 2012.

http://en.wikipedia.org/wiki/Ember_days : May 16, 2012.

http://en.wikipedia.org/wiki/First_man_or_woman : April 30, 2012.

http://en.wikipedia.org/wiki/Epic_of_Gilgamesh : May 22, 2012.

http://en.wikipedia.org/wiki/Noah#Comparisons_in_other_religions : May 22, 2012.

http://en.wikipedia.org/wiki/Noah : May 22, 2012.

http://en.wikipedia.org/wiki/Queen_of_Sheba : May 22, 2012.

http://en.wikipedia.org/wiki/Beheading_of_St._John_the_Baptist : May 22, 2012.

http://en.wikipedia.org/wiki/Herodias : May 22, 2012.

http://en.wikipedia.org/wiki/Cult_of_Herodias : May 22, 2012.

http://en.wikipedia.org/wiki/Raziel : May 22, 2012.

http://en.wikipedia.org/wiki/Hercules : May 22, 2012.

http://www.lightspill.com/poetry/oe/wanderer.html : May 22, 2012.

http://en.wikipedia.org/wiki/The_Wanderer_(poem) : May 22, 2012.

http://en.wikipedia.org/wiki/Leonora_Piper : June 15, 2012.

http://en.wikipedia.org/wiki/Emma_Hardinge_Britten : June 15, 2012.

http://www.fst.org/piper.htm : June 15, 2012.

INDEX

ABOUT THE AUTHOR

Christopher Penczak is an award-winning author, teacher, and healing practitioner. As an advocate for the timeless perennial wisdom of the ages, he is rooted in the traditions of modern Witchcraft and Earth-based religions, but draws from a wide range of spiritual traditions including shamanism, alchemy, herbalism, Theosophy, and Hermetic Qabalah to forge his own magickal traditions. His many books include *Magick of Reiki, The Mystic Foundation, The Three Rays of Witchcraft,* and *The Inner Temple of Witchcraft.* He is the co-founder of the Temple of Witchcraft tradition, a non-profit religious organization to advance the spiritual traditions of Witchcraft, as well as a co-founder of Copper Cauldron Publishing, a company dedicated to producing books, recordings, and tools for magickal inspiration and evolution. He maintains a teaching and healing practice in New England, but travels extensively to teach. More information can be found at *www.christopherpenczak.com* and *www.templeofwitchcraft.org.*

The Temple of Witchcraft
MYSTERY SCHOOL AND SEMINARY

Witchcraft is a tradition of experience, and the best way to experience the path of the Witch is to actively train in its magickal and spiritual lessons. The Temple of Witchcraft provides a complete system of training and tradition, with four degrees found in the Mystery School for personal and magickal development and a fifth degree in the Seminary for the training of High Priestesses and High Priests interested in serving the gods, spirits, and community as ministers. Teachings are divided by degree into the Oracular, Fertility, Ecstatic, Gnostic, and Resurrection Mysteries. Training emphasizes the ability to look within, awaken your own gifts and abilities, and perform both lesser and greater magicks for your own evolution and the betterment of the world around you. The Temple of Witchcraft offers both in-person and online courses with direct teaching and mentorship. Classes use the *Temple of Witchcraft* series of books and CD Companions as primary texts, supplemented monthly with information from the Temple's Book of Shadows, MP3 recordings of lectures and meditations from our founders, social support through group discussion with classmates, and direct individual feedback from a mentor.

For more information and current schedules, please visit the Temple of Witchcraft website: *www.templeofwitchcraft.org*.